Sarah Tuke Grubb

Some account of the life and religious labours of Sarah Grubb

Sarah Tuke Grubb

Some account of the life and religious labours of Sarah Grubb

ISBN/EAN: 9783337132101

Printed in Europe, USA, Canada, Australia, Japan

Cover: Foto ©Lupo / pixelio.de

More available books at **www.hansebooks.com**

SOME ACCOUNT OF THE LIFE AND RELIGIOUS LABOURS OF SARAH GRUBB.

WITH AN APPENDIX,

CONTAINING AN ACCOUNT

OF THE

SCHOOLS AT ACKWORTH AND YORK,

OBSERVATIONS ON CHRISTIAN DISCIPLINE,

AND

EXTRACTS

FROM MANY OF HER

LETTERS.

JOHN vi. 12.
——— Gather up the Fragments that remain, that Nothing be lost.

DUBLIN:

PRINTED FOR R. JACKSON, No. 20, MEATH-STREET.

M,DCC,XCII.

CONTENTS.

CHAP. I.

Her Education.—Divine Visitations.—Conflict arising from her natural Vivacity, &c.—Solid State of her Mind in the early Part of Life.—Exercises about the Time of her first Appearance in the Ministry.—Visit to Part of the Counties of Westmoreland and Cumberland.—Visit to the Meetings of Cheshire and a Part of those in Lancashire, &c. Page 1

CHAP. II.

Her Marriage—and Journey into Scotland, Cumberland, &c. 43

CHAP. III.

Visit to her Husband's Relations in Ireland.—Journey into Norfolk, &c.—Visit to the Meetings of Friends in Ireland. 78

CHAP. IV.

Visit to some of the Western Counties of England. 114

CHAP. V.

Family Visit at Sheffield.—Illness there.—Consideration of removing into Ireland.—Journey into Lincolnshire.—Removal to Ireland.—Journey into Holland, Germany, and France. 145

CHAP. VI.

Her Concern respecting a Boarding School for Female Youth.—Visit to Friends Families in Cork.—Journey to London.—Visit to Dunkirk, Holland, Pyrmont, &c.—Her Return—and Decease.—Testimonies concerning her. 183

INTRODUCTION.

AS few lives have exhibited a more pure example of piety and virtue, than that which is set forth in the ensuing pages, it has been thought right to bring it forward to general notice; under a hope, that an account of this humble, self-denying, and dedicated servant, will prove the means of instructing others; and of strengthening their faith in the efficacy of that Divine Principle, "which wrought all her works in her."

It will be proper to inform the reader, that the materials from which this work is composed, consist of journals written by herself of her travels through Scotland, Ireland, and some of the western counties in England, and of a considerable number of letters to some of her intimate friends. From these last have been extracted such parts, as were descriptive of her other labours and travels, or likely to be of public use. A connexion of the different events and circumstances, has been made throughout, by short narratives or explanations; but great care has been taken to preserve, as much as could be, her own words and arrangements.

Those extracts of letters which do not appear to have a peculiar connexion with the narrative, and which could not have been regularly introduced there, have been collected together, and are, nearly in the order of time, inserted in the Appendix. The importance of their subjects, and their instructive tendency, it is apprehended, will render them an acceptable addition to the other part of the work. Although, from the time of her engagement in the ministry, she was greatly dedicated, and much employed in various religious services during the remainder of her days; yet, for want of materials left by herself, an account of many of these is omitted in the following work; which it seemed proper to confine, almost throughout, to such part of her life and labours as could be collected from her own writings. It may not be improper to observe also, that this mode of composing a narrative, by extracts from letters, will sometimes be, unavoidably attended with a want of close connexion, and with a degree of repetition: but as this was the only way by which a material part of her labours could be brought into view, it is hoped that these circumstances will not be deemed of much consequence; and that the deeply instructive nature of her literary correspondence, will sufficiently warrant its publication.

THE LIFE OF SARAH GRUBB.

CHAP. I.

Her Education.—Divine Visitations.—Conflict arising from her natural Vivacity, &c.—Solid State of her Mind in the early Part of Life.—Exercises about the Time of her first Appearance in the Ministry.—Visit to Part of the Counties of Westmoreland and Cumberland.—Visit to the Meetings of Cheshire, and a Part of those in Lancashire, &c.

SARAH GRUBB, daughter of William and Elizabeth Tuke, was born at York in Great Britain, 20th of 6th month, in the year 1756.

In her tender years, she was deprived of her mother, who was removed from her by death, before she was five years old: but her father marrying again about the tenth year of her age, this loſs was, from that time, abundantly compenſated by the maternal care and regard of a ſecond mother; of whoſe tenderneſs, and ſolicitude for her beſt welfare, ſhe has left many grateful and affectionate teſtimonials.

The watchful and religious education with which ſhe was favoured, proved as a hedge round about her, and, under divine care, preſerved her during that dangerous ſeaſon of life, from the many corruptions and follies, that abound in the world, and to which unguarded young people are ſorrowfully expoſed. In the days of her youth, ſhe was often made ſenſible of the goodneſs of her heavenly Father, and her eyes anointed to ſee the emptineſs and deluſion of all worldly enjoyments, and to behold the beauty which there is in the truth; and ſtrong deſires were often raiſed in her mind, that ſhe might be thoroughly refined, and, even at the loſs of every thing elſe, be made to poſſeſs the pearl of great price.

Theſe gracious extenſions of divine regard met with great oppoſition from the livelineſs of her diſpoſition, and the ſtrength of her natural powers; which occaſioned the ſelf denying meekneſs and ſimplicity of the chriſtian life, to be to her an hard attainment; and many painful ſtruggles ſhe experienced, before ſhe was made willing to yield up every ſacrifice, and to follow her Lord whitherſoever he might be pleaſed to lead.

During the laſt illneſs of that eminent miniſter, John Woolman, ſhe was, at times, favoured to wait upon and affift him. His faith and patience, with the fweet favour of his pure fpirit, made a deep and profitable impreffion on her mind; exemplifying the power and goodnefs of that divine hand, which fhe felt fecretly at work in her own heart, calling her to newnefs of life, and holinefs before the Lord. It was to her that this valuable friend, when near the clofe of life, addreffed thofe comfortable expreffions, which, indeed, may be called a bleffing: " My child, thou feems very kind to me, a poor creature ; the Lord will reward thee for it."

A deep fenfe of the purity of the divine life, and a lively feeling of her own frailties, joined to an earneft concern that fhe might become fully purified in heart and life, caufed great circumfpection and fear, and made her often go mourning on her way. This appears from the following extracts of divers letters to her friends, written in early life, which, in fome meafure, fhow the exercife, and ftate of her mind, at that period; and which may be acceptable, as they ferve to exhibit the beginnings and gradations of that work, which confpicuoufly marked the future periods of her life.

1772.———" I feel thy bearing with my weakneffes, and thy candor in judging of them, which makes me the more ready to communicate what I feel. Oh could I tell thee, it would be comfortable ! But that which is felt and not underftood, cannot be defcribed; and, indeed, I begin to think a ftate of infenfibility to what is good is approaching. I may truly fay I dread it. May I, by that fear, guard the more; yet my infirmities feem fo juft a cause, that they are numerous enough to depress the little life that is left."

1772.————" Thine has excited in me the warmest wishes for the extendings of divine bounty, to be enabled, with resignation and fortitude, to do, bear, or suffer, whatever it may please the Father of spirits to inflict upon me. Yet I cannot but, with conscious sorrow, own the truth of thy remark, concerning a too great anxiety for a larger portion of the descendings of the Father's love, than is suitable in the sight of an omnifcient Deity."

1773.————" I seem recovering from my late illness, and have favourable symptoms for life; but for what kind of a one I know not. I am at a loss to say whether it is a pleasing, or a painful prospect. I feel the effects of both, and am ready to countenance the latter, knowing there is something in my nature, which is loth to be subjected under that power, which ought to actuate every part of our demeanour; and there is nothing, that I know of, so contrary to my natural will, as that patiently waiting, and quietly hoping, which thou mentions; it being, certainly, preparatory to the work of reformation in us; and if this be rightly performed, no mundane enjoyment would be adequate to the foretaste of that consummate felicity, which I believe is the result of so desirable a work: and, indeed, without some degree of that blessing, even in my unworthy state, this life, would be little superior to that for which I should look. But O this glimpse of hope, how ready are we to catch, though the twig be ever so tender, and the prospect ever so faint! yet there is a danger of being deluded, as the Adversary is ever ready to attack the weak part, and that is one which is generally exposed, there being room in the human breast for such prepossessions. I acquiesce with thee, that it is in silence we enjoy advantage, and in solitude we muse the wonders of unsearchable wisdom. Could we but partake of a larger share of retirement, I am sensible the works of an almighty hand would have a greater influence, and the mind would not be so alienated from this source, this pleasing source of every joy."

1773.————"Surely the commemoration of the goodness of infinite wisdom, in favouring a large share of the youth of our society with a virtuous and sober education, ought to inspire us with a willingness to imitate the bright examples we have, rather than those, whose loss we should compassionate; for many are the irreligious principles, that the Adversary is endeavouring to suggest in the minds of youth, more especially when they are exposed to the tempestuous billows of an unstable world; but happy is it for those that resist the temptations, and surmount the difficulties: if any may look to the recompense of reward, 'tis certainly they. But for my part, I am often afraid lest I should grow like the heath in the desert, that knoweth not when good cometh; or that the manifold favours should prove, as water spilt upon a stone; for I am sure there is a hardness in the natural heart, not easily penetrated; and though I experimentally confess it, yet I hope there are many, on the other hand, who can say, they witness the returning from their gatherings with friends, as arising from the washing pool."

1774.———" We certainly reap the greatest advantages from a friend, when the mind and natural flow of spirits are most depressed. It is at these seasons we hear the intelligible language of sympathy, in its pleasing notes, and look upon friendship in its exalted station. A view of these enjoyments excited me to taste their fruits, (which are the disclosure of our minds) by opening the fountain of sorrows, and unlocking the spring of painful feelings. That they may overflow the banks of my pleasures, and bring down the tall cedars of Lebanon, laying waste the hills and the mountains, and establishing in the room, that Rock whereon the church must be built, is the swaying inclination of my heart. But how apt are we to turn our feet from the path which is narrow; being unwilling to make straight steps, a thing most repugnant to our unregenerate wills! We therefore cull out every discouragement, and stumble at the smallest stone; each prospect appearing in its gloomiest colours, or rather, our eyes being dimmed by the glitter of worldly objects, and inexperienced in the joys accruing from faithfulness, we see them not."

1775.———" Though trials and conflicts are allotted to the faithful followers, yet they rise, as with stones of memorial, from the bottom of Jordan; when alas! I, and such like, instead of being benefitted by these baptisms, find them unpleasing and contrary to our natural propensities, and so shun them, for a more easy way to peace; but cannot such be met with in a straight place, where neither the devices of the creature, nor the pleasures of the world, can rescue them from the pains of a wounded conscience? When I look at these things, and consider how intricate the path to our real happiness is, it makes me frequently say in my heart, " blessed are the dead that have died in the Lord."

1775.———" My mind was often with you yesterday, though I could not thereby partake of the valuable company of our dear friends; but I hope many that are more worthy did: for certainly the society of those labourers in the great vineyard, must be pleasing and instructive; yet, at times, we feel a mortification in their absence, which, if suffered to have its proper effect, might be a means of exciting us to seek after an inward communion with the source of all good, the spirit of truth, which is pure and unmixed with human propensities. But I am afraid that I am speaking more from hearing the experiences of others, than from my own; for I know the language of this internal monitor is not intelligible, without the mind be prepared by the subjection of its will, and all its powers yield to the Supreme: and this state I am so often deprived of, by the predominance of self, that it seems hard to say, whether I ever rightly enjoy this divine privilege."

1777.———" When we are favoured to feel an internal communion, an intercourse incomprehensible, 'tis indeed attended with rejoicing of heart. A state which I can impute to no good cause, frequently accompanies me, in which it would be hard for me to say, I love my friends; but perhaps it is a constitutional stupidity, which nothing but the immediate operations of truth can divest of; and it is only during the overshadowings thereof, that the useful faculties of my mind are applied to good purposes; for the spring of thy S. T.'s machinery are indeed weak, and daily require a supernatural aid; but when wisdom utters her voice, when the gentle movings of uncreated purity have gained our ear, what obduracy does it require to resist its energetic language, and lightly esteem the offers of permanent peace! My heart glows with an earnest solicitude, that we, my dear friend, may never faint in our pursuit after celestial treasure, but resignedly surrender our whole affections to the gracious disposer, and preserver of his people; then, I doubt not, our union will increase, in the increase of purity, and our joy and rejoicing in the fruition of reward, will be of that nature with which the stranger doth not intermeddle."

In the twenty third year of her age, she appeared in the ministry. For this awful service she had been prepared, by the great head of the church, with deep and humbling baptisms of spirit. But as she continued patient and faithful, under this proving dispensation, she experienced divine support, was graciously brought through all, and enabled to stand acceptably for the cause of truth and righteousness on earth.

The close trials and humiliations of her spirit about this time, are, in some degree testified, by the following selections from her letters, to some of her near, sympathizing friends. And though these extracts are of considerable extent, it is hoped their instructive tendency will warrant the insertion of them thus at large.

1778.———" I don't know but a little love for my friends, and sensibility of their favours, are the only virtues I possess, and, consequently, all that I can derive any good from: for to my dear friend, to whom my heart hath ever been open, I may confess, that whatever has heretofore felt like life, or been a participation of eternal substance, (though always small, and no doubt the food convenient for me) is now entirely extinguished; and the law, the testimony, and the effusions of some little secret devotion, are all as springs shut up, and fountains sealed. Thou art experienced, and tried with many deep baptisms, with wants and with aboundings; but perhaps such a state of insensibility to, and desertion of, all that seems good and valuable, was never seen meet for thee; thy resignedness rather bringing thee its rewards, those of true obedience, which have built up and compacted as a Jerusalem, the foundations whereof are sure. But if thou knew the different situation of my poor tossed mind, it would, I believe, excite a degree of thy sympathy, and fear that the Tempter will wholly overcome: for now, in this time of deep poverty, the world has indeed occupied much room, and what may be called the enjoyments of it, are as clay fettering that part appointed for immortality."——" I often wonder when better times will come; when, in truth, we can adopt the language of the juſt to their ancient ſource: " ſpring up, O well, ſing ye unto it!" But how can my humiliation be deep enough, when I confeſs, that this fountain appears to be to me, neither ancient nor new?"

1778.——" There is, I believe, an holy intercourſe and communion experienced by thoſe whoſe language is ſimilar and pure, whoſe feet are eſtabliſhed upon the immovable Rock, and whoſe teacher and ſtrength is the ſovereign Lord. This is, I doubt not, one of their rewards; but its ſanctity, its refined and exalted nature, ſeems to exclude me from the participation thereof; for I may confeſs, the painful experience of my mind is often under ſuch a ſtate of deſertion from infinite goodneſs, that I ſcarce dare look towards his holy temple, or addreſs him, but in ſighs unutterable."

1778.——" Let us travel, unitedly travel forward in the path of humble obedience, which tho' tribulated, and thoſe that walk in it have often to experience a ſhare of this legacy, " In the world ye ſhall have trouble," yet the annexed peace, the bread that is handed in ſecret, and the joy with which a ſtranger doth not intermeddle, are ſurely ſufficient rewards in this life, and an earneſt of that which is to come, that glorious reſerve of immortal bliſs. I feel a greater ſolicitude than words can deſcribe, that we may, unitedly, be entitled to it, and partake thereof, and that we may feel this certain mark, that we love one another, even with that love which will subsist beyond the grave. But I wonder how arose these sensations, for I daily conclude myself destitute of any that are good; and in the absence of him whom I wish to be to me the chief of ten thousand, I implore the path of obscurity, and, with the mournful prophet, exclaim in my lonesome habitation, the secret of my heart, " Oh that I had in the wilderness a lodging place! but alas! this will not do, this is not the will of him who desires, not to take us out of the world, but to preserve us from the evil that is therein. It is the path of suffering, it is the cross and the shame that we recoil at; and for want of true dedication of heart, many deep and hidden sorrows are ours."

1779.————" To inform thee, my dear friend, of the secret path I have trod of late, is a thing which I know thy good sense, and experience in the mysteries of godliness, will prevent thy requiring. In the sacred union, we see the necessity of the leaven being hid, which cements together and brings our nature into a oneness, till the whole lump is sanctified. Under this apprehension, I have of late been led to endure many new and severe conflicts, without daring to seek consolation, save from that fountain, which issues in the right time, an inexhaustible stream; but to which I am ready to conclude, I am not entitled to approach."

1779.————"I lately thought the blessing that was craved for us, was abundantly shed, and our walking seemed, a little, as if it was by the pillar and the cloud; but now, the sun and the moon, even those

heavenly bodies which are univerfally diffufed, have, from our eye, withdrawn their light. For my part, I have feveral times concluded, the work is done; and if it be fufficiently, I am glad; but when it feels like the defcription of meat and drink, there wants, not only patience, but refignation; an attainment which appears to me to be a degree harder than the other. Oh may we walk in the way caft up for us, and may we, now our Mofes is withdrawn, be preferved from making a likenefs!"——
" A fouth land" will, I hope, yield thee " fprings of water:" they require hard digging for here; but the fountain is found to be fo deep when come at, that we need not be afraid of the labour. But I have nothing to boaft of, for the refrefhing influence of the waters of this fountain, has, I doubt not, been wifely withheld from me; and to have a channel ready for their return, is, what I endeavour, though feebly, to preferve."

1779.————" My mind has been, for fome time, incapable of deriving any fatisfaction, from either the intercourfe with, or confolation of a friend. And not having any defire to feek comfort, or have any, but from the fountain of it, filence was not only moft confiftent with my judgment, but moft eafy to myfelf, if I found any thing that could bear that character. Floods of diftrefs have indeed nearly overwhelmed me, and I know not where to turn, or where to look; I abhorred myfelf, and beheld not the power that could purify. " When I looked for good, then evil came; and for light, behold, there was darknefs."

1779.———" I went to meeting yesterday morning, with, I thought, some degree of devotedness, and for some time sat in darkness; but after a deep labour of mind, there felt something to gather about me; and with it came my deep rooted dislike to the work; which so strove with the other, that for a time, enduring a state of agony, the meeting broke up. On going in the afternoon, I concluded myself given up, and little expected to feel any thing again at that time : but after sitting a while, the matter again returned, and would, I believe, have terminated the same way, had not a friend stood up with the passage, "He that knew his Lord's will and prepared not himself, neither did according to his will, shall be beaten with many stripes." This did indeed come home, and so operated with what was already kindled, that; after such a conflict as I have cause ever to remember, I ventured upon my knees, and, in a manner I believe scarcely intelligible, poured out a few petitions. Now I feel in such a state of humiliation and fear, as I never before experienced; and my strength, both natural and spiritual, so low, that the floods are ready to come upon me again."

1780.———" I often keep silence, and find myself a subject copious enough for meditation, which is not always of the pleasing kind; but I endeavour to pass along as quietly as I can; it being seldom my lot to experience much sympathy or fellowship with my friends, and, consequently, I cannot expect to derive much from theirs. And yet for all this, I do not mean to complain, but am abundantly convinced, that I lived upon this pleasant fruit, this sensible union, long enough; and to know the want of it, is, I doubt not, sometimes as necessary as its free circulation, which may perhaps return in its season, when it may prove like the dew of Hermon."

1780.———" I cannot but fear thy apprehensions of my alliance to a state of properly attained peace, arise more from thy good wishes to me, as an individual, and from that universal love, which is imprest with a sense of the benevolent extendings of divine regard, that desires all may partake as at the river of life freely, than from a just sense of the real situation of my mind; which has not yet cast its sackcloth covering, nor received a garment of praise. And as this change cannot be effected, but by the miraculous power of the divine arm, I wish only to seek for it from this source of strength; and if it be my lot to go softly all the days of my life, in the bitterness of my soul, I wish to submit to this allotment, and endure the necessary turnings of the divine hand: but Oh! that I had in the wilderness a lodging place, that no eye might see, nor ear hear, the imperfect state of a heart, the depths of whose distress, omnipotence only can fathom."

1780.———" When thy letter, before this last reached me, it was my full intention to have replied to it very soon; but in this, as in the most important and necessary pursuits the human mind can have, the spirit of procrastination prevailed; which I generally find is the case, when the first ability the mind poffeffes to do good, is not accepted. This is a reflection I have often painfully to make, becaufe its fubject never fails to impart a feeling fenfe of weaknefs; and when we confider it properly, that our being here is uncertain, and that the time, wherein we can acquire durable riches, is, though fufficient for the work defigned us, fhort and fleeting, we can fcarce quench an impulfe to vigilance, or view ourfelves in any other light, than fojourners in a land of exile, where the fpirit that is pure, and the light which is the life of men, is oppreffed and rejected, becaufe to the natural eye, it hath neither form nor comelinefs. I may, to my dear friend confefs, that my travel hath long been through a wafte howling wildernefs, where, (though furrounded with innumerable bleffings) my mind hath been led moftly to feel itfelf like a pelican, and to wifh for an outward fituation fimilarly obfcure, that I might for ever be hid from the eyes of men, of whom I often feel a fear that baffles defcription; but as this allotment has not fallen out for me, there feems no way, but fimply to attend to that impulfe which I have apprehended to be divine, and at the fame time am thoroughly willing to be convinced, is not. Thy wifh, that faith may be equal to the trials of my day, was peculiarly applicable; for could I give thee an idea, how often I am ready to fink in the depths of diftrefs, when the weeds are indeed wrapped about my head, and all fupports are either refufed or withdrawn, thou would readily conclude me fhort of faith, and patience too. But no language is able to fet forth that fituation of mind, when the wifdom which is from above, and that which is from beneath are ſtruggling for victory. It is truly a fiery trial, but one which I fear will never in me conſume all the reprobate ſilver. I have ſtumbled on a ſubject, which I had no thoughts of even hinting at, when I began; but in confidence and freedom I have often been led to open my mind to thee, and I truſt That, wherein we were heretofore united, will not fail to ſtrengthen our bond, and open to us a channel of converſe, more hidden and pure than we have yet altogether experienced; and a fellowſhip which is only underſtood, when the myſteries of the true church are opened. Tell me, my beloved friend! art thou paſſing through this wilderneſs, and often ready to faint for want of water? If ſo, allow me to ſay, prolong not thy journey there, through a fearfulneſs of taking thy poſſeſſions in the promiſed land, nor of the inhabitants which are to be ſubdued before it can be enjoyed; for I truſt no tranſient, fading joy, can yield thy mind that peace it deſires: wherefore let not thy hands hang down, but rather put on ſtrength, in the name of him who is able to help, and in whom is the fulneſs of power, and be ſtrong and work; for I believe it is a day, in which this command is gone forth to thoſe whoſe hands are not polluted, and whoſe language is not that of confuſion. Deep are the baptiſms of ſuch, or how could they be fitted to ſtand in that day of trial which is, with a gradual and ſteady pace approaching, if not rooted and eſtabliſhed upon that Rock, againſt which the gates of hell can never prevail. And though theſe, for the preſent, have to drink of that cup of adverfity, whereof our holy pattern firft tafted, and have to be baptized with the baptifm he was baptized with, yet, in the immediate revival of his promifes, from that comforter which he has fent, there remains to be confolation."

In the 4th month 1780, with the approbation of the monthly meeting, and in company with her mother, fhe was engaged in a religious vifit to friends in the counties of Weftmoreland and Cumberland.

The following extracts contain the material parts of what are collected, from her own account of her concern in this vifit.

———"The meeting at Bowes was trying, though I believe fatisfactory to my mother. For my part, I had deep heart-felt mortification, (which I have been very little free from fince) and went very much fatigued to bed, it being ten at night when the meeting broke up, and we had a hard day's work in travelling. Next morning, we fat a little with a fchoolmafter and his wife, to whom there was much opennefs to communicate clofe counfel, as well as encouragement. Next day we went to Penrith, where we ftaid over firft day, and had two fuffering meetings; in both which I felt a greater unwillingnefs to fubmit to a neceffary wading of fpirit, than I can defcribe; for really, the fpring of life requires fuch digging for, in places where the fubftance of religion is departed from, and only the image retained, that, in this exercife, I frequently felt ready to faint, and always engage with it in great dread; becaufe it oppofes that natural part, which would keep the house in peace, and be free from all these troubles. However, I felt more ease of mind in the evening than I could have expected, having drank tea at the house of a widow friend, and had an open, favoured opportunity amongst her daughters, several of whom appear to be under a fresh visitation. We were at the monthly meeting at ———— and a most painful, trying time it was: but after much labour, and deep suffering, the right thing got uppermost, and though the other was not slain, it was a favour that it did not altogether rule. Oh the untempered mortar there is in that place, and the unsoundness almost from the crown of the head, to the sole of the foot! I ventured to stammer out what appeared, though in a manner scarcely intelligible, and in great fear, having previously had specimens of offerings, which carried not the evidence of having been prepared at the altar, and which indeed often create the query, " who shall stand?"

————" Longtown* was, as I expected, a place of some suffering to me; but I could not have expected to have felt myself such a speckled bird as I did, though I kept myself much to myself: but it was impossible to keep as retired as was desirable, nor were my motives for it justifiable, being only to shun the appearance of a fool, amongst a set of wise and fine folks, whom we had at our inn. Indeed, a state of deep heartfelt mortification has been my lot, mostly, since I saw you; but as the cause, without doubt, originates in the impurity of my own mind, I ought to be thankful for dispensations so ne-

* The northern yearly meeting was then held there.

cessary, though hard to bear; for surely there never was any, to whom the simplicity of truth was so irksome, and who caused themselves such deep and hidden conflicts as myself. When one is got over, and another approaches, that disposition, which loves not sorrow, but would walk easily through life, is ready, in the remembrance of what it has suffered, to say, like the king appointed for destruction, I thought the bitterness of death was past; but Oh! how many strokes do I need to accomplish this death! It has been hard for me to have my mind bent under any degree of that weight and suffering, which are generally necessary to feel, before the spring is found to be opened, or any circulation of divine life experienced: because flesh and blood cannot aid in this labour, and, its strength being set at nought, it wars with the spirit: in the feeling whereof, I am often ready to faint. Oh! that my feet may stand fast in the bottom of Jordan; that I may neither flinch from a necessary wading of spirit, nor be overpowered with the floods of the mighty deep; and, above all, that I may be preserved from uttering words without life, for truly, "'I am a child!'"

———" When I wrote you last, my mind was indeed in a sad spot; the billows seemed to go over my head, and life felt almost to be a burden; for I could not at that time, look at our going to Whitehaven without the view of visiting the families, and that work appeared so ungrateful to me, that I could not bear the thoughts of having any thing to do in it. However, I endeavoured to forget it, and to consider that if the thing was right, it would be got through, and that somebody, better able and better skilled than myself, would have the burden to bear, and the work to do; and that if I got mortified with having something to do, now and then, the visit might be of as much benefit to me as to the whole meeting besides. Thus I endeavoured to rest it, when my mind would submit to think coolly on the subject; and indeed I had almost lost the painful impression when we got to Whitehaven, till we both felt it in the forenoon meeting on 1st day, with this conclusion, that to yield was the only way to leave the place in peace. My mother having previous to her view of this visit, concluded to have a meeting at Maryport on 3d day, found herself most easy to pursue that plan, and accordingly we went on 2d day afternoon. We found that the right time was fixed on for Maryport, and a favoured meeting it was, there being much openness to labour, indeed far more than in some places where a greater appearance is retained; but where, it is sorrowfully to be felt, the mighty are fallen, and tribes are lacking amongst them. There are many such places in this county, as well as in ours; and under a sense thereof, we have known a going bowed down all the day long. After this meeting, we returned to, and proceeded in, the work at Whitehaven. The labours in this visit were of the mortifying kind, and required a continual exercise of both faith and patience: because we had generally to sit where the people sat, which was often in dismal places; but being, I trust, in the right line, it will be made more profitable than could then be seen. It got finished on 6th day, and in the evening there was a meeting appointed to begin at 5 o'clock; which was, like all the visit before, a suffering meeting; but I hope the rightly concerned in that place, will reap the benefit of it, for it was, though painful, a remarkable time. It is with a degree of thankfulness I may acknowledge, that I felt in this visit, a greater resignation to what I apprehended was the divine will, than I ever experienced before; and I can, now it is over, cheerfully submit to the belief, that I was of no use, (if even preserved from doing harm) but that the thing was made useful to me, in subjecting my own mind, and teaching me, by a little more experience, the true way to wisdom, which is first becoming a fool. This state of preparation I expect to be in, all my life long; but I wish, (with a fear) that it may be so abode in, as to obtain the prize at last. Well, this trial is over, with being refused, reviled, and fought with as by beasts at Ephesus; yet these are small troubles indeed, when compared with the enemies of our own houses, that host of opposition which is often hard to press through. This woe is past, and I pray in my heart that another of the same kind may not soon come; for though I was favoured to feel it made much easier to me than I could have expected, yet the work of visiting families has always, since I was led seriously to consider it, appeared to be so awful, and to require the royal signet to be so evidently affixed, that the fear is great, of either moving without it, or being concerned in so momentous a work, when there is not strength enough to support, and wisdom to teach."

On their way home, they felt a concern to visit the families of friends at Kendal; near the conclusion of which, she says, "The spirits and body seem both ready to fail under the present exercise; but we have no reason to repent engaging with it; for, thus far, we have experienced strength sufficient for the day." Soon after her return from this journey, she writes concerning it as follows: " After many close exercises and deep trials, mine chiefly of my own making, we are now enjoying a good degree of peaceful serenity, and though (I think) sufficiently stripped, yet we seem pretty clear of any painful reflections on the past allotment.

Towards the latter end of the year 1780, she came under a religious concern to join her friend and relative T. Hoyland, in a visit to the meetings of Cheshire, and a part of those in Lancashire. And having the concurrence of the monthly meeting, and a certificate thereof, she set forward to engage in this service, in the 12th month. The ensuing parts of her letters on the subject, afford some account of this journey, and shew the situation of her mind, under the prospect of the work before her, and in the prosecution and completion thereof.

————" Cheshire has long attracted my mind, and of late more than usual; and on my cousin T. H. laying a similar concern before me, those feelings revived with some weight; and not without a great fear lest, (though the impulse might be right) the time and companion might not be in the fame appointment: and hence appeared the necessity of having it hewed and squared.

————" It is only in a little faith that I look towards the journey in prospect, and at the rectitude of it; and though I fear it is not equal to a grain of mustard seed, yet I think I am thankful for this little: and since it has been received, and the affair mentioned, a degree of peacefulness and quietude hath attended my mind, which is all the light I find upon it; and which requires sometimes, all my vigilance to retain, lest the floods from the mouth of the dragon should overwhelm, and cast away that little strength that is at present afforded; and instead of adding thereto by devotedness, to be any thing or nothing, leave me tossed upon the unstable element, where neither rock nor shore can sometimes be perceived."

————" It was not indeed the least of my concern, or rather dislike, to submit to the thoughts of going to some places in Lancashire, which I had in view; for, indeed, that seemed not much less than giving up my life: and this proceeded from considerations which I think thou canst hardly share, having surmounted many of the difficulties and mortifications which appear very formidable to me. But when we have suffered for disobedience, and are favoured with a view of the rewards of the faithful, and are likewise convinced of the importance of our duties, though ever so small in appearance; when our nothingness is sufficiently felt, and our minds impressed with the awfulness of the divine requirings; life itself looks but a small sacrifice, and so reasonable, that there is no excuse for withholding it, especially that inward existence which does not co-work with the life of true religion".

————" From Ackworth, I had a companion who imparted some good and wholesome counsel to me, and more encouragement, than I could have looked for; but my secret sitting was in the dust, and much gloom seemed to cover my little views. I reflected on the preceding evening, and found its enjoyment was then like manna two days old, having lost both favour and nourishment; and instead of a renewal of the same, a fast was dispensed, the cause of which I must leave; but it is a painful one, and if I had felt myself before I left home, as I have done since, it is much if the venture had been made. Could I believe that this is any thing like going forth without either scrip or purse, I should perhaps be more reconciled. I am thankful that, in every state I have some degree of the comfortable impression, that unity is good; and though mine is not of the most expansive kind, yet in a renewed feeling of my little, I cannot but wish, that we may be so willing to suffer together, and frequently to go down to the potter's house, to be there fashioned and formed either for vessels of honour or dishonour, (as may best please him who hath power over the clay) that we may also experience an humble ascent to the house of true prayer, and a rejoicing together. My heart is too full for words to relieve, but being convinced that there is a better and more refined intercourse than this, a communion which, proportioned to our obedience, is pure and edifying, I wish in that to remember, and be remembered."

——"We went to Lowlayton on 6th day, and found there but one family of friends, who came in by convincement. It was a comfortable place; for their simplicity and integrity rendered their cottage an agreeable mansion, in which there was nothing painful to be felt. The meeting there next day, was much larger than we looked for, many people in the neighbourhood coming in, whose solid, innocent countenances, were, I thought, as likely to do us good, as we to do them any. It was a satisfactory meeting, and afforded some encouragement to proceed. We went to Stockport on 7th day afternoon; the meeting on first day was a painful, trying one, and yet strength was not withheld. From Macclesfield we came to Leek, and have just finished (except one family) a visit to the families here. We have had eight sittings to day, besides the weekday meeting, which has been close work. We are however (and have cause to be) thankful, that strength equal to the undertaking has been afforded; and though we have been deeply tried, yet, upon the whole, I believe we may acknowledge, that we have lacked nothing, and have been much united to a few in this place. This work of visiting families, is the last I should choose for myself, if I might be my own chooser; but as it is wrong to desire that indulgence, I see I may as well give myself up to what appears in the line of duty.—It is with thankfulness of heart, that I acknowledge myself in a tolerable degree of health, through many different dispensations which have fallen to my lot since I saw you; for there have been experienced a wanting, and a sufficient abounding; but I wish I could add, that in every state I have learned to be content. Great indeed hath been the condescension of him who is pleased to make use of poor, weak instruments, and by things which not only appear low and contemptible, but are so in reality, to bring to nought, and reduce things that are mountains in prospect; proving to us a present help in every needful time, and, by his invisible power, strengthening us when we are ready to faint in our minds. And still greater, I may acknowledge, hath appeared his wisdom in deeply trying us, or however myself, with the most abject poverty and strippedness of mind; indeed so much so, that I think I never before experienced such humility, in a sense of myself, and, under the convincing proof, that of ourselves we can do nothing. This is a situation wherein we see whence all good comes, and the necessity of casting ourselves so wholly upon the divine arm, as to have no confidence in the flesh. No dispensation, however desirable the enjoyment of good may be, seems so much to drive us to the root of life, if we endeavour sufficiently to profit by it; and consequently, none that we ought to be so thankful for, when our hearts are capable of feeling true gratitude; for he who knows the weakness of our frames, and is touched with a feeling of our infirmities, sees what we can bear, and knows how frail we are. Thus have I, in this little journey, been wisely taught, through many trials, to live by faith; and thus far, in reflecting on the past, to own I have lacked nothing. But we are abundantly convinced, that they who are sent out in this day, to a people who have, in a great measure, forsaken both law and testimony, and what is still worse, see not their states, but are secure in themselves, have not to eat much pleasant bread: for I think I may say, it hath often been our lots to go bowed down all the day long, and to mourn in a deep sense of the great desolation which overspreads the society: insomuch, that we often admire that there should be any sent out to visit them, and that the feet of those that are rightly shod, should not more generally be turned to others: for from these, there are the greatest hopes in this county, which is likely, in many places, to be left desolate of friends who keep their places. We have, however, in a few of the meetings which we have last attended, been agreeably disappointed, in finding more preserved or quickened by the life of religion, than we expected; and it hath been our lot to visit these, as well as a very contrary sort, by families. A very trying work it hath been, and it is not yet done. In it I have often lamented, lest for want of that spirit of discerning, with which the prophet was endued, when he went to anoint one of the sons of Jesse, there should not be a right division of the word, and thereby much harm be done. And under this consideration, great abasedness hath attended my mind, and a desire that the fleece may be tried both wet and dry. We left Namptwich undone, and hoped, nay even refolved, to return to it no more; but now I have to confefs, we are on our way thither. It is however a favour, that, through all, we are led to feel and fympathize one with another; I mean my companion and felf, and that our little fervices have been harmonious; and if we keep near that preferving arm which hath been with us, I doubt not but this ftrength will continue and increafe; for in unity, if it be of the right kind, there is certainly ftrength."———" We got to Manchefter, after a week of many probations, which ended better than we could have looked for, at the beginning of it, when our hearts were ready to faint, and the billows feemed to run over our heads, in the feeling of what we had already fuffered, in remembering the affliction and diftrefs, the wormwood and the gall. Our minds were humbled in the profpect of an opening field; but I truft it was He who commanded the waves to be ftill, that calmed thefe floods, and renewed a degree of faith and patience to perfevere in the tribulated way. What need there is to keep near to the fountain of life, and to receive our refrefhment folely from it! becaufe from thence only, arife our frefh fprings, and immortal food; which, though the bread of adverfity and the water of affliction, yet coming from this fource, it is no lefs efficacious to the nourifhing, ftrengthening, and building us up, than the fenfible union with divine purity. Our hearts are very incapable of judging, concerning the virtue of the difpenfations of providence; we know not ourfelves, and confequently, cannot prefcribe for ourfelves. How paffive then, and how like little children, should we be to him that searcheth the heart? but I am often afraid, lest, by indulging my own ideas of what is good, and not labouring after a total resignation of mind, but wanting to have things in my own way, I should frustrate the divine intention, which may be to humble and reduce self, more than flesh and blood would point out. The great meetings we meet with, are almost overmuch for us, and what made it still worse to us at Liverpool, was a funeral in the afternoon, and a vast number of people. We little thought when we fixed to stay over 2d day at Manchester, that we should have one to attend there, which is the case this afternoon, and how it will be got over, I know not. If we may but be favoured to be rightly quiet, it is all we desire; and if we cannot be that, it is certainly our best way, as far as we are able, to take up the cross, and despise the shame; which sometimes feels great, and at others, I may thankfully acknowledge, is in a great measure removed: but then, what need there is of care not to overrun the guide, and work without the power of the word? Dangers surround us on every hand, and our standing often seems as on a sea of glass."

————" With satisfaction and pleasure, I have lately looked towards home; indeed with so much, that a fear sometimes strikes me, lest in wisdom some unforeseen affliction should be sent to moderate it. According to my present feelings, I am returning peaceful and easy; and though we have missed some meetings, which I own I had a view of, yet it was with a full belief, that they will not be laid to my charge. I wish that we may be thankful enough for the favours we have received divers ways, since we left home; and, what appears to me no small one, for the readiness of my beloved connections, in making every thing as easy as outward means can possibly do, and affording accommodations, for want of which many lie under very great difficulties. The consideration of these things often affects my mind."

Bradford, 19th of 1st month 1781.

———" I thought, when we left Manchester, that it was a strange thing if we did not return to it again; yet I had since lost the impression, further than wondering why such a thought should then have struck me; and even the concern about many meetings, which I thought we had missed, was so much gone off my mind, (where it had dwelt with some weight) that I seemed perfectly easy, under the belief that the concern would devolve on my companion, but little expected it was so soon to be evinced: for after much secret sorrow, which I perceived, but durst not pronounce my apprehensions of the cause, she disclosed last night her uneasiness, and desire to return to the places we passed by, as well as to go to some others in this county. On looking a little seriously at it, (indeed not a little, for we had nearly a sleepless night) I could not see that it was less than my duty to return with her; not only from having had a view of the same places, but as a companion, which, if truly one, cannot leave in the day of trouble. I wish myself better qualified to sympathize with her in this trial, which is a very great one, and requires all the alleviations that are in my power to bestow. I believe her willingness is now so great, that, for the purchase of a little peace, she would return to all the places, to do the things which appeared needful, and were not fully joined in with; but when this great sacrifice of the will is completely made, I trust some ram will be caught in the thicket, or some smaller offering accepted. Home now looks at a great distance, and I find that it will contribute most to my peace, to think as little of it as I well can; and if it had been less in my mind of late, this turn in our affairs, would by me, have been less felt. We find ourselves after the meeting to-day, in a very gloomy situation of mind; as it was a suffering time, and we thought left us with the sentence of death in ourselves; perhaps that we may not trust in ourselves, which I ardently wish we may be preserved from. We intend going to Leeds to-morrow evening; we dread it not a little, and this day's work increases the apprehension of very great suffering; but it often seems best to leave, or draw the mind from future trials, and endeavour, as well as we can, to bear those of the present day, which are generally found to be sufficient."

Manchester, 4th of 2d month 1781.

―――"Our minds are often bowed down, under a sense of the awfulness of our engagements, and dismayed at the sight; nor need I say how closely our time is filled up therewith; for after sitting with seven or eight families, we are generally ready for rest. I have the very great satisfaction now to say, that, except one family, we have finished in this place; have had four to day, beside the two meetings, and upwards of forty since we began, with putting now and then two together. We were at Stockport on 4th day, and had it unexpectedly in our power, to pay off a small debt, which we contracted when there before. It has been wonderful to us, how we have been, and are likely to be, turned to places, and thrown in the way of doing our first works; which we cannot but view, as a mark of divine condescension to our infant state: Indeed it hath been manifested to us, far beyond what we could have looked for, in the course of this journey throughout; and not less so since we came into this place, where instruction hath been daily administered from different sources; some of which have proved deeply trying to flesh and blood; but being, I trust, in the ordering of unerring wisdom, I wish (perhaps more than I endeavour) to profit patiently thereby, and value the rod as well as the staff. It is indeed high time to number our blessings. They are truly many, and we cannot fail of seeing and feeling them; that of having the parental care and solicitude of several of our much honoured and valued friends, is not small in our estimation."

————" We have now got to Warrington, and are endeavouring to keep ourselves quiet, and, as much as we can, labour to feel what is the divine will concerning us; which, with respect to our coming here, hath been much a myftery. The profpect almoft difmays us, attended with a fear, that we may now be in danger of compaffing a mountain in the wildernefs, and engage in a fervice, for which our ftrength is not proportioned; and fo, notwithftanding we have been favoured with divine condefcenfion to our ftates heretofore, bring upon ourfelves unneceffary trials, and thereby pierce our minds, in future, with many forrows. It is no fmall concern to us to find, with the prefent view of things, every qualification wanting for fuch a fervice; and our minds greatly ftripped of ftrength and clear difcerning: and to move without a renewal of thefe, we dare not. When my companion firft propofed our return, the evidence I thought was fo ftrong, that I cheerfully complied; yet feelings very unlike thefe enfued, even a ftate of deep diftrefs and mortification, when I found we muft turn our backs on home, and return from whence we came, to do our firft works. Great was our pain, from, I believe, an unfubjected will; but great likewife and evident, was the operation of the divine hand, in judgment upon us for the paft, and, no doubt, as a preparation for the future; for it never appeared clearer to me, than when under this difpenfation, that for every frefh fervice and work in the church, we muft experience a renewed baptifm of fpirit, and purification of the gift; and that the more we have of the drofs, or the reprobate filver, the more frequently muft we pafs through the r ... ing fire. Notwithftanding I was, fometimes, ...

impatience of my heart, ready to query as the children of Israel did, "were there not graves enough in Egypt, that we are brought hither to die;" yet there were times, when all that was within me, was prostrated under the chastising hand, and sought that it might not spare. How preferable is it to all secondary administrations of judgment, when, with David, we wish rather to fall into the Lord's hands, than into the hands of man! and surely, the more we seek to derive our instruction and food from the fountain of good, the less we shall be subject to instrumental means."

————" I never felt myself under such complicated discouragements at any time; and Oh! that we may both be enabled to bear these fiery trials, with resignation to the divine will, and seek to profit by them, that the state of a weaned child may become our experience."

————" As I make no doubt it will be acceptable to thee to hear from two poor pilgrims, who are almost worn out with things that appear too mighty for them, I just embrace a little vacant time, to hint how we have fared; and may in the first place say, that the present engagement hath been the most trying of the kind we ever experienced. It hath been frequently our lot, to go down as to the bottom of the mountains, where the earth with her bars, was about us; under this pressure, our minds have been secretly clad with sackcloth and deep mourning, when it has evidently appeared, that the pure life of religion is in a state of bondage, and that it sensibly utters the language, "I am oppressed under you, as a cart with sheaves." To visit this seed of the kingdom, we find to be no light matter, especially when hid under the briers and thorns, and then plumed with human wisdom; who indeed is sufficient for these things? I often lament, and with reason, that my heart is not more bound to the cause, and more willing to suffer for it; and I fully believe, that until this is more experienced, there will remain to be, as there have already been, many trials and afflictions, which originate not in the divine will; for it is still a truth, that our greatest enemies are those of our own houses, and that to endeavour to subdue these, is our indispensable duty: but oh! what strokes are in wisdom administered to us, to destroy that life which hath no existence in the divine purity; and except we be faithful unto this death, we can with no probability look for the crown immortal. We have frequently had to recur to the moving cause of this journey, and, as an additional trial, found the feeling sense of that withdrawn from us; but all these things teach us where to place our present dependance; and notwithstanding dispensations thus painful have been our portion, we have great cause, thankfully to commemorate the blessings of the divine and bountiful hand, which hath been strength in our weakness, riches in our poverty, and a present helper in the needful time; and hath refreshed our drooping spirits, insomuch that, with alacrity of heart, we have pursued the path cast up for us, and have been favoured to see the great necessity of passing frequently through the furnace; and oh! saith my heart, that I may be willing to descend again and again, till He whose invisible arm sustaineth us there, is pleased to say, " it is enough."

———" We have now finished, for what we know, our engagement at Warrington. We wound up all in this family last evening; but oh what a day was yesterday! my companion's situation and mine were very different, though both trying; and the more so, because we were not alike led; but still there is a secret trust, that we were both in our places. The meeting was held at Penketh, and being the preparative meeting, was very large. The first meeting was so low and painful in the forepart, that I was glad secretly to offer myself to do any thing, if light might but shine upon my dwelling. In this situation, I soon saw that we had nothing to do in that sitting; but it seemed as if I heard a voice, " visit the men and women when separated, for they require different food." The evidence was, I thought, so strong, that I earnestly desired to be preserved faithful, however hard it might be to the creature, lest a worse state should befal me. When the meetings parted, I just requested my companion, to feel if it might not be best to go into the men's meeting: her reply was, " she had seen nothing of it, but would go with me." This greatly increased the burden that was upon my mind, but remembering my recent view and request, I durst not, after all the favours I had received at the divine hand, in our late probationary visit, refuse a compliance with this intimation of duty; and finding I had a little strength, was made willing, with that, to become still more a spectacle to angels and to men, than before in this place.—I believe I had my companion's sympathy, but she said she had nothing to do; which I own, so discouraged me, with the painful apprehension that I had been out of my place, led by an unsanctified zeal, or, at least, had so imprudently administered the right thing, that I had already done more harm than good; so that, though there was a covering of good over the women's meeting, and a little ability to relieve my own mind at least, I so lost faith, and gave way so much, to thinking myself quite spent and exhausted, that I managed to bring my load away with me; which, added to the mortifying remembrance of what I had done, nearly sunk me for a time into the deepest distress. But by endeavouring to keep it to myself, (my greatest discouragements however) and to recur to what I apprehended, was the moving cause of my doing and leaving undone, there ensued a little quietness, and a small, but comfortable evidence, that the offering of obedience, as far as it had been made, was acceptable; and that what was omitted, was viewed with divine, compassionate regard to the weakness, and not wilfulness, of my poor depressed mind. And notwithstanding we had three sittings afterwards, and my body almost as ill as I thought it could be, to bear up, yet there felt to me full as much strength and life, as I have found before in this place; and this morning I feel so refreshed with the foregoing, and a good night's rest, that I don't know that I have a complaint of any sort; only I could wish for a little more clearness respecting some approaching days. Thus I comfortably and thankfully experience, that though forrow has come for a long night in this place, joy fprings in the morning. When the fun of righteoufnefs, in any degree, arifes, and the mind feels its refrefhing influence, how does it encourage to prefs forward, and to think nothing too hard to fubmit to, for this excellent appearance! but how ready, like the difciples, are we to folicit that our tabernacles may be built here, and we not defcend into the lower parts of the earth again, there to be covered with its bars, and feel ourfelves as at the bottom of the mountains; though it is from thence, we are led to look for a better habitation, and to labour that the pure life may arife, and we be favoured to dwell with it, though feldom in a ftate of dominion, remembering for our inftruction, that Aaron the great high-prieft, was permitted to enter into the holy of holies but once a year, for his common fervice was in the tabernacle. —I cannot but look upon this morning, which feels pleafanter than many, to be perhaps the opening of another tribulating day; for it does not appear a time for fuch as are, in the fmalleft degree, able to be baptized into the prefent ftate of the church, to eat much pleafant bread: but I wifh I was more preferved from thofe infirmities of darkening counfel, &c. in times of proving, when a gulf feems to open for prefent deftruction. Oh what a trial, or trials of this fort have we had in this place! but I wifh to forget thefe toils, and rather feek for greater wifdom to bear the future. It is marvellous to me, how things are brought about, that we have had views of, but no probability of being effected; and particularly with refpect to this monthly meeting, which I thought I faw, before we fet off from home, and often wondered when we were leaving Lancafhire, how fuch things could be? and fometimes, on that account, was ready to call all in queftion; finding many fuch caufes of difcouragement, which now feem gradually removing."

Liverpool, 20th of 2d month, 1781.

———" The fellowfhip and tendernefs of our friends was never more defirable, than in thefe days of deep probation and inftruction. Wonders are indeed yet manifefted in the deeps, where, finding the demonftration of the fpirit and power, even my ftrong heart has, to my own admiration, been made willing to receive the bittereft of cups; and all that is within me, has bowed and done obeifance to him, before whom I have had daily and piercingly to abhor myfelf; under renewed, powerful, evidences, that without the frequent adminiftration of the holy Ghoft and fire, and repeatedly defcending to the wafhing pool, there is no offering an acceptable facrifice; and that this muft be a difpenfation for life, if ever any offering is found to be without blemifh, which I fear it never will; but if preferved with fpiritual fight, and a neceffary jealoufy over myfelf, I fhall, I truft, fo far deem myfelf bleffed.—How are fuch as move in this line to be pitied! their ftanding cannot be better defcribed, than as being on a fea of glafs, mingled with fire. But I would not fay any thing to difcourage, nor would I wifh to be like the evil fpies; therefore may add, that from what I have feen of the good land, attainable at times in this work, it is well worth our preffing after, and its fruit is fo pleafant, that it amply refreshes the weary traveller. I could, yefterday morning, fet my feal to the truth of this; but alas! the fcene then has, fince changed much. We were at the monthly meeting at Hartfhaw to day, for which we have both caufe to be thankful; not becaufe the food was pleafant, but becaufe it was, we truft, wholefome; and this evening we are come to this place, to which we fet off in the bitternefs of our fpirits. It looks indeed often to my mind, as if a fingular vifitation is renewedly extended to our fociety; but there is a painful fear, that the day will pafs over the heads of many: yet, with it, a hope fprings, that there are others who will be purified, tried, and made white."

York, 3d of 3d month, 1781.

————" Many of our late tribulations appear to me, more and more, to have been in the orderings of divine wifdom; and fuch as have more evidently arifen from our unwillingnefs to fubmit to the humbling power of the crofs, will furely be profitably remembered by us, and gradually work that patience and pure refignation of heart, which can enable us, in holy confidence, to rejoice, and count it all joy, when we fall into divers temptations and tribulations, for the trial and refinement of our faith in him, who was made perfect through fu fering. My mind, has, in general, fince my return home, felt a state of deep prostration, and humble gratitude to that all-ruling power, which hath, I fully believe, helped us in our late engagements, and would more eminently have done it, if our minds had borne a greater similarity to the passive clay. Great instruction arises in the commemoration of these things. To feel our minds centred in a quiet submission to the present allotment, now we are returned, and a willingness either to do or suffer, appears the most desirable state for us, and is what I hope thou largely experiencest."

In the twelfth month 1781, with the approbation of the monthly meeting, she was concerned in a religious visit, to a part of the families within the monthly meeting of Owstwick and Cave. Although her steppings along in this service, were attended with close trials, yet she was enabled to perform it, with a degree of peace and satisfaction; which appears from her own expressions on this occasion: " We have got along as well as we could have looked for, considering the prevailing declension and weakness of the present day; which in these, as well as in many other places, widely spread themselves. Deep suffering, and a painful exercise of mind, are often our lot; but being, I trust, in a good degree resigned thereto, they are, at times succeeded with a calm, and a little evidence, that the servant is not wholly disunited from the master."

She was engaged, in the 1st month 1782, in a visit to some families, which had not been visited by the friends who had lately been concerned in a family-visit in that quarter. At the conclusion of this visit, she remarks as follows, "It was, I think, the most trying service of the kind that I ever had any sense of; the general unfeelingness and impenetrableness of the visited, rendered the labour almost without hope. So greatly departed are many amongst us, from the virtue of heavenly dew, that it is now deemed an unnecessary attainment."

CHAP. II.

Her Marriage—and Journey into Scotland, Cumberland, &c.

IN the 4th month 1782, she was married to our friend Robert Grubb, of Clonmel in Ireland, who had for some time resided at York; to whom she was a faithful and tender companion, and a sympathizing, strengthening helpmeet, in the various probations of their spiritual pilgrimage. On this subject, the following instructive letter, written some months afterwards, appears to be worthy of insertion."

―――" It was an awful thing to me, to enter into this new sphere. I am now blessed with all, and more than I had any right to ask for in it. I wish to number these blessings, and approve myself worthy of them. This belief ever accompanies my mind, that if we wrest not ourselves out of the divine hand, whose fatherly care and protection is over us, our cup of life will be so blended, as to prevent our sitting down in outward enjoyments. Few and fleeting are the days of our pilgrimage; and every additional experience confirms the sentiment, that our solid satisfaction depends not on our possessing all that the unmortified part in us can desire; for there still remains, in the immortal part, a void, which immortal substance only, can satisfy. To have this supplied with wholesome food, and every other gratification to stand subordinate thereto, is the present secret breathing of my spirit: that so, the blessing of preservation may attend us, and patience have its perfect work, till the burning of the Lord's day hath done its office, and a quiet centre in everlasting repose, is obtained."

About two weeks after this event, she entered on a religious visit to friends in Scotland, in company with her friend Mary Proud; having previously obtained a certificate of concurrence from the monthly meeting. This concern had, for many months, dwelt frequently on her mind, and had now matured so, that she thought it her duty to engage in it, at this time. Her feelings under the view of it, and in the prospect of her marriage, with her resignation to the service, and desires for divine preservation and direction; are, in some measure, set forth, by the following extracts from some of her letters, written on those occasions.—" I cannot be on the verge of such important, and some new, concerns, without feeling deep anxiety, and many fears: my mind is often so deeply oppressed with my present load, that I feel continually bowed down under it, and not very fit for this employ. The mind and body seldom suffer alone, and it is comfortable to believe, that they are not intended to be always, or long companions. I have not been very well of late, which is not to be wondered at, nor is it worth much attention."

————" The sentiment thou drops respecting Scotland, is so exactly similar to my own, that it was like a little strength handed in the time of need; and I greatly wish, if the thing be proved to be right, to be enabled to make a sacrifice of every selfish inclination; that my offerings and prayers, in this one step, may be pure and acceptable to Him who sees in secret. But I often feelingly remember a saying of M. Peisley's, that she was " torn as between heaven and earth;" and it many times is matter of doubt, in which I shall centre. I have as much nature as most, and as great an aptness to cover myself with it, and live upon it; and though to be thus drawn from such a source, is cause of thankfulness, yet it seems like the pangs of death, and I sometimes query, whether my natural body will not fall under the operation. Was it not for, now and then, experiencing my strength a little renewed, and my mind clothed with the quietness of that habitation, which the arrows of the archers cannot penetrate, I must fall to the opposition of the enemy in myself; but when the arm of power is felt to be near, then it is, that we rejoice in the means of our salvation."

————" There is still a secret belief, that the growth and cultivation of my views respecting a northern journey, were, by that hand, from which I have apprehended my most important engagements have proceeded; and though it has, for many months, dwelt frequently upon my mind, yet I cherished a belief, that it was very far off; till the prospect of settling in a new line of life drew nearer, and then, this distant view as fast approached. It was afresh revived when I wrote to thee last; but I wished to try it still a little longer, if, in the kindness of Him, who knows my great unfitness for an engagement so important, my resignation to it might be an acceptable sacrifice. Instead of this, the weight increased, and I found, on complying with some early proceedings in another affair, that my peace materially depended, on having thee informed of what I had in view; that thereby this concern might keep pace with the other, and I attend to what may appear to be my own business, no further, than resignation to a superior service was experienced. My dear friend knows the necessity of an entire surrender of ourselves, to what appears, in the pointings of duty, to be our proper business, and of keeping our eye as steadily to that as we can; that so, by its singleness, we may have light sufficient for the work of our day. And as, without this quiet attention, we are often led into doubts, fears, and many reasonings, so we are frequently found to require provings of mind, strippings, and many baptisms, in order to fit us for the state, in which alone there is safety; a truly humble, dependant state, reduced of ourselves, and seeking that honour, which cometh from God only. It is with great awfulness I look at the work before us, and under a deep sense, how unable we are of ourselves, at all to help forward the cause, wherein we desire to be engaged, or to bring honour to that name (either amongst us as a society, or those who are not of our fold) to which the nations may yet be seen to gather. It is desirable, however, that our dwelling may be deep, that the wisdom and instruction we receive, may, (though small) be pure; that if we venture to move, the cloud may sensibly be taken off the tabernacle, and we careful to follow the appointed guide, for our days and nights, and be favoured, in this day of deep degeneracy, with an evidence, that we have done what we could."

The following is an account of her journey through Scotland, &c. taken from a short journal written by herself, and found amongst her papers.

―――" 'The twentieth of the fourth month, 1782, I left York, with my friend M. Proud, for the yearly meeting at Edinburgh, intending from thence, to visit the friends in Scotland, Cumberland, &c. We were at Thirsk on first day, the twenty first, where we sensibly felt the pure life of religion to be at a low ebb, though the professors thereof are numerous; and such as have been anointed for, and employed in, the Lord's work, dwell amongst them. But these being only standard-bearers, whilst they continue exercised in the Lamb's war, and prove their loyalty to the King of kings, by their careful attention to his pointings, and humble walking before him, have need to live under an awful sense of the importance of that service, to which they are called: that so, their spirits may be kept savoury, their conversation, likewise, seasoned with the heavenly salt, ministering grace to those that hear. For want of the Lord's servants, or those in the foremost ranks of the people, being thus preserved near that power, in which their life and their strength consist, great declension has happened to us, as a people; and those, who have been looking for the substantial part of religion in them, have, instead of finding its influence, received, by the lightness of the conduct of such, a warrant for their own propensities. Under the consideration of these things, I was affected, and feeling the aptness of my disposition to yield to the like infirmities, I was led, renewedly, to beg for strength. Notwithstanding we had to suffer with the seed in this place, and to behold the breaches which are made as in the walls of the royal city, yet, a renewed visitation was extended to many, and especially to the youth; and our minds were a little encouraged to press forward in the work before us, under a fresh sense of divine regard. The next day, we left Thirsk, and my husband, who had accompanied us thus far, went with us a few miles further on this day's journey; and after we parted, my mind felt a covering of divine love to replenish it, with faith and patience; and, from a little sensible experience, I could thankfully say, with a disciple formerly, "I have left all to follow thee." And under a renewed sense of this holy attachment, and of my own unfitness for the service before me, without frequent baptisms of spirit, and the sanctifying power thereof, I was inwardly favoured with some new instructions, respecting the office of a minister of Christ, and openings how to fulfil that office: and thus, I was led to acknowledge, that he who had called is faithful, and his grace is fufficient for us, as our dependance is placed thereon, and all confidence in ourfelves removed. We attended a meeting on third day, and had, painfully, to feel the ftate of things amongft them; and it appeared clear to my mind, that the work was in the Lord's hands, and that he will, in his own time, make manifeft the hidden things of darknefs; when thofe that retain a little life amongft them, will be enabled to renew their ftrength, and fhew themfelves on the Lord's fide, though their numbers may be few. We were favoured in fome degree, to relieve our own minds, and left them that afternoon.

The next day we were at a meeting which, for fome time, was a painful fitting, under a fenfe that the leaders of the people caufed them to err, and were crying, "the word of the Lord," when the Lord had not fent them. But after experiencing fomething of the baptifm unto death, with our holy High Prieft, we were favoured to feel the refurrection of life; in which, judgment was placed on the head of the tranfgrefling nature, and the minds that were defirous to know fomething of the work of religion for themfelves, were pointed to the means of redemption from fin. From thence we went to Newcaftle, and were at their week-day meeting on fifth day, where truth, meafurably, prevailed. On fixth and feventh days, being the twenty-fixth and twenty-feventh of the month, we travelled from Newcaftle to Kelfo, and were at their meetings on firft day, which are very fmall of friends, but many others came in, especially in the afternoon; and though, at first, they appeared rude and ignorant, yet the power of truth, in which the authority is felt, rose so into dominion, that it became a solemn opportunity. And thus we had fresh cause to observe, that it is only by divine strength, that we can run through a troop, or leap over the walls of opposition. On second day, we went to Edinburgh, where, on third we rested, and on fourth and fifth attended the yearly meeting, which was but small, there being very few members of society of that nation then present. There were several, who, through neglect of christian discipline, think they have a claim to the society, as being the offspring of friends; others were like the Philistines in whose hands the ark of the testimony is fallen, and esteemed by them as a contemptible thing; there were also present a number of students from distant parts, whose parents are not only members of society, but some of them useful therein. On account of all these, our minds were painfully exercised: and notwithstanding the public meetings were large, and owned with divine favour, in covering these assemblies with a degree of holy awe, and the minds of some of his servants with gospel power and authority, to declare the way of life and salvation: yet through all, the sense of deep, hidden, as well as flagrant corruption, so impressed my mind, that I was led to believe, truth will never prosper in this place, nor the excellency of it appear unveiled, till, not only the branches of the corrupt tree are cut off, but the root so dug up that the remembrance thereof may rot; and then, there is a hope that the present planting may get watered the ground renewedly cultivated, and fruits appear to the praise of the great Husbandman. Deep discouragement attends the Lord's exercised servants in this day, when labour is added to labour, baptism to baptism, for those that are dead in trespasses and sins, and for those that are unacquainted, in their own experience, with the glad tidings of the gospel; so that, if they were not at times refreshed with a little bread handed in secret, and their evidence confirmed, that the foundation of God stands sure, having this seal that the Lord knows them that are his, they would be ready to faint in the work, and to shrink in the day of battle, when the arrows of the archers surround, and the spirits of the people are opposing sound doctrine, and crying "prophesy unto us smooth things." But I have had frequently of late, under these discouraging views, to remember the prophet when he mournfully exclaimed; "I have laboured in vain, and spent my strength for nought;" yet recollecting himself in holy confidence in, and interest with, invisible and divine justice, he added, "but surely my judgment is with the Lord, and my work with my God." From some necessary baptisms of mind, and renewed evidences that this is enough for any true minister of the gospel to desire, I have been led awfully and humbly to implore increasing strength and ability, to walk before that gracious eye that sees in secret, without seeking the praise, or regarding the censure of men who are not circumcised in heart and ears, and who cannot discern, or value, sound uncondemnable words, but want their sensual wisdom and depraved ideas gratified with the divinations of men, and approbation of themselves. We had an exercising, close, and searching opportunity on fifth day evening (after the public meetings were over) with those under profession with us, and particularly the students; to whom divine regard was eminently manifested, and a powerful call extended, to close in with the present visitation and day of salvation that is offered; whereby they would be redeemed from that wisdom which separates them from the pure fear of God, and the tree of immortal life; and also preserved from going down to the chambers of death, by falling in with those snares and gilded pollutions, with which the unwearied enemy of our souls is seeking to entrap and defile us. Their minds were sensibly affected, at that time, under the power of truth; and he who was pleased thus to influence their spirits, is alone able to prosper the work*. The next morning

---

* It is difficult to suppress a remark, respecting young men of our society being sent to complete their education at this place; which is, that the advantages of medical improvement are, beyond all comparison, outballanced by the pernicious principles of infidelity which are imbibed there. Several young persons, religiously hopeful at the time of commencing their studies, have returned from thence deeply poisoned in their religious principles; and some who have not been altogether slain in the contest, have, it is feared, become so much

we went to Kirkaldie, (by Queen's Ferry) where we had a meeting with the town's people, some of whom behaved well, the glad tidings of the gospel were preached; and a satisfactory meeting it was. From hence we went that evening one stage further, and purposed next day for Montrose, forty-nine miles. The first stage in the morning was to Coupar in Fife, where we felt a considerable openness for a meeting, but having too much, in our own inclination, fixed our work for this day, we put by this simple feeling, and thought that, if way opened, we would give up to it in our return. A few hours convinced us that our plans were frustrated; for when we arrived at Dundee Ferry, we found ourselves about half an hour too late for the tide, so that our horses could not be taken over till about that time in the evening, at which we should have been there, had we staid and had a meeting at Coupar in Fife. From Dundee we went to Aberbrothick, which we left next morning for Montrose, where we had a meeting in the evening with the town's peo-

wounded, as to endanger their going halting all their days. It is of unspeakable importance for parents and guardians solidly to consider, in their disposal of youth, the danger not only of this, but of every other exposed situation in life. No professional advantages, or qualifications whatever, can be put in competition with the loss or injury of that pure faith and principle, which is our unerring guide, our support and comfort through time.

ple, who behaved well, and to whom divine regard was powerfully manifested.

From hence we went to Inverbervy, a little seaport between Montrose and Aberdeen. Here we found we could not get away, without a meeting amongst the town's people, which was readily provided for, and a very solid company attended; whose minds seemed like the good ground cultivated by the divine hand, for the reception of the feed of the kingdom. Divine aid was eminently extended to us, and to the people, and we were led, publicly and secretly, to return the gratitude of our hearts to him whose works alone can praise him, and who, in infinite wisdom, after these favoured opportunities, is sometimes pleased to lead his poor, weak, servants, as from the holy mountain, and from tasting the animating wine of the kingdom, into the wilderness; and to cause them, like their Master, to experience something of the forty days fast, and the power of the Tempter; that so, their own inability may be proved, their humble confidence renewed in the divine arm, they drawn from having any confidence in the flesh, and taught not to live by bread alone. From hence we proceeded to Stonehaven, and sat with the few friends there, in whom the life of religion is weak. We went to Aberdeen that evening, and next day had a close time with the friends there. The same afternoon we reached Old-meldrum, and next day sat a meeting with them, where we found we could not get away without sitting in the families, and having a public meeting with the town's people; the first we set about the same day, and had a satisfactory meeting with the people in the evening. We found things very low amongst the friends, but a comfortable hope, that of the youth would be raised up such as would be qualified to support the cause of truth, which is ready to fall in the streets, and the principles thereof almost forgotten by those that profess them, particularly in departing from the plain language, and losing the distinguishing marks of their profession; whereby the cross is evaded, and the people's minds become like the high-way ground. We finished the visit to the families at Kilmuck, and went from thence on seventh day evening for Aberdeen, and staid there the next day. My companion attended the meetings, where she had good service, and many people of the town came in. I had been unwell for some time before with pain in my face and teeth, which had now so increased upon me, with fresh cold, that, feeling no particular draft to the friends or people, and scarce being fit to move, I staid in the house that day, in order to use some means for recovery, which were not ineffectual, and next morning we set forward for Urie. Here the friends of Stonehaven met us, but it was a painful opportunity, and little of the divine life to be felt. We reached Montrose in the evening, and next day went to Aberbrothick, where we used some means to obtain a meeting, but they not been effectual, we were easy to leave the place; and went forward, without any other meeting in the way, to Edinburgh, where we arrived on fifth day evening, the fifteenth of the month *. The next evening we reached Kelso, and Morpeth on the seventeenth, from whence we went next morning to Newcastle to breakfast, and attended both their meetings; in which we had deep,

* From Aberbrothick she writes thus to a friend: " The minds of many of the people in this land seem preparing, like the good ground, to receive, in childlike simplicity, the ingrafted word; and though it may be long before fruits appear, yet if those that come this way, follow the simple openings of truth, in their stoppings at places where there are no friends, and get baptized into the states of the people, it appears clear to us, that such will be instrumental in helping forward the light of the perfect day of the gospel, which has dawned in many of these parts; but it is under present chastisement for neglect of duty, that I acknowledge we have not sufficiently trod this path. One material omission the week before last, has laid a foundation for repentance through this land, if not through time, unless our Master sometime sends us again to pay debt and interest; because, from that one neglect, has proceeded many entanglements, and preventions of doing right. We have great cause to believe and acknowledge, that the divine aid which hath been afforded, particularly in this land, hath been great; and though it may have been chiefly on account of the people, yet gratitude hath covered our minds for it, and it occasions us to feel more deeply any want of faithfulness."

The following letters were written a few days after her getting out of Scotland.

" It is a favour when we are at liberty to feel one another, in the cementing bond of pure love and unchangeable fellowship; for, really, in journeys of this kind, our minds are often so stripped of satisfactions like these, that instead of feeling as if we belong to any

searching, but honest labour; and a degree of quietude, resignation, and serenity of mind, closed the day. The next day we rested, and on third were at Shields, fourth at Sunderland, fifth at Benfieldside,

body, or have any outward source of comfort, the state of the pelican in the wilderness seems most similar to ours; and, no doubt, for wise ends, our minds are thus clothed with abstractedness, and separated from domestic blessings: for our eye then being single, and we considering ourselves servants that have need to watch every pointing of the Master, we are in the greater fitness to receive that divine light, in which, and by which only, every service in the church can be rightly accomplished."

―――― "We are convinced it is right for those who go into Scotland, to go without plans, or fixed times for things, and simply to attend, day by day, to the openings of truth, giving up their time freely, and considering themselves in no respect their own. Such as thus faithfully visit Scotland, and get deep enough in their minds to bring up such weapons as will penetrate the minds of the people, and reach the divine life, rather than aim merely at convincing the judgment, will have, I am persuaded, great service in that land, and find the free dedication of their time to be an acceptable sacrifice."

―――― "We have now got as into our own camp, where close painful labour is often our lot; which being almost continual, and without apparent effects, we are sometimes ready to shrink from the work, and turn our faces homeward, considering ourselves, in every sense of the word, unprofitable servants. But I have thus far found, that when we have been so reduced, as hath been the case, that we durst not look for great things, divine strength hath been most administered, and the blessings that

sixth at Newbiggin, seventh at Allondale, first at Alston, and second at Cornwood: at all which, the effects of an inattention to the unerring spiritual guide, were deeply felt by us; and, from place to place, our spirits were pained in viewing the declension and desolation which have spread themselves, even amongst the foremost classes of the people; so that some of those who have appeared as shepherds over the flock, have been overtaken therewith, smitten by the hand of the enemy, and proved their disqualification for service; whereby many that knew not the sure foundation, but whose eyes

attend our thus dwelling in the deeps, have been couched under these feelings; and the spirit of discernment hath so proceeded therefrom, that we have had humbly to admire the dealings of the divine hand, which, by reducing his servants, exalteth his own cause. When self is most brought down, there is least anxiety about the fruits of our labour; they are left to the great Husbandman, who causeth the rain to descend on the just, and on the unjust; and surely it is enough for us to experience our meat and our drink to be an obedience to the will of our heavenly Father: for thereby, we get food that the world knows not of, and feel ourselves bound to his truth, though many may forsake it. We are reconciled to suffer therewith, seeing with an eye of faith, that notwithstanding the declension amongst us, the smiting of the shepherds, some in being happily removed from the evil to come, and others by the hand of the enemy, and the scattering of the sheep, yet the promise will be fulfilled, upon the little ones: and these keeping to their Judge and Lawgiver, they shall with the Lamb, experience a victory."

were fixt upon man, and whose walking was circumscribed by the appearance of others, have been scattered from the place of true feeding, and thus want an anchor to their souls in the time of trial. This the spirit of truth would have amply supplied, had it been made the object of their researches, instead of the honour, the wisdom, and the complicated gratifications of man in his depraved state. But in the course of these meetings, particularly at Newbiggin, Allondale, and Cornwood, we felt an evidence that the divine promise will be fulfilled upon the little ones, and that there are of this number, who, if they keep faithful under the preparing hand, will be raised up to be standard-bearers in the work and house of their God. But oh the danger of even these, that have been several times dipt as in Jordan, not abiding the day of further trial, wherein nothing but the pure gold will stand; because the fiery baptism of the spirit, is so superior to every thing but what is of its own durable nature, that whatever has been mixed with it must, in this test, be swept away; that the vessel which is formed of the residue, may be so pure as to be entitled to the inscription of, "holiness unto the Lord." As it is for want of this patient dedication of heart to the operation of truth, that many vessels amongst us have been little better than sounding brass or tinkling cymbals to the people, having no authority from that of which they spoke, nor discovering an alliance to the master by following his holy pattern, my heart has been led fervently to implore for myself, and for a number of these, to whom I felt united in our heavenly Father's love, that whatsoever may be the sufferings of the present day, and howsoever one may fall on one hand, and another on another, our eye may be fixed on the Rock of our strength, and our faith so replenished, that though the feet may be placed as in the very bottom of Jordan, we may not flinch therefrom, nor seek an easier path than that which the wrestling seed of Jacob have ever trod; nor have any greater joy than to be united by an exercise of spirit to our holy Head, whether in suffering or in rejoicing. We had, in all these places, the renewed assistance of that spirit which helpeth our infirmities, teacheth how to pray and travail in spirit, and how to minister to the states of the people; whereby some of the hidden things of darkness were searched out, the strayed of the flock invited to the fold, and the little travailing remnant were encouraged to go forward on their way. We had a uniting season at Cornwood, in that pure fellowship of spirit, which supplieth every member in the body with fresh vigour to perform its function.—From hence, with our friends M. J. and J. W. we went to a meeting in Cumberland: it was a time of deep exercise of mind, but in faithfulness thereto, the power of truth rose into dominion, and we had reason to hope it was a profitable time to divers. We left this place, and in the afternoon were at another meeting, which was, for a time, painful beyond description; but by an humble waiting, it was discovered that the people were fed with unsound ministry, that the ark was taken into the hands of the uncircumcised, and that there was a number who loved to have it so. The power and authority of truth arose, by which we were enabled to place judgment on that spirit, which was seeking to support the testimony with unsanctified hands, and to have their honour from men, forgetting that holy anointing and preparation of heart, whereby the Lord becomes sanctified in all those that draw nigh unto him, and the bread that he gives them to break receives a blessing upon it, in that it shall not be void, but prove a visitation of his love to those to whom it is sent, whether they will hear or forbear. Here we had afresh to observe, that where ministers maintain their inward exercise, and keep near to their gifts, the spirit of true discernment, which searcheth all things, is not wanting to prove, from the line in which it leads them, the rectitude of their ministry to the living and wise in heart; who judge not by the sight of the eye, or the hearing of the ear, but by the unerring evidence of truth, which remains to be the favour of life unto life. Our minds were thankful, under the fresh sense of divine favour and strength, in being found worthy to suffer with the suffering seed, and with the little remnant that are thus exercised, and who belong to this meeting: to these, though they are weak, the bread of encouragement was broken.

Next morning we set forward, and on our way, I received an account from my husband who was then in London, of the death of his father, and that he purposed going over with the friends who had attended the yearly meeting, to accompany his sister, and to pay a visit to his mother and friends, on this affecting occasion; reasons with which my judgment led me to coincide, though I felt myself deeply affected with so unexpected a circumstance; and having received a letter conveying sorrowful intelligence on various subjects, I was ready, with the additional concern of the important service in which we were engaged, to sink under the general pressure of my mind. But, in this situation, I had fresh cause to recur to that divine and invisible arm which drew me out; and in the feeling whereof I could then say, with a degree of holy confidence, " Lord I have left all to follow thee," to that station into which I apprehended myself called, though but a child, and to nothing short of a disciple of the Lamb, to fight under his banner, and to prefer his work to every gratification or concern of my own. I found it was an easy thing to say, I will follow thee wheresoever thou leadest; but when our fidelity is tried with cross occurrences in our natural feelings, united to the fresh painful sense, that the foxes have holes, &c. then are we ready to shrink, and desire that the cup may pass from us, forgetting that all must be left to the great Disposer of all things; that so, with holy confidence, our resolutions may be, " though thou slay me, yet will I trust in thee." Under this dispensation, I was afresh stripped, and became a suppliant at wisdom's gate; where, I found, I had nothing to receive for my help, but a patient submission to the divine will, and renewed strength, simply and singly, to wait, not only respecting circumstances relating to my social concerns, but in the line of my religious duty, and in the exercise of the gift; seeing that it is only when the eye is single, that the body is full of light. We attended the next meeting, which for a time was inexpressibly dark and painful; but being engaged fervently to travail for the resurrection of life, we had renewedly to acknowledge, that our labours were blessed, and strength afforded for that time, to awaken a number from a state of spiritual death, and to shew them the deplorable situations they were in. We proceeded to another meeting, and on first day attended both the meetings there; in the first of which we were enabled to relieve our minds from the weight which, in the forepart, deeply affected us, and it was a time of renewed favour. Numbers will not hear either the Master or the servant when sound doctrine is delivered unto them: but the most fine gold becoming changed, and they remembering something of the work of the Refiner, but not keeping under it themselves, are making somewhat for the people which is specious, and feeds their itching ears, but which at the same time is putting death into the pot: so that for want of those that hear recurring to the witness for God, the true spirit of prophecy, the seed of the kingdom becomes stifled, and total insensibility ensues; a state over which, in this county, we had deeply to mourn. The meeting in the afternoon was silent, and our minds preserved in great resignation. On 3d day following we went to Moorhouse and Kirkbride, on 4th at Wigton and Bolton, on 5th at Berkfoot and at Maryport, and on 6th at Allonby and Broughton. The closeness of the exercise in meetings, and in travelling, had by this time sensibly affected or reduced our strength and spirits; but resting on 7th day with a friend helped to restore us a little: yet the wounded and captivated state of us as a people, and especially in this county, renders a little present rest, like the eating of the passover, with bitter herbs; for how can the servant rejoice where the Master reigns not! On 1st day we sat with the friends at Pardshaw, where divine regard was renewedly extended to us and to them, in opening the book of His law, and discovering the transgressions of the professors thereof. The same evening we rode to Whitehaven, and had a meeting there the next day the 10th, which was painful; but a little oppressed remnant were strengthened; for which thankfulness ought to arise, and gratitude cover our spirits, notwithstanding we, as the poor servants and off-scouring of all things, are often abased under the sense of our own nothingness, and of our omissions and commissions; for on these the compassionate eye of the Master condescends to look, when we see ourselves, and are prostrate before him, under the sense of how liable we are to swerve to the right hand or to the left, from the clear and pure openings of truth in our religious services, without a close attention of mind thereto. This requires a previous strippedness, and baptism of spirit, that our own activity may be reduced, and subjected to the Power that quickeneth and giveth life, and that, likewise, unprofitable timidity and fear of man, may become so removed, that we can, with finglenefs, and refignation, depend folely upon the fimple revelation of the divine will. For though it is needful for our refinement, and fitnefs for fervice, to be clothed with the fenfe of our weaknefs, and the infufficiency of our wifdom and difcernment in the myfteries of the kingdom, and in performing the leaft work for the fpiritual building; yet on this, when called to labour, our eye fhould not be fixed, but reft, with faith, on the invifible arm of divine power; that being in a fituation ready to receive help from it, we may be therewith content, and favoured with that bleffing which renders acceptable the fmalleft offering, or the bread that may be compared but to the barley loaf. We went to another meeting, where things are very low, fome of the members being fo weak as to let fall fome of the fundamental principles of our profeffion; whereby the few that are faithful are oppreffed with the feed, and are ready to fink under difcouragements, and alfo with fome appearances in the miniftry, concerning which we felt no anfwer of life as unto life. Here we lodged at the houfe of our valuable friends J. and B. D. who, next day accompanied us, with fome other friends, to Kefwick, where we had a pretty large and fatisfactory meeting amongft the town's people. On fifth day the thirteenth, we attended the week day meeting, and monthly felect meeting at Greyfouthen, where gracious condefcenfion was eminently extended to us, and to the members thereof; and we parted with many of our friends on that fide, in much affectionate fellowfhip, and fympathy with each others' tried situations, arising from the deep declension and desolation which widely spread over us as a people. Next morning we rode to Isell meeting, in a very stormy, tempestuous day, so much so, that the friends belonging to the meeting durst not venture out, except three men, for whom, in a cold damp meeting-house, we waited in our wet cloaths three quarters of an hour; having no better accommodations for ourselves or horses, than a bare shelter from the heavy rain that fell here. We sat down with the few that came, and our guides, ready to conclude that, under these circumstances, it would be an unavailing attempt to have our minds properly stayed; but he who mercifully condescends to visit the two or three that gather in his name, was pleased eminently to own us that day. I remembered, and had to open the passage, " Blessed is that servant that watcheth, and keepeth his garment, and who, when his Lord cometh, is found ready." It appeared to my mind that all those who have enlisted under the spiritual, unconquered Captain, have received a mark thereof, a change of heart, an awful covering of spirit, a loving one another, and means whereby such might stand in readiness for the word of command; and that therefore the peculiar blessing of the divine hand rests upon these faithful servants, who when not actually in service, so remember their office, as to be fit, when called thereto, to step into it, and move only in that raiment, and with that armour, which the master gives them. For want of this watchful, attentive care, in times of withdrawing, many amongſt us, when there has been an opening for labour, have not been found ready, nor approved worthy, to advocate the heavenly cauſe; and thus the warfare has not been maintained, but the battle is retarded, Iſrael falls before his enemies, and the accurſed thing is in the tribe of Judah. At the cloſe of this meeting, where my mind had been led to centre to a quiet dependance on the ſmalleſt evidence of the divine will, after ſome days of deep probation, and frequent deſertion of ſpirit, the aforeſaid paſſage, "bleſſed is that ſervant, &c." powerfully revived and ſpread before me, and, with a voice intelligible to my ſpiritual ear, applied it to myſelf; which introduced ſuch a calm over my mind, and ſeparation from the natural feelings thereof, as I never before experienced. Under this ſenſe, I concluded it was the laſt meeting I ſhould ever be at; that the dedication of my heart, and ſome afflictive diſpenſations that were paſt, had proved acceptable, and that now there was no obſtruction to my final diſſolution; nor an attachment in me to any thing below: a ſituation of mind ſo different from what I uſually felt, when I have feared that the cloſeneſs of my connections had the aſcendency over my love, and travail of ſpirit for the cauſe of truth, that I wondered at the change. I looked towards my friends, ſaw ſome of them in their places, and feeling myſelf in my own, without a cord to break, I apprehended that, in a very little time, I ſhould be gathered to that eternal habitation of reſt, whereinto I never before ſo ſenſibly entered, and of which I had never ſuch a foretaſte. It was nothing that elated me, my natural ideas were dormant, but what I experienced seemed solid substantial truth. After the meeting broke up, and I was making the necessary preparations for proceeding to the next meeting, there was no interruption to my mind, till riding along the road, with a fresh, awful application to the Lord, and breathing that I might not rest too much under this impression, and that if there was any other end to answer than what I had seen, it might be discovered; lest by looking too much at an opening so comfortable to myself, I should be in danger of neglecting a continued exercise of spirit, and the service I might be called to from place to place; and thereby render that which was intended a blessing, a block in my way in pressing after so desirable an end as had opened therein: thus waiting to see further the way cast up for me, I thought I clearly discovered, that it was a mark of divine regard at that time extended, in order to shew me the excellent, ultimate, effect of what I had had to open to others; and the need there was for me to attend to it myself, during the course of my own pilgrimage; and also to remove an idea, that the ties of nature are so interwoven with my attachment to eternal excellency and purity, that the separation must be, like the furnace being heated seven times hotter than it had before been experienced. Instead of this, I had to behold, in humble admiration, the works of an almighty hand in the deeps, and how, when our hearts are upright before him, he invisibly works our deliverance, by means which the unenlightened underſtanding of man cannot comprehend. When the power of truth predominates, we fee, in the viſion of light, its ſuperiority to every natural endowment or gratification; ſo that the inſurmountable difficulties that are beheld by the natural eye, are ſubjected, and the mountain of the Lord is exalted on the top of all the hills. In commemoration of this token of divine regard, my mind is bowed, under the ſenſe of my own unworthineſs, and how unable I am, notwithſtanding this view, to dwell in a ſtate of preſervation and acceptance, without wreſtling, from time to time, for that faith which overcometh, and that patience whereby we are kept in the hour of temptation: for if the Lord keep not the city, the watchman watcheth but in vain. After the meeting at Iſell we went to Coldbeck, where we had a ſuffering time, but were enabled in a good degree to ſearch out the cauſe. Next day we attended a meeting at Moſedale, where we had comfortably to obſerve that the Maſter's feet had been, though in general things are very low. On firſt day, the ſixteenth, we were at both their meetings at Penrith, where we painfully felt the oppreſſion of the ſeed, as in many other places. That evening we rode to Terril, and next morning had a meeting there; where the neceſſity of thoſe who are called to the miniſtry ſitting looſe from outward connections and profits, and following the Maſter whitherſoever he leads them, was clearly ſet forth. From hence we went to Strickland meeting, and on our way, I had a fall from my horſe, with which I was hurt, but attended the meeting, which was favoured, and I gradually recovered. From Strickland we went to Hawkshead, and from thence to Swarthmore, where many not of our society attended; and it proved an eminently favoured season. Our next meeting was at Height which was a low time. We then proceeded to another meeting, rested and wrote on 7th day; and on first sat both their meetings, where we had secretly to mourn over, and publicly to discover, the affecting situation of those who, from year to year, have been divinely favoured, and, like the vineyard we read of, dug about, fenced, and visited by the good Husbandman: but oh, the falling short! one may plant, and another may water, yet as the increase is of the Lord, and He not being devotedly sought unto, for that dew of heaven which renders us fruitful, and that pruning hand which would keep the branches clean, numbers, after having been planted choice vines, have become the degenerate plants of a strange vine unto the Lord; and notwithstanding they keep a greenness, and an appearance of life, it was clear to the view of our minds, that if there was not a getting deeper, even to the washing pool, and being stripped of themselves, the princes also arising from the dust of the earth and anointing the shield, that spiritual death will greatly increase amongst them, and the judgments of the Lord for disobedience will ensue. We took the week following, Preston, Grayrig, Sedberg, Dent, Garsdale, Ravenstonedale, and Lartington; and also had a satisfactory meeting at Bowes, where are none of our society; and at the others, we were favoured with strength for the exercise that fell to our lot therein. The first day following, we attended the meeting at Staindrop, and another in the evening at Bishop Aukland; on second day we went to Durham to their quarterly meeting, attended the several sittings thereof: in all which we were enabled, far beyond our expectation, to relieve our minds, by honestly, in the fear of the Lord, and not of man, expressing our sense of the state of things amongst them; and it was a time of renewed favour. From thence we went forward, and at a meeting wherein the uncircumcised spirit was painfully felt to prevail in the forepart thereof, but our help and safety depending upon our going down to the brook, we were engaged patiently to wait for divine clothing, knowing that it would be dangerous to go against them in untried armour, notwithstanding the cause might be good: and we may thankfully say, that good is the word of the Lord, and efficacious to the smiting of the Goliahs of this day."

Her own account of this journey ends here; but it appears that she proceeded from this place, and visited the meetings at Stockton, and Yarm, back to Benfieldside, then Ayton, Bilsdale, and Kirby, and returned home about the middle of the seventh month.

After she had got out of Scotland, she and her companion felt their minds disposed to salute the friends of the monthly meeting of Old Meldrum with an epistle; a copy whereof follows.

Dear Friends!

"As in our travelling along, we have frequently felt our minds covered with an earnest engagement for your preservation, and a sense of the love of our heavenly Father towards you, which engaged us to pay you a visit, we are drawn in the renewed extendings thereof, to salute you with a few lines, and, according to the ability received, to strengthen the little life that is amongst you; that the elders may be gathered to the true place of feeding, the middle-aged arising may become men and women of valour for God, and the youth having examples set before their eyes of a steady circumspect walking, seasoned with divine virtue, may be engaged, by the efficacy of the same holy principle, to succeed their parents, and the faithful in all ages, in carrying forward the Lord's work, and in His name, which is His power, setting up their banners. But, dear friends, as there are many impediments which have hindered us as a people, both in this land and in yours, from advancing in our spiritual progress, and increasing our strength in the Lord, let us enquire into the cause whence they have come, and to what they will tend; for if we had kept to the sure foundation, and in all things considered ourselves the followers of a crucified Lord, rather than nominal members of a religious society; and been concerned to walk even as He walked; the snares of the enemy would not have prevailed to have led so many captives into a strange land; because, against the Rock of ages, whereon we might have been built, the gates of hell shall never be able to prevail. But for want of keeping an eye open to this preserving Power, a spirit of indifferency hath crept in, and, whilst many have slept, tares have been sown; which, as they spring up, have had a tendency to choak the good seed, those tender impressions, and reproofs of instruction, which would have prepared our spirits, and have bound them to the holy law and testimonies of truth. Thus, strength hath been wanting to maintain the discipline of the church, in that purity wherein it was first established; and a door hath opened for encreasing liberties. Hence, hath ensued a mixing with the spirit, and customs of the world; so that those who have not been taught the same doctrines, but are looking upon us, may query, " where is your God?" seeing, that though we profess to be led and guided by the spirit of truth, our fruits differ not from theirs; but the cross is removed out of the way. As one deviation from the path our predecessors walked in, conformable to the precepts of Christ, painfully affected our minds, both when our lot was cast amongst you, and since; we feel not easy without renewedly observing, that, in the promise of the restoration to Israel, it was said, " I will turn to the people a pure language;" and knowing that this gospel day is still more glorious than that, if we did but live in the light thereof, which would clearly discover to us the corrupt source of flattering titles, and seeking to gratify the vain mind of man, how can we, without sacrificing the principle of truth, which leads and guides into all truth, give up that pure language to which our forefathers were turned, and adopt the unfound words of You to a single person; and calling the days of the week and months by the heathen names; and those, our masters and mistresses, who are not really so; forgetting the command to call no man, master. Is not this returning to the night of apostasy, and in our dealings and converse with men, crucifying afresh the Son of God, and putting him to open shame, by thus denying, or refusing to bear his cross and testimony to the world?

"We believe there is a number amongst you, who, by example, have been trained in a deviation from our holy profession; and these we tenderly address, and exhort to feel for themselves after the influence of that holy spirit, which leads its followers in the same path, however remote from outward help their situations in life may be; for the peculiar privilege of these is, they need not that any man teach them, but as this same divine anointing teacheth them all things. Though you may have but few to strengthen your hands, by their example and sympathy with you in your honest endeavours to break down the partition walls, which the enemy has raised to prevent your advancement to the perfect day of God; yet be not dismayed in your labours; but remember the fervent zeal of our predecessors in the truth; how they endured the persecutions of that day, and how, with unconquerable fortitude and resignation to the Lord's will, they steadily pursued the path of true self-denial, and fought the good fight of faith. And if we, in this day of deep declenfion, look to the Rock of our ftrength, we cannot fail to find that it is a day which calls for diligence; and that whatever pointings of duty we are favoured with, our prefervation depends upon a faithfulnefs thereto. And therefore, beloved friends, be ye engaged to fee what it is that keeps you in a ftate of weaknefs, and prevents your feeling the ftrengthening and confolating influence of the fpirit of Chrift; that fo, you may be enabled to remove the impediment out of the way, be faithful to the Lord, and ftand in the authority of his truth; that endeavouring to rule your own houfes well, and to have your children in fubjection with all gravity, you may know his baptizing power upon your fpirits, in your affembling together; and your fecret proftration and fervent breathings, will be acceptable to his holy eye, and bleffed by his bountiful hand; and in your meetings for difcipline, you will likewife be feafoned with the falt of the covenant, and by your honeft endeavours to keep the camp clean from all diforderly walkers, you will grow ftronger and ftronger, and your minds become united together in the bond of true peace. Thus, may it pleafe the Lord to operate upon your fpirits, and to influence the youth amongft you to a watchful attention to their thoughts, their words, and actions; that being preferved from mixing with thofe, who would draw away their minds from the difcoveries of truth, and centre them in the corrupt language, and changeable customs of the world, they may prefer a religious awfulness upon their spirits, and seek for that pure fear of the Lord which is a fountain of life, preserving from the snares of death, and securing a safe hiding-place in the day of trouble. With satisfaction we acknowledge, that we felt, whilst with you, that the hand of the Lord has been at work upon the minds of the youth, and that some of these have submitted thereto; to whom our spirits were, and are led into near sympathy, and filled with an earnest desire for their preservation and progress in that good work which is begun in their hearts. Be encouraged, beloved friends, to hold on your way, and more fully to submit your necks to the holy yoke; that thereby you may be made willing to suffer for the cause of truth; and though you may not have many examples and helpers in the Lord, yet being engaged to dwell near the Root of divine life, and seeking for strength therefrom, you will feel the progressive dispensation of the heavenly Visitant, and grow in stature, from the state of children, to young men in the Lord; let situations be what they may, and outward advantages ever so great, we are abundantly convinced, that whoever experience an inheritance in the truth, and an establishment therein, must purchase it for themselves, learn to live on manna of their own gathering, and know from whence all their fresh springs proceed. And now, dear friends, the fervent desire of our spirits is, that you may be stirred up to a renewed sense of the declension of the present day, and under it, be engaged to seek for strength to stablish you in every good word and work; that being clothed with a zeal according to knowledge, for the prosperity of Zion, and the enlargement of her borders, you may become established as a city set upon a hill, having the light of the gospel day upon your dwellings.

Benfieldside, 7th month 7th, 1782.

CHAP. III.

Visit to her Husband's Relatives in Ireland.—Journey into Norfolk, &c.—Visit to the Meetings of Friends in Ireland.

IN the 11th month 1782, she felt an inclination and freedom of mind, to accompany her husband into Ireland, on a visit to their relations. The deeply instructive exercises which she met with previous to her landing in Ireland; with her humble, watchful state of mind and engagements there, may in part be collected from the following letters, which, except the first, she wrote in that land.

————" This place (Holyhead) is uncomfortable to stay at, amongst a great deal of company, and no woman but myself; and though it is made easier by their great civility, yet the journey altogether is an awful thing. On surveying my inducements for coming and impartially examining myself, I have not yet found any uneasiness, though I am low, and our present situation is a trial of both faith and patience. Indeed the many rocks and shoals attending us in our religious and civil concerns through this trying pilgrimage, will, I apprehend, ever prove a trial of these; and therefore, by the direction of the Best of Pilots, to guard against them, and to steer wisely through life, is the work of our day; and will open most clearly the prospect of the haven of durable rest."

———" I was greatly pleased when we got to Holyhead, hoping soon to be in Dublin, and dreading the water but little. Here our disappointments began. We went out to sea next day, were tossed about for fourteen hours, and I then returned extremely ill; so much so, that it became a matter of doubt to my husband whether he should not have to bury me there. I thought as soon as my head was laid after our return, that I perceived a cup bitterer than death; for that death, except on R. G.'s account, 'I should not have regretted, so shaded are all the domestic enjoyments and temporal blessings of life, when, abstracted from them, we are called upon, faithfully and with singleness of heart, to do the will of our heavenly Father. To have a meeting at Holyhead presented with great weight, and at the same time the appearance of things told me that, on various accounts, (my own bodily weakness not the least) it was an impossibility. I was afraid, but I think I was not rebellious. In the depth of distress, I offered myself as one unable to answer the requiring, hoping the offering would be accepted, and that some ram would be caught in the thicket; here the call seemed renewed to obedience, and not sacrifice; and I saw that if any thing short of the demand was offered, tho' I even exerted myself in faithfulness in Ireland, as I promised to do, I might be suffered to fall into a snare, and return from thence, instead of the reward of peace, with the query, Who hath required this at thy hands? Present obedience, and subservience to the operation of truth on our minds, is no doubt what will preserve us on this sea of glass mingled with fire; for if we keep with the life, and move therein, it will keep us humble, reduce our confidence in the flesh, and draw us down into suffering with it. When our dwelling is as amongst the pots, and no goodliness remaineth in us, then we know in whom is eternal help, and the travail of our spirits is for ability to look towards his holy habitation. Our first failing was on fourth day, and by sixth day I was got something better, when the captain, and a great number of passengers were disposed to sail, and none of them more so than ourselves, if the wind would take us, which, according to the feelings of my mind, I believed would not; but I have no cause to think it was unacceptable to try the fleece again; which we did, and after getting out of the harbour, the wind turned against us, and grew very rough. The vessel was violently tossed, and at one time we were in great danger of foundering. I lay quietly as I could, beholding the wonders of an almighty hand concerning us; and in the deeps, both spiritually and temporally, I felt myself a Jonah, when the people were crying, that there was one on board; and all was tremendous about me. The danger we were in was evident, but my hope never failed me; which I esteemed an unspeakable favour, and which led me to a greater willingness than I had before felt, to give up to the meeting, or any thing else that was required. We were out this time but about four hours, and after we landed, a large merchant ship was wrecked in our sight, but no lives lost. My situation now became awful; there seemed no way but resignedness to the meeting, and that I could not see was to be till first day. My husband I perceived was afraid, for he considered us accountable for whatever the cause suffered by us, especially as there never was a meeting there before. On first day morning we were tried again, for the wind being fair, we prepared for sailing, and when all was ready for going on board, a storm came on, and the captain durst not venture to loose the ship in the harbour, believing that if he did it would be soon wrecked. We then returned again, and the time came on for the people to go to some place of worship; when finding an empty house near the inn, we engaged it, and felt most easy to give notice to but a few, that we were going to sit in our usual manner to worship, and that if they, or any others, chose to accompany us, we had no objection. Before we got to the place, many were there, and more followed; and to our humble admiration, divine assistance was near, and wonderfully helped us over that sitting. At the conclusion, the people were desirous of another in the evening, which, when we had considered it, we consented to; and if I may venture to say, it was crowned with good, and the melting operation of truth appeared to be experienced by many of the people, who behaved with great solidity. The next evening tide suited for our passage, and with peaceful minds we embarked, and were but nine hours from bay to bay. Thus have we cause to turn back to this page of our lives, with humble gratitude of mind, and to acknowledge that a simple pointing of duty, and a simple discharge thereof, is productive of solid satisfaction, when, on the other hand, no exertion or anxiety of our own, can furnish us with one grain of it, nor can we, by taking thought, add one cubit to our stature!"

———" Often, very often, since I saw your faces, has my mind visited you in affectionate nearness; but I have seldom felt greater inability, than since I came into this land, thus to converse with my friends; for as our coming was sudden, it has occasioned deep searchings of heart, for preservation, and direction how to move in the line of wisdom.

" We met with a very cordial reception in Ireland; the hospitality and affection of our friends were not unacceptable to a poor stranger like me; nevertheless my mind has not seemed at liberty, as I could have wished, to enjoy that society which is gratifying to self. It is good for us renewedly to feel ourselves not our own, to stand resigned to the divine will, and to know it to be our meat and drink to do it. Every little additional experience tends to convince us, that herein consists our most solid and permanent satisfaction; and were our disposition of resistance to the painful preparation for devotedness removed, we should more often have feelingly to acknowledge, that with the divine blessings, there is added no sorrow; but we make sorrows for ourselves, we add that which our gracious Benefactor hath not in store for us. A path exempt from trials is what I have no right to expect, and what I hope I am learning not to desire. A patient submission to every divine dispensation, is what I wish for an encrease of; that so, the mingled cup of life may prove a profitable draught, and impress me, more and more, with an humble sense of the multiplied blessings bestowed upon me: for by this means, I believe we shall encrease in knowledge how to move and conduct ourselves, amidst the various temptations, besetments, and cross occurrences, incident to this probationary state.

"We went pretty directly from Dublin for Clonmel, after the half-year's meeting, and spent two days very much to my instruction, at Ballitore. We staid about ten days amongst our relations, who are valuable and kind, and then went for Carlow quarterly meeting, where were Robert Valentine and his companion, &c. I think, upon the whole, it was a very favoured gathering, though here, as in our land, the world and its spirit has made great devastation and scattering amongst the gathered tribes."

————"We look with a degree of satisfaction at our return. A little rest to body and mind will be truly acceptable, as our visit to our relations seems now completed. Our passage through this land has been encumbered with many thorns, and attended with many trials unforeseen by us. It is a day of deep humiliation, and it sometimes looks as if our judgment was taken away. I want not to make complaints; I wish rather to profit by what I have suffered, and reap instruction from every renewed dispensation of infinite kindness; feeling myself unworthy of the least of His benefits, and that, without His peculiar care, I shall be overwhelmed, and warped aside from the stability of the truth: but by being baptized into a deep sense of my own weakness and frailty, I have been led to acknowledge, that even the bitter things are sweet; seeing, that in infinite wisdom, they are ordered for the strengthening of our spiritual appetite, and bringing down that part in us which is at enmity with the cross, and loves not its government in the mind."

Her home for several years after her marriage, was at Foston, a village ten miles from York. This was to her a comfortable retirement, when not engaged abroad in the service of truth. But though gratifying to nature, and a desirable resting place, her concern for the advancement of her great Master's cause, which was her most desired meat and drink, often called her from this abode, so that she seldom resided there for a month together. It appeared, indeed, that she was unwearied in promoting the cause of truth and righteousness, and willing to spend and be spent for the great Name's sake.

In the spring of the year 1784, she appears to have been engaged in a visit to the meetings and some families of friends, in Norfolk, and to divers other meetings, as she proceeded to the yearly meeting at London. Of this religious engagement, no regular accounts of her own, have been discovered; the following are the material parts of all that have been collected from her letters.

————" We had nine meetings last week, at eight different places, beside private opportunities in families, which we durst not avoid; finding the declension to be so great in almost every one, where we have come, and so few who seem to know it, that we are ready to say, For Zion's sake we cannot rest nor hold our peace, till at least they are informed of their state."————" We attended their week day meeting at this place, with which we were well satisfied, it being a time of much instruction, however to my mind; finding by a degree of living experience, that there is indeed a Minister of ministers, on whom we have great cause to wait to be instructed ourselves, in our private, as well as public duty; that, in all things, we may approve ourseves obedient servants, and good examples to the flock. It was my lot to sit in silence, viewing the great, and almost general insensibility to true religion."

————" We have not only travelled hard, but found much work at places where we have come, finding it rather more than usual in the line of our duty, to bear a testimony, not only to the truth, but against the numerous evils and inconsistencies, which have generally overspread the professors in these parts; and as our peace much depends, in our passing along, in being honest, and speaking the truth without parabies, we have been enabled, pretty tolerably, to discharge our duty, and to shew them how far they are from what they pretend to be; though 'tis hard work, and we find that the more abundantly we manifest our love in this way, the less we are loved by many who have been used to smooth things, and have sought to make the truth conform to them, instead of this conduct being brought to, and regulated by the truth. So that indeed many are blind in error, and those that see, will not exert themselves to search their own houses, and remove the inconsistencies that are in them. A mournful prospect appears in these, as well as many other parts; no likelihood of a succession in the truth, and even the present standard-bearers ready to faint. Under these impressions, we seek not great things for ourselves, but rather are disposed to consider it a favour, (great enough for us to expect) if we have our lives for a prey, from one place to another.

"We have little expectation, that in any sittings, our minds will get above the spirits of this people; and till that strength arises which puts the armies of aliens to flight, I trust our lips will be sealed, and we content therewith; for indeed, it is not an easy task to minister to this degenerate age, who think they know all things, and, like the magicians in Egypt, can account for all the works of the divine hand: but what a favour it is, that there is still extended to us as a people, that power which confounds the wisdom of these, and brings to nought their great understanding."

————"We have been much engaged the few days we have staid at Norwich. It has been to our minds a suffering time, during our stay in that place; but though we have mourned, and perhaps rather murmured at times, yet we have great cause to be thankful for the help wherewith, in infinite kindness, we have been helped. It is a day of great discouragement, and I think I was never more ready to lay down my armour, than in silence this day at meeting. The situation of mind I was in, I found tended to humble and reduce the creature; and as my soul was hungry, even the bitter food I partook of, became sweet, and I saw the profit of these seasons."

────"We left Norwich on seventh day, were at Yarmouth on first, Pakefield on second, Becles on third, Leiston fourth, and Woodbridge to day, where, as at some other places, we sat in mournful, but I trust instructive silence. What falls at times to our lots in meetings, and sometimes in conversations out of them, seems much like pulling down old houses, and we are often afraid of being choaked in the dust; for indeed most of the buildings we see are painfully superficial, and our little labour has been deeply distressing; so that the language of my heart often is, "Who hath believed our report?" but I am thankful in feeling the burden decreasing, as our work seems closing."

In the year following she felt a religious concern to join her friend Rebecca Jones, on a visit to the meetings of friends in Ireland, &c. and having laid the same before the monthly meeting, with the approbation thereof, and the concurrence of the quarterly meeting, she set forward on this journey in the 7th month, 1785. Of this visit there is preserved a short journal written by herself, which is as follows.

"I left home the 13th of 7th month 1785, and spent two nights at York, in order to allow a comfortable opportunity of taking a solid and affectionate leave of my connections there; and on the 15th, went with my husband to Bradford, where, next day, I parted with him, he returning to York, and I proceeding with my cousin W. M. (who was to accompany me to Ireland) for Manchester.

"We staid there the next day, being the first of the week, and I was at both their meetings; which savoured to my mind of that righteousness and wisdom of man, which never can work the righteousness of God nor favour the things that pertain to His kingdom.

"But there is a precious suffering seed in that place, to which my spirit was renewedly united in the covenant of light and life. On second day we went, with many friends, down the water to Warrington, where, on the 19th was held their monthly meeting, which I felt most easy to attend, though I might thereby miss an opportunity of crossing the water, so early as I otherwise might choose; and I was comfortably satisfied with this little dedication by the way. I went that evening to Liverpool, and waited till 6th day for a suitable wind for sailing. During this time, was their week day meeting, and my spirit was there deeply exercised, on account of some who were substituting their own righteousness for the righteousness of God, which is inherited in pure faith, in the virtue and power of that creative Word, by which all things were made, that were made in the spiritual creation, and by which, through the reduction of the natural will and wisdom of men, they can no more worship the work of their own hands: and in the strength with which my spirit was renewedly supplied, I attempted to express somewhat on this subject, for which I felt peace. We next day embarked for Dublin, in the Hawke packet, and had a very tedious and distressing voyage, being uncomfortably detained, in part for want of wind, and in part by its being contrary; the latter occasioning us to put into the Isle of Man, where we staid two nights, and found a very courteous and hospitable reception from the inhabitants. My mind was attached to them, in the secret effusion of gospel love, but feeling abundant weakness in myself, and wanting that united exercise which is received by fellow labourers, I did not perceive it to be my woe if I preached not the gospel; and therefore, in an humble trust that the great Shepherd of Israel would send more suitable servants for that work in that isle, and not put my omission in the balance against me, I embarked again with the rest of our company, save one, whom we left dead on the island. Being out longer than we expected, by two days, our provisions were exhausted; and though through divine protection we did not suffer much from want, yet it was a favour gratefully to be commemorated, that we were enabled through some difficulty to land when we did; which, with the instruction conveyed to my mind, under deep discouragement, and close searching of heart, when all human consolations stood afar off, afforded humble cause to believe, that this trying dispensation was intended as a necessary baptism of my spirit into the service before me*. On our landing, I soon met

---

* A more particular account of this voyage, with several additional instructive remarks, are contained in the following selections from her letters.———" It is very unexpected to me to write from this port; but so little do we know what, in the course of divine wisdom, shall fall to our lot, that every encrease of experience convinces us, there is no safer or easier situation of mind, than a daily dependance on, and quiet resignation to, Him who knows what is best for us, and what will tend most to His own honour. We sailed last sixth day from Liverpool, having got there on third, but the wind not being very fair when we set out, and turning more against us afterwards, occasioned a troublesome and wearisome passage thus far, not only by contrary winds, and severe sickness, but by the almost intolerable stench and suffocating closeness of our cabin and lodgings, and the continual wicked, obscene, conversation of our passengers, who are seventy in number. Sometimes, I was afraid it would overcome me, both in body and mind; when recalling to my remembrance the poor Negroes, (who, added to what I have mentioned, in a far worse degree, are chained together, under the load of that anguish naturally attendant on a forced separation from the nearest connections in life, and with the prospect of perpetual bondage under cruel taskmasters) my small trials in this line, and indeed in every other, diminished in my view; and the multitude of blessings, in infinite mercy, showered down, so crowded in their place, that at times, instead of repining, I saw abundant cause to enquire, " what am I, that thou art thus mindful of me, and what shall I render unto thee?"

with our honourable friend Samuel Emlen, whose animating company and fatherly kindness, greatly revived me, and helped me to leave the things

We put in at the Isle of Man, and were hospitably received by the inhabitants, whose engaging simplicity, and religious zeal, have attached my mind to them. I am sincerely desirous that if I do nothing for the truth, I may do nothing against it; and when I look thus, I feel a comfortable belief, that even this care shall tend to the furtherance of the gospel, and that it will somewhat open the way for future service in this place; for if the sense that attends my mind be right, when the feet of the messengers are more eminently turned into the way of the Gentiles, to Pul and Lud, &c. and to the isles afar off, this little place will not be forgot, but offerings will be brought here to the mountain of the Lord's holiness, and His glory shall break forth."

———" I am safe arrived in this land, and have humbly to commemorate divine protection, and secret supporting goodness in my passage hither. The ways of the Most High remain to be ways of wonders, and his acts are past finding out; nevertheless, he still revealeth secrets, as he did unto Abraham, when a degree of the same faithfulness is, through His humbling power, attained to; and without it, how little do we know, even when we think we know most? Never did I so sensibly enjoy the bosom of the church, which, I may humbly acknowledge, was cordial to receive me; but how much more excellent is that pure faith, which reveals itself when all human consolations stand afar off, and by centreing our spirits therein, wonderfully convinces us, that it is the " substance of things hoped for, the evidence of things not seen."

———" I feel myself much recovered from fatigue, and have gratefully to commemorate divine protection, and secret sustaining help, when the feeble efforts of

that are behind, and to press forward in prospect to a degree of humble dedication to the renewed pointings of duty. My beloved friend R. J. with G. Dillwyn and wife, having performed a family visit to friends in Dublin, were gone to Ballitore, where they found a similar engagement to that in which they had been employed; and when I reached them, they had nearly finished, and were almost ready to proceed. In a few days we accordingly set forward together, viz. G. D. R. J. and myself; our prospects comfortably corresponding one with

bodily strength and natural fortitude, seemed unequal to render me that support, which one grain of living faith affords. Oh! what abundant reason we have, not to trust in ourselves, but in Him who died for us, to whose death, if we are not conformable, we cannot fully experience the prevailing power of eternal life."

———" I trust the probation my spirit experienced in our passage here, will not prove altogether an unprofitable dispensation, on entering a service, the right performance whereof depends on our being baptized enough, and weaned enough; so that whatever is brought forth may be of the new creation, unconnected with all old heavens, and old earth. And indeed I may say that, before I left home, though my mind was much stripped and tried, I often suspected whether I had fully partaken of the necessary cup of suffering, preparatory to such an undertaking as the present; and believed I should have a trying baptism to pass through before I entered upon it; though I now have no doubt but my movings this way, were in the right time. It is an unspeakable blessing to meet with the crucifying power of truth by the way; and the desire of my heart often is, to be more and more in love therewith."

another, we cheerfully concurred therewith, to travel in company. On the 4th day following we went to Chriſtians Town, and in the evening viſited a family of young people, one of whom was in a declining ſtate of health; to whom, with the reſt, inſtruction and encouragement were handed, to prefer the humbling diſpenſations of infinite wiſdom, to all temporal gratifications. We then returned to our lodgings, and ſat with the family; where my beloved companion was enabled, in awful ſupplication, to breathe for continued ſupport, and preſervation in the path of obedience; which comfortably cemented our ſpirits together. Next day we went to Rathangan, where we had to travail for the ariſings of pure life, under the diſcouraging apprehenſion of its being very low in that place; but infinite kindneſs vouchſafed to own the deep exerciſe, and gracioufly ſent forth His light and truth, whereby the way to His holy hill was opened in the demonſtration of the ſpirit and power, and the meeting ended under an humbling commemoration of his goodneſs. In the evening we went to New Park, and next morning to the meeting at Timahoa, which was ſmall, and the public ſervice rather laborious, becauſe of the unfitneſs of many of the profeſſors to receive ſpiritual things. In the afternoon we went to Proſperous, a new ſettled town, where there are no members of our religious ſociety. We had a meeting there much to the ſatisfaction of viſitors and viſited; the people behaved well, and we had reaſon to believe, by the ownings of truth, that there is a precious ſeed there. We went to New

Park again to lodge, and in the morning fat with the family and others then prefent, and fome profitable counfel opened. From thence we went to Edenderry; and next day, being the firft of the week, we ftaid, and were at their own meeting, their preparative meeting, a public meeting in the afternoon, and in the evening fat with their minifters and elders; at all which, merciful help was near in the needful time, and enabled to difcharge our feveral duties in fimplicity, for which the reward of peace and quietude was not withheld. On fecond day the 8th of 8th month, we came to Oldcaftle, and were at their meeting next day, where many people not of our fociety attended; amongft whom there was opennefs to labour. After meeting we ftaid with thofe few in profeffion with us, when their low eftate was felt, fympathized with, and counfel flowed thereto.

On 4th day we went to Cootehill, where are very few friends; they are in a poor fhattered fituation as to the life of religion, and fcarce able to keep up their meetings. Many of the town's people came to the meeting, and it was a folid favoured opportunity; and a comfortable belief attended our minds, that there is a precious feed in that place; but the profeffors of truth are ftumbling blocks. We fat down with them felect at the conclufion of the meeting, and found it exercifing work to vifit the feed in them, but were enabled honeftly to difcharge our feveral duties*. From thence we went to

---

* In a letter dated the next day, fhe writes: " Through divine fupport, mercifully vouchfafed from day to day,

Caſtleſhane, a place very like Cootehill; and in the evening after the meeting there, reached Grange, near Charlemount, and lodged at the houſe of ——— a viſited young man, who, with two others in his family, afford a comfortable proſpect of a revival of ancient ſimplicity, and right zeal in that place. Our ſpirits were nearly united to them, and the ſtreams of encouraging counſel flowed freely for their refreſhment and ſtrength. We were at their meeting next day, being the firſt of the week, which was a ſuffering time; and in the evening, had a very large and ſatisfactory meeting of the country people not in profeſſion with us, who behaved well, and in many of whom the witneſs of truth was raiſed. Next day we proceeded to go round Lough-Neagh, by taking Toberhead, Colerain, Ballynacree, Ballimena, Grange, and Antrim; at all which places, we had deeply to lament the low declined ſtate of the profeſſors of truth, not only as to numbers, but in a departure from the precious, preſerving, principle of light and life; whereby the living members of the church are kept in their lots, and enabled to ſtand with firmneſs, as a city ſet on a hill,

we have been enabled to diſcharge the miſſions committed, ſo as to leave each place with a good degree of peace. Indeed it is a relieving conſideration, under the diſcouragements that poor travellers often meet with, that the work is not ours, and that an inſtrument has only to be paſſive in the hand of him that uſeth it, leaving its proſperity, and the honour of the cauſe, to the all ſufficiency of the divine arm, which can work with us or without us."

to the praife of His grace who hath called them out of the world, into His marvellous light. The country people coming in at the aforefaid places, tended to the more free circulation of life, wherein the fpring of gofpel miniftry was fometimes opened; but it was my lot to pafs along in gloomy fuffering, and, at times, inftructive filence. After meeting at Antrim, the 21ft of 8th month, being met by a friend and his wife, we returned home with them, and refted next day; on the evening of which my dear hufband came to us from England, and after ftaying in the neighbourhood where we were, and falling in at divers meetings for difcipline with us, he went to Clonmel, and ftaid till we came near that place before we faw him again. On the 23d we went to Newtown, and next day had a meeting with the few friends there. The knowledge and virtue of true religion feemed very low amongft them, and it was hard work, by deep and fecret exercife, to minifter to the pure life. From hence we returned to Lifburn, and attended their monthly meeting, wherein a little ftrength feemed given me for fome public labour; but my dear companions were filently baptized under a concern to vifit the families of friends in that place, though the time did not appear to be then come. After being at Hillfborough, Lurgan, Ballyhagan, Moyallen, and Ballinderry meetings, we returned to Lifburn, and in about a week performed the fervice; the Minifter of minifters being near to hand forth in the needful time (often after long fuffering filence) fuitable inftruction and confolation to the vifited.

Great indifference and infenfibility, as to the knowledge of the Lord's dealings with His people, prevail in that place, though a little tried remnant dwell amongft them *. At the clofe of this vifit, came on the quarterly meeting at Ballinderry for the province of Ulfter, which was rather a low fuffering time. Here we met with our friend Zachariah Dicks from North Carolina, who was come over on a religious vifit to this land, and who was in fome expectation of our companion G. D—— joining him ; but not feeling releafed one from another in the fervice wherein we were joined, it was judged moft prudent to wait for the openings of truth, as much in our feparation, as we had endeavoured to attend to

---

* The following is extracted from a letter bearing date the 1ft of 9th month, 1785. " Such is the ftate of our fociety in thefe parts, as well as in divers places in our land, that it is hard dragging along for poor travellers ; the prevailing death is ready to fwallow them up, and fo put a ftop to all circulation of life. Well ! drooping as our fpirits often are, we have no where elfe to go but to the fountain, which is, at times, when faith and patience are at the loweft ebb, unexpectedly opened for our renewed refrefhment, and encouragement to truft a little longer. Here are, notwithftanding, in the North of this nation where we have been, a few beautiful plants amongft the young and younger men, whofe roots are, I truft, deepening in the heavenly foil ; but in the profpect of their future trials, if they are faithful, I am almoft ready to tremble, there is fuch a hoft of oppofition for them to prefs through, in reviving the purity of the gofpel. We are nearly united to them, and to find them was like meeting with near kindred.

them in joining. We left this Province pretty directly after the quarterly meeting, and set off towards Dublin, taking Rathfriland meeting in our way, to which many town's people came, and it was a large and favoured meeting. We reached Dublin the 15th of 9th month, where we staid near a week, and sat several meetings, under great oppression and discouragement of mind, and without much relief saw an opening to leave the place and go to Timahoe. Here we visited their families and had peace therein. From thence we set off for Edenderry; and going by way of Rathangan, an opening which had been put by when we were there before, of having a public meeting amongst the town's people, presented again; and we had cause to admire, how providentially we were cast in the way of performing such pointings of duty, as had been, more from diffidence than a rebellious mind, passed over. Here we staid over first day, and had a large crowded meeting in the evening, which was considerably disturbed by some rude people in liquor, but divers were very solid, and it ended well. From Rathangan we pursued our journey to Edenderry, Tullamore, Moat, Ballimurry, Birr*, Killconnenmore,

---

* From this place, she writes as follows: "Gloomy is the prospect that opens in many places, and yet, by getting low enough, we sometimes find to our refreshment, that there is, in most places, a hidden suffering seed, with which we have sympathized, and in the extendings of renewed strength, been led to visit, though it is but little known or valued by the easy carnally minded professors; and I have sometimes thought, that

and Roscrea; in all which a degree of painful exercise was our lot, under the feeling sense of the general departure of the professors of truth, from that ancient, righteous zeal and primitive simplicity, which the people of God who walked faithfully before Him, were, in all ages, conspicuous for. But He who never said to the wrestling seed of Jacob, "seek ye my face in vain," graciously condescended to reward the travail of our spirits, by arising for His own name's sake, and giving strength to lift the standard of righteousness, and furnishing with an invitation to the youth to repair to it, and so inherit the blessed effects thereof.

We went to Limerick from Roscrea, and staid there over first and second days. The public meetings were low, distressing opportunities, and little ability to labour amongst that people, who seem much under the influence of the god of this world: but on first day evening, a number of youth being present at T. M's and a few honest-hearted friends more advanced in years, we had a very favoured season of retirement, and the streams of love and life, through instructive, consolating ministry, ran freely. On third day we left Limerick for Youghall; my mind was dipped into a sense of my own weakness, and great discouragement and dismay sur-

if our coming answers no other end than to strengthen a few, weak hands, and be instrumental in reviving the hope of the humble, tried children in the family, it will be enough, though the reward to ourselves may be but small."

rounded me. I saw the necessity of an encreasing labour to dwell near the pure gift in myself, which I have ever found to be the most effectual preservation, in the conflicting work of purification and faithfulness in more public service; for when it reduces the mind, and brings it down as into the bottom of Jordan, it likewise stays the billows thereof by pure faith, and succours by the incomes of patience, whereby every divine dispensation is rendered profitable, and every bitter thing sweet; centring us out of the reach of fleshy confidence, in that state of abasedness to which divine compassion is most eminently extended. We lodged one night at an inn, and on fourth day reached Youghall, where, on fifth, we had two large and favoured meetings. Next day we got to Springmount near Cork, to the house of our dear and honourable friend S. N. Here I heard of the decease of our beloved friend, Robert Walker, who departed this life at Tottenham, near London, after having paid an acceptable religious visit to friends of that city and its neighbourhood. He was a man who having passed through deep baptisms of spirit, in preparation for the work of the ministry, became eminent therein. The multitude could not judge, neither did they know, his frequent, suffering descendings with the seed, when crucified in the hearts of the people, as in the streets of spiritual Sodom and Egypt; and considering himself as an unworthy minister thereto, he was clothed with resignation to the dispensation of the day. Great was his industry, and yet many were the trials of his faith for the supply of temporal things. Though unadorned with human literature, he was instructed in the school of Christ, as a good Scribe to whom was committed the knowledge of the mysteries of the kingdom, wherein all necessary accomplishments were acquired, and displayed in gospel simplicity.

Since my coming into this Province, the subject which has for some time been under my consideration, of settling in these parts, has often presented to my mind; with an anxious desire, that the most endeared companion of my life, may, with myself, be kept single in all our views, and resigned in our spirits to whatever infinite wisdom sees meet to do with us; that the way before us, though it be strait and narrow, may not be made more difficult, by any willings and runnings of our own. I am often afraid of myself in this respect; I feel, when unsupported by best help, a partial attachment to my native land; and to part with my connections, and some to whom I am closely united in spirit, at times appears hard: but even on this footing, I find a counterpoising weight on my husband's side, who has also valuable relations, and many friends in the best sense, with temporal concerns and conveniencies more suitable than elsewhere. Oh then, may divine counsel influence our spirits, in the consideration, and determination of this important step! Thou knowest O Lord! the fervency and exercise of my spirit herein; thou knowest, that, above all things I wish to serve thee, with the dedication of all that I have, when thou callest for it; and as by thy power only, an holy compliance is wrought; O withhold it not in the needful time! Suffer not our feet to flide from the ancient foundation, but with the right arm of thy ftrength, enable us to make war in righteoufnefs, in the lot thou affigneft! O fhew us the lot! Suffer us not to wander in the dark, but be thou gracioufly pleafed fpiritually to lead us, by the cloud and pillar of fire, certain tokens of thy holy approbation of the way that we take!

At Cork we ftaid, (except going one day to Bandon, and returning the next) eleven days, and attended nine meetings, and many private opportunities in friend's families, where counfel and encouragement often unexpectedly opened; which were miniftered under the precious influence of divine love and life; wherein the fpirits of a remnant were cemented together, in a degree of holy fellowfhip, and an exercife generally prevailed to help one another forward in the new and living way; which in many places lies much unoccupied, the travellers having got into paths fo widely different, that it is fometimes difficult to find it, and when found, fo to believe in its rectitude, as to make ftraight fteps therein.

During my ftay in and about Cork, I had frequent occafions humbly to commemorate the wifdom, mercy, and power, of our gracious Helper, who, in a time of deep humiliation and adverfity, fuftained my poor toffed foul; and, by a portion of that holy faith which I knew to be his own immediate gift, gave me to fee his all-fufficiency, and my own nothingnefs; and after melting all that was within me, by his humbling difpenfations, faw meet again to renew his image upon my heart, and to cause me to experience more largely the work of the new creation, and the necessity of ever abiding in lowliness of mind, and treading the courts of the Lord with holiness and fear. O! said my soul, withhold not from me whatever hath this tendency; let the voice of the Holy One go forth, which saith, " cut down the tree," rather than it should overspread, and bring forth fruit, to dishonour the great and excellent Name: nevertheless, may that which is pure be fastened, as with a band of iron in the tender grass of the field, that so, humility and simplicity may spring, and more loudly acknowledge, that the Most High reigns in the kingdoms of men, and giveth of his own precious gifts and favours to whomsoever he will.

We went from Cork to the house of a friend who, for some months past, has been in a low dejected state of mind; and in the evening my dear companion R. J. was dipt into his situation, and her mouth was opened in living counsel and encouragement, which for a time seemed to revive him. Here I met with my dear husband, to our mutual consolation; and from hence, after attending a meeting next day at Garryroan, which was rather a low time, we went to Clonmel to our mother's there, and rested one day before the quarterly meeting for Munster province came on. Our minds were measurably baptized for the approaching solemnity, particularly that of my beloved friend R. J. who with dear G. D. had good service; and the meetings, though laborious, were eminently owned with the extenſion of divine good, and friends were renewedly encouraged to faithfulneſs in their reſpective lots. I ſat all the meetings ſilently, not without a fellow-feeling and travail with thoſe engaged in turning the battle to the gate; but my ſpirit was ſo clothed with the garment of mourning, and the ſenſe of my own inſufficiency, that I was ready to ſay, with the Prophet, " I will ſpeak no more in Thy Name." Yet to be preſerved in a ſtate of patient exerciſe, and in reſignation to what might be the allotted portion of ſuffering in this day of trial, was the fervent deſire of my mind. In this frame, I have often known the moſt ſenſible incomes of holy help, and been more enabled from thence to bring up ſtones of memorial, than when the travail of my ſoul has been more ſhallow, and the ſtreams of the miniſtry have lain nearer the ſurface of the people's ſpirits; and O! that, in all ſeaſons of proving, I may never ſhrink from under that mournful covering, till the ſenſe of what I am, and a degree of living faith in the immediate teachings of divine wiſdom, are not only raiſed, but prevail in my heart; that ſo, the creature, its wiſdom and activity, may die daily, under that Power which crucifies all that is of the fleſh, and ſanctifies throughout. After the quarterly meeting was over, we were moſt eaſy to ſit with the friends of that particular meeting; where I felt an openneſs for ſome religious communication; and it was a cloſe, but favoured time; nevertheleſs a degree of ſadneſs remained with me. After this meeting was over, and partaking of a cup of heavenly consolation in the family of a relation, we went down to Anner Mills that night, and next day set off for Dublin, in order to attend the half year's meeting, held in the eleventh month. It was rather a low time, but holy help was near (according to ancient declaration) to the Poor in Spirit, the exercised wrestling seed, of which, through preserving goodness, there is a remnant in this land; with whose tribulated path I have often been dipped into near sympathy, and was renewedly so at this time: nevertheless, we had unitedly to believe, that if some of these persisted in unfaithfulness to the manifestations of duty, concerning their religious services, they were in danger of occasioning to themselves such a wilderness travel, as might prove very difficult for them to be delivered from. These were fervently and honestly laboured with, "to offer to the Lord the sacrifice of thanksgiving, and to pay all their vows;" that so, a generation might be raised up more zealous for the honour and promulgation of the great Name, than many of later times have been. My mind was greatly depressed in this city, and I found it conduce to my safety, to weigh well what I apprehended to be the motions of truth. The meetings were large, and my beloved companions being not only better qualified for service therein, but coming from so distant a part of the world as Pensylvania in America, and there being little or no prospect of their ever having another opportunity, of so fully relieving their minds to friends in this land, I sought for obscurity: which is always most desirable to my own mind, knowing that safety attends it; and that it requires deep baptisms, and a close dwelling with the gift, rightly to minister life, and visit the seed in large mixed congregations. Without an extraordinary degree of these, it seldom happens that the appearances of those who are young in experience, afford satisfaction to the true church of Christ, or that they reap the reward of solid instructive peace in their own minds; and often feeling that I am one of these, the prayer of my spirit has been, that I may be kept under the humbling sense thereof, and be preserved from burdening the living by being too shallow in my spirit, or spreading too much into fruitless branches; that so, the great and excellent cause of truth may never be dishonoured by or through me. Infinite wisdom is, nevertheless, to direct and go before us, in the line of His own appointment: and under an apprehension of the puttings forth of the heavenly Shepherd, I ventured to step forward in two large meetings; and through his sustaining goodness, I was enabled to relieve my own mind in a good degree; for which with many gracious assistances, from time to time dispensed, may my soul bow in humble gratitude and awful fear, through the continued stages of my tried pilgrimage. My dear friends R. J. and G. D. had great and good service in the course of these meetings; and R. J. feeling an engagement to have a meeting with the women friends, (none being held for discipline for them at that season of the year) after laying it before friends, it was cheerfully complied with, and a solid profitable meeting it proved.

R. J. and myself, feeling something more than a freedom to sit with a committee of men friends, appointed by the national meeting to consider the state of society, and complying with it, we were enabled to feel with friends thereon, and to lay down our respective burdens. The evening preceding our leaving the city, and after the meetings were over, many friends being collected at our lodgings, we had a refreshing, instructive, opportunity of retirement; wherein counsel and encouragement were ministered, and friends parted under a living sense of the extension of divine favour to His church and family. Next day we went to Baltiboys, a very poor small meeting; after which we proceeded about five miles further, intending next morning to set off for Mountmellick; but when all was ready for our departure, a hesitation sprang, and spread, respecting the propriety of our pursuing the intended plan; and the more it was looked at, the more clearly it appeared best to sit with the few friends select, there having been many not of our profession at meeting the day before. One of our guides, therefore, kindly undertook to collect the members of that meeting together; which was done, and we had no cause to repent our stay, but were rather encouraged to trust in future to the turnings of the spiritual guide, who requires that we should be followers, and not leaders, if we pursue the path of true peace. Instead of going to Mountmellick from Baltiboys, we went to Ballitore that night, and next day to Athy meeting; then to Mountmellick, Mentrath, Knockballymaher, Ballynakill, and to

Carlow to the quarterly meeting for Leinster Province held there. It was a remarkably low time, and the minds of many were baptized into a feeling sense of the coolness and indifferency, that prevails amongst the professors of truth in these parts, and silent sadness was much our lot. Intending from hence for Waterford, and the counties of Wexford and Wicklow, we first paid a visit to the little meeting at Castledermot; it was small, but divine goodness was near. My mind, in time of silence, was comfortably gathered from some buffetings, doubtings, and dismay; and the language of the apostle sweetly passed through, and settled me in an humble confidence and calm; be patient, establish your hearts, for the day of the Lord draweth nigh. We returned to Carlow and next day attended their week day meeting; after which we went to Ballydarton belonging to Kilconner meeting, which I was prevented from attending by a pain in my head and teeth; but was enabled to proceed with my companions to Ross next day, where growing worse, they were under the necessity of leaving me, after they had sat with the few friends there, in order to attend the first day meetings at Waterford; where my husband and divers of our relations from Clonmel came to meet us. My R. G. came to me, and was a truly acceptable guest, my mind having sunk, and my strength seeming to be exhausted with the pain. I was so much relieved as to be able to go next day to Waterford, to rejoin my beloved friends R. J. and G. D. whose company and services have been, through the course of this journey, instructive and strengthening to my often doubting mind. When through the descending of heavenly virtue, my spirit has been cemented with theirs, and in the unity and covenant of life, an harmonious exercise has prevailed in me, either in public or in secret, I have had renewedly to admire the gracious condescension of our holy Head and High Priest, in anointing, in any degree, for a work so great and awful, and leading into this excellent fellowship. At Waterford we staid their week day meeting on third day, which was a favoured time; and after having likewise divers comfortable religious opportunities with friends of that place, (there being a quickened remnant growing in the spiritual life) we took leave of them under a precious sense of divine superintending care, and went to Forest, Cooladine, Randal's Mills, Ballinclay, Ballicane and Wicklow; and found an honest-hearted set of friends, who are preserved in a good degree of consistency with the principles we profess: yet there are others who widely differ in this respect. Our kind friend J. W. having met us at Ballicane, we went in company with him to Dublin on the seventh day of the week, and next day attended their meetings in Meath-street and Sycamore-alley; at both which my companions were silent. My mind was deeply exercised in them, and as I perceived some little opening for public labour, I gave up thereto under many discouraging impressions; in part the effects of a reasoning disposition, and unprofitably ruminating on the repeated labours of more qualified instruments, and the unsuccessfulness of many of them; and in part, I trust, of a right and necessary jealousy over myself, lest I should be the means of conveying a lifeless multiplicity of words, or be found feeding the people, when the divine word might proclaim a fast. But it awfully sprang in my mind, that if ever so small a warning was given me to deliver, and I concealed it, the blood of those for whom it was intended might, according to the declaration of the Most High to the Prophet, be required at my hands. As this visit to the nation was closing, a secret prayer was begotten in me, that we might be enabled, as faithfully and willingly to finish the work, as, through humbling operations, we were resigned to begin it; which, to the praise of His grace who puts forth and goes before His own sheep, we were strengthened to do, and had afresh to discover that His ways are not as our ways, nor His thoughts as our thoughts. When we apprehended ourselves at liberty to sail from that city, and had agreed with a captain bound for Whitehaven for our passage there, the wind proved contrary, and we found it safe to look around us, that if any little service was omitted, it might then be performed. This we were ready to think was not much the case, having attended their men's and women's meetings on third day, where, through divine ability graciously afforded, we had a close, searching, and humbling season: but now standing in the resignation, not being detained of ourselves, divers opportunities for public and private labour unexpectedly opened, generally tending to invite the ignorant, and to encourage the sincere and drooping minds to a faith in the sufficiency of the gift of God in themselves, for the sanctification of the soul, and the necessary supply of every spiritual enjoyment, and qualification acceptably to worship; which must now, as formerly, be sought for, in the beauty of holiness, and in newness of life. The wind proving contrary, we staid over another first day, when my companions G. D and R. J. were enabled to bring up living stones of memorial, to the sealing I trust of their testimony on the spirits of many; and my cup of affectionate fellowship seemed to overflow in secret. The next day a gale rose in our favour, which we thankfully accepted, and were gently wafted over by it in twenty five hours, having had as pleasant a voyage as we could wish for, sickness excepted; and for the holy directing and protecting power of immortal goodness, we were gratefully humbled. We staid one night at Whitehaven after our landing, and next day attended their week-day meeting, which was a low time. Soon after it closed, we set off for Greysouthen, where R. J. and I staid that night. Our much loved friend and companion G. D. and his wife (who had been with us ever since we were at Cooladine) finding it conduce most to their peace to stay the quarterly meeting for Cumberland, to be held the week after; and we having a prospect of attending the quarterly meeting for the county of York, to be held at Leeds; we found the time for our separation was come; and had to commemorate the kindness of infinite wisdom, in so casting us together, and cementing us, according to our measures, in the hidden life. Here we took an affecting and affectionate farewell of each other.

We stopped at Cockermouth in our way to Kendal, and spent a few hours very agreeably with our friends J. and B. D. and their children; and before we left them, the spring of heavenly consolation arose, and refreshed both visitors and visited; and with grateful hearts we set off, and reached Keswick that night; and next day, having a pleasant ride among the mountains, we were favoured in good time to get to Kendal, where my dear companion had an opportunity of visiting J. and R. W.'s children, who, since she was there before, had lost their honourable father, and it was a humbling favoured opportunity. Finding ourselves at liberty to leave that place, and R. J. having passed by Wray and Bentham meetings when she was that way before, and now feeling a draft towards them, we went next day, the twenty fourth of the twelfth month, to Wray, and in the evening had a good meeting with the few friends there, and some others who came in. Next morning we went to Bentham meeting, which was an exercising time, but ended in awful supplication, wherein my beloved companion was publicly engaged. Having an evening meeting appointed at Settle, we reached there in time, and it proved a solid, instructive, season. From thence on first day, the twenty sixth, we got to Leeds, and there met with my dear father and mother, to our mutual satisfaction. The quarterly meeting came on next day, and held till the evening of the twenty ninth. Through the several sittings thereof, I had undoubtedly to believe that my companion was in her right place; and was thankful, under the confideration that we were there in better wifdom than our own, and were found worthy to bear a fhare in the weight of fufferings, which generally attend thefe large affemblies. Rebecca Jones being difpofed to fpend a little time in reft with our mutual friend C. H. we parted after our quarterly meeting, and I came homewards, with a defire rightly to feel my way, whether to continue a while longer with this my endeared friend, in her religious fervice, or to give up and furrender my certificate: for though I had a profpect, when I left home, of vifiting the weftern part of this nation, to which my certificate was alfo addreffed, yet if the commiffion fhould clofe fooner than I looked for, my compliance therewith appears as neceffary, as it would be if it fhould extend further; feeing that the virtue of all our religious movements confifts in the divine putting forth, and the continuation of holy anointing; which we have abundant caufe to acknowledge, is not at our command.

CHAP. IV.

Account of her Visit to some of the western Counties of England.

A FEW months after her return from Ireland, she felt a renewed engagement to accompany her friend R. Jones, on a visit to some parts of the western counties in England. Of the principal parts of this visit, she has left the following journal.

After my return from Ireland, my beloved companion R. J. being detained in Yorkshire, on divers accounts, for three months, I was thereby set at liberty to adjust some family concerns at home, and pay some visits to neighbouring meetings as truth appeared to open the way; especially to Whitby, Scarborough, Bridlington, Hornsea, and Hull; in the course of which my mind was, in the needful time, mercifully supported with renewed supplies of holy help, though, in general, in a low and stripped state; fearing lest, in the exercise of the gift, a zeal which is not according to true knowledge, nor originating in that baptism of spirit wherein the creature is humbled, should so mix with the divine openings, as to carry away the feet of the mind from that safe standing in the deeps, which is justly compared to the bottom of Jordan. Here, it is necessary for true gospel ministers, steadily to abide, with the weight of the service they are engaged in upon their shoulders, till the spirits of the assembled are, in some degree, attracted to the promised land, the new heaven and the new earth, wherein dwelleth the righteousness of faith, and where spiritual worship is rightly performed, in the beauty of holiness and newness of life. To be instrumental in the divine hand of thus, in any measure, converting the spirits of those to whom we may be led to minister, requires an unction altogether unmixed; but when revolt, backsliding, and a superficial spirit, have been necessarily unveiled, I have, sometimes, distressingly found, that some of my armour was carnal; and O! how hath all that was within me been humbled at the discovery, that the Lord's righteous controversy with the works of darkness, had not been righteously upheld, nor the door of escape therefrom wisely opened. An encrease of experience convinces me, that preaching is a mystery which every one exercised therein, has need to be often industriously, and impartially learning, as far as concerns themselves; and where this is the case, I am abundantly persuaded, that our dependance must be drawn from the sentiments of those friends to whose judgment we are most attached, in order rightly to distinguish betwixt the unity of the one infallible spirit, and their partiality to us, and to be weighed in the just balance of the sanctuary, where we are sometimes found defective, even when all around us speak peace.

"My dear husband accompanied me in this little round: his sympathizing mind, and care for my preservation every way, was truly strengthening, and afforded frequent occasions of humble thankfulness to the Author of all good, who had so bountifully provided for me, both in spiritual and temporal things. After our return home we gave up housekeeping, not with a conclusion that we should remove from England, but under an apprehension that it was right to take that step, as the way opened for my being again united in service with my beloved companion R. J. and my husband had no prospect of being settled during my absence. We therefore removed our furniture, and ourselves to York, the quarterly meeting there being at hand; after which, the 1st of 4th month, 1786, I went to Ackworth to meet my companion, who had gone there the day before. We staid there on first day, and found some close and necessary labour, not only in public, but in private opportunities, amongst the masters, mistresses, and servants, severally; for the Enemy of all good hath proved himself busy, in endeavouring to sow his tares amongst the good seed in that institution and family; and unless those on whom the weight and care of it most devolves, keep in view the necessity of attending more to the holy Oracle in their movements, than to the strength of their own wisdom and understanding, it will lose the lustre that truth would put upon it, and become the nursery of a worldly spirit, though disguised with an appearance of religious form. There is in that family a suffering, wrestling seed, an exercised remnant, which though small, is a means, under the divine blessing, of keeping open the spring of life; and if such keep their places, there is reason to hope that more will be added to their number, and, through the influence of their example, the truth, in its own simplicity, gain ground, instead of the disguised spirit of error. A salutation of love flowed to such, under a sense whereof we left them, save our worthy friend W. S. who went with us to Wakefield, where divers are under convincement, and some of them appear to be rightly so. Here we had an open, instructive opportunity; and from thence went to Bradford, and next day proceeded to Manchester, where we attended their week day meeting; in which my companion was greatly favoured to dip into the state of the seed, and profitably to visit it, and silence was I believe rightly my lot. From Manchester we went to Stockport, Macclesfield, Morley, and so to Warrington, to the monthly meeting there; where again I thought my companion had eminent service, and close searching labour, wherewith I felt a spiritual travail, and sympathetic mourning over the great carnality, and departure from the way of peace, which greatly prevail in that, and the neighbouring places. Though there is a peculiar people, and a royal priesthood, in that monthly meeting, yet as the number in a very different spirit, is great, the pure life is prevented from circulating, and purifying the temple. So that the prospect, amongst the youth especially, is exceedingly discouraging; dissipation, or the gilded corruptions of human nature, having possession, and, like the strong man armed, keeping the house and all the goods thereof in peace: and 'till a stronger than he, by the spirit of judgment and of burning, dislodges him of his hold, casts him out, and spoils all his goods, there is but little room to expect such to demonstrate unto others, by the liveliness of their spirits, the circumspection of their conduct, and a rightly seasoned conversation, that they are acquainted with the efficacious virtue of true religion. From Warrington, my husband returned to Yorkshire, in company with William Rotch of Nantucket, and we back into Cheshire. It was rather a gloomy parting to me, being very unwell with a rheumatic complaint in my head, and more depressed in mind than I was free to express to any; which is often the case with me, when under a sense of the awfulness of the work I am embarked in, of the little effect it has on the minds of many, and of my own exceeding great weakness, and apparent unfitness for engaging with sacred things; so that my way oft seems to lie by the valley and shadow of death; where I feel myself subject to fearful apprehensions, and a deep and gloomy exercise. Nevertheless, to the praise of the divine grace, my soul can thankfully and humbly acknowledge that, through what appeared the smallest grain of faith, preservation hath been experienced, and strength to ascend, in the Lord's time, that holy mountain where nothing can hurt or destroy; because the creature, and its attendant evils are subjected, and access to the feast of fat things, and of wine well refined, is graciously afforded, to the renewed support of the drooping mind, which was ready, but a little before, to cast away its confidence, and say, " the Lord hath forgotten me." Thus, as by a tender father, are we dealt with, under those proving dispensations, which are essentially necessary for carrying forward the work of sanctification in the soul, and a preparation to receive the inscription of, " Holiness unto the Lord." When I consider the necessity hereof, a fear, on the other hand, often arises lest it should be partially or superficially effected; and a fervent craving of spirit, that the refining operations of the Holy Ghost and Fire, may so perform their assigned office, as that every specious appearance of self-love may be consumed, and the spring of action, in the performance of both religious and moral duties, rendered pure. Thus variously, is the attention of the travailing soul turned; and if the pure discoveries of truth are but the object singly sought for, He who created light out of darkness, and hath sown it for the righteous, doth, in times of our greatest extremity reveal himself to be the Lord Almighty. From Warrington we went to Sutton, Franley, Newton, Chester, Nantwich, and Middlewich, when our visit to Cheshire seemed ended, where, as in other places, we had to view, and mourn over, the desolation which hath prevailed amongst the professors of truth; so that the Heathen may query, " Where is their God ?"

Our next stage was to Leek, and so to Colebrook Dale; we had meetings both at the New and Old Dale, which were favoured, strengthening seasons; by ability being graciously afforded and accepted, to sink down deep into suffering with the precious seed; and a little exercised remnant were found wrestling in spirit for the divine blessing, who were visited in the renewings of life, and instructive counsel flowed towards them. Divers of the younger sort amongst them, have been visited by affliction; the day of the Lord hath come upon all that was lifted up, and the projects, like the ships of Tarshish, which were intended to go to fetch gold, have been broken early in their setting out, as at Eziongeber, and all their pleasant pictures spoiled; which have evidently been permitted in mercy, that their affections might be loosened from things transient and perishing; and, instead thereof, durable riches and righteousness become their inheritance. But as this work is great and glorious, and cannot be effected, save by the humbling processes of the work of sanctification in the soul, a deep engagement dwelt upon my mind, that those in whom this work is begun, may by preserved from flinching under it, or taking themselves, or one another, as out of the furnace, before it effect the great end for which it was prepared; and that, being redeemed from the superficies of religious experience, to an entire dependance on the holy purifying spring of immortal life, they may approve themselves the humble followers of Christ; and, through the efficacy of his own spirit, be qualified to advocate the cause of truth and righteousness. From hence we went to Shrewsbury, and were at two meetings there on first day, which were favoured opportunities; the latter was public, and a great many of the town's people attended. There are some visited young people in this place, and a prospect of a revival comfortably affected our minds. It was here to be determined whether we should turn towards Worcestershire, Herefordshire, &c. or into Wales, which was occasion of deep enquiry to find out the good and acceptable way; and as our minds were single herein, we were favoured to unite in the conclusion, that it was better now to turn into Wales, a step we had no reason to repent on any account, finding a peaceful serenity attending our minds through the course of a solitary travel therein; and such a supply of strength to dip into, and visit the seed in those parts, as was cause of humble thankfulness to the Author of every good and spiritual gift. His eye perceives the most obscure parts of his own creation, and graciously compassionates His humble suppliant children, who, under a sense of their own wants, are casting all their care upon him, and looking singly to his bountiful hand for food convenient for them, both spiritual and temporal, in preference to the luxurious enjoyment of transitory things; desiring that blessing which makes truly rich, and whereunto no deadly sorrow is added. We were comforted in finding a number of this sort in Wales, particularly at Tuthynigarrig and Llanidloes; though, at the former, amongst divers of their members, a worldly spirit and lukewarmness about the best things prevail. We were also at Eskergoch, a very poor desolate place every way; but some solid people not professing with us, attending the meeting, were

G

a help to it; and my beloved companion was drawn in the language of confolation to vifit fome of thefe, who were as fheep wandering upon the mountains, and panting after a fhepherd. It was from this place we went to Llanidloes, where we had a large public meeting, and from thence to Rayadar, a place where there are no friends, but where we had a fatisfactory meeting amongft the town's people, in one of the rooms of the inn; and after it went to Pales, and were at meeting there next day, which was a laborious, fearching opportunity, many diforderly walkers being there. We then ftept out of Wales, and vifited the few friends at Almilly and Leominfter, in Herefordfhire. The firft is very fmall, having fcarce any weight to fupport a meeting; but many folid neighbours attending, it was a precious lively opportunity, and my fpirit was humbled, and awfully reverenced the condefcending goodnefs of our Almighty Helper, whofe loving kindnefs is better than life, and the lifting up of the light of his countenance, than great riches. The meeting at Leominfter was low and trying. We went from hence to Troy near Monmouth in South Wales: here we lodged one night, and next morning fet off for Pontipool to the quarterly meeting, which was to be held there the firft day following. Our dear and much valued friends T. Corbyn, H. Wilkins and T. H. overtook us upon the road; we were mutually glad to fee each other, and alfo to feel each others fpirits in the meetings we attended together at Pontipool and Cardiff, whither we went (after the quarterly meeting was ended) to attend the Welch yearly meeting there. My mind, on drawing near to that place, was awfully affected, in a renewed fenfe of the important ftation of a gofpel minifter, which, the more my underftanding is opened, the more I perceive it to call for a watchful care to keep in the ftation, and to preferve it unblameable, by endeavouring to dwell low enough with the gift, fo as rightly to diftinguifh between a filent union with the feed in meetings, (wherein we fometimes fympathize with the concerns of others), and our own public fervice for the caufe. And I was thankful in feeling my fpirit humbly contrited, under a fenfe of my own weaknefs, and the commemoration of infinite kindnefs in times paft; and I fecretly fupplicated that the approaching folemnity might be gracioufly owned with the virtue of divine life, immediately imparted from the great Minifter of minifters; whereby I felt, in a good degree, ftrengthened for my own meafure of exercife, which proved altogether in filence. But this was not the cafe with fome others; with a few of whom a fenfe of near unity attended my fpirit, both in a fecret travail of fpirit, and in the exercife of their gifts; never that I remember, being fo fenfible of the purity of that life which, and which only, quickens fervices in the church, and qualifies the centred mind, to judge righteoufly concerning public offerings in meetings. Whatever has a tendency to clofe up the fpring of this life, by cafting rubbifh thereinto, inftead of induftrioufly removing it, fuch as the fhallow, fuperficial judgment of the natural mind, its old experiences and wisdom, which are held out of the life, can never availingly invite the wrestling soul, that is panting after the pure milk of the divine word, to the fountain of spiritual consolation, or refresh the christian pilgrim in his journey heavenwards. O the purity of that life which is hid with Christ in God! It cannot be supported but by the flesh and blood, the virtue or divine nature of the Son; nor can it unite with that which is not congenial to itself. There is a ministry which, like the whirlwind, the earthquake, and the fire, makes apparent effects upon nature, shakes it, throws it into confusion, and kindles it with untempered zeal; but proves very deficient in settling it upon the sure foundation; or introducing it into that rest which is prepared for the people of God, who cease from all their own works; or teaching it to distinguish between the voice of the Shepherd, and the voice of the stranger. Hence, many, otherwise well disposed minds, have got bewildered, their attention diverted from the one great Object, and fixed upon sacrifices of their own; which, in time, are so depended upon for righteousness, that the hunger which was once begotten decreases, and the state of the church of Laodicea becomes theirs; growing rich and full, increasing with goods and in need of nothing; when alas! though specious their appearance, their situation is most wretched, and, in the light of truth, they are discovered to stand in need of every thing. Under these considerations, my mind is often instructed in the necessity of confiding only in the Spring of life itfelf, and approving nothing as religious, but what comes from it, or is under its preparing, fanctifying power: and for this end, it is neceffary to be very watchful over the activity of felf, that the fpirits may be tried, and my faith proved, whether it is grounded and eftablifhed upon the right foundation, or is of that fort that wavers and floats upon any imaginary prefentation, whereby I may be rendered of thofe who are not to expect any thing at the hand of God, James, i. 6, 7. There are fo many ways for the mind, when it is off its guard, to be enfnared either into fenfible darknefs, or a righteoufnefs of its own, which is worft of all, that, when cloathed with a fenfe of my infirmity and weaknefs, I mourn in fpirit; and am thankful when, in a grain of unadulterated faith, I can fay, " if thou wilt, thou canft " make me clean," and breathe for the blessing of prefervation. From a fear of being inftrumental in fettling down young people efpecially, in the form of godlinefs without the power; and urging them to an appearance which might create felf-complacence, and reconcile them to an apprehenfion, that they are further advanced in the work of religion than is really the cafe; I have often forborne to drop fuch advice upon the fubject of drefs, amongft thofe who were inconfiftent in their appearance, as, fometimes, I felt the teftimony of truth to dictate; a departure from true fimplicity herein being generally obvious. At large meetings particularly, where friends from diftant parts are collected, there is a considerable appearance of inconsistency in clothing and demeanour, which, with many other things, indicate a love of the world, and a fellowship with its spirit; but though a regulation herein is only a small part of the fruit of the good Tree, yet it is as assuredly a part, as the more striking constituents of a christian. " Whatsoever is not of faith is sin," is a comprehensive truth, which neither approves an inconsistent, nor a plausible appearance and conduct, merely as such; but wholly condemns every part of our lives which is not governed by the redeeming Spirit of truth, wherein our faith should stand: so that, to attain this state, to live under the righteous controul of divine monition, is I apprehend to be a follower of Christ, under whose spiritual baptism the precious is separated from the vile, and by whose fan, the chaff, to which the vanities of this life may be compared, will flee, and leave the wheat, for divine protection, in the heavenly garner. Feeling my mind drawn to a little solid conversation with a young woman, to whom I had felt near unity, and whom I believed to be under the preparing hand for service, but diffident in spirit, and a suitable opportunity offering, I accepted it; wherein I dropped a little matter by way of encouragement to her, in her silent steppings and hidden exercises; taking occasion to observe, that as she had hitherto been preserved, in a good measure, independant of human consolations, so I wished her to continue, believing that the arm of omnipotence was most eminently revealed to us in this state of singleness, under such spiritual provings and conflicts as are essentially necessary for sanctification. It was a time of mutual comfort, and I was thankful that I gave up to it.

At Cardiff we met again our beloved brother G. D. which both he and we rejoiced at. He was much favoured in several of the meetings, especially the public ones, which were large; but my dear companion had not much openness for public labour, till the last opportunity with friends select; when she was strengthened to visit the members of our society in a memorable manner; which with some, will I trust, be as a nail fastened in a sure place. In our way from Cardiff to Bristol, to which we were bound, we stopped at Newport to breakfast, where my companion and G. D. felt an inclination to have a public meeting, which was readily complied with, and held in a room in the inn; many came to it, and it was a favoured opportunity. We then proceeded on our journey, crossed what is called the new passage, and reached Bristol late that night. We met with a hospitable reception from Lydia Hawksworth, with whom we sojourned, and next day I went with my companion and Lydia to see our beloved, honoured friend, C. Phillips, then at J. Hipsley's at Congersbury. She was in a languid state of health, which in some degree occasioned a depression of spirits, but her best life was strong, though hid from herself with Christ in God. She hath been a faithful, laborious servant in the church, especially under the exercise of her gift, which was eminent for its purity, its copiousness, and clearness; distinguishing the good and evil trees by representing their fruits in their true light. Her ministry had a tendency, to raise into dominion the pure life, and in supplication she hath been often wonderfully favoured with near access, and enabled to cast down every crown, and to ascribe worship and praise, salvation and strength, to the Lord God and the Lamb. Since my mind has been graciously visited with a sense of truth, such hath been my sentiment concerning this great and good woman: but about two years ago, to my humble admiration, in a season of great proving of spirit, it was so renewed and sealed to me, the inward attraction so strong, and the evidence that she was a faithful follower of the Lamb, so undoubted, (a language sweetly flowing through my mind, " I have chosen her and she is mine") that I not only rejoiced, and was strengthened, but saw the abundant superiority of the unfoldings of truth, to all the prepossession we can receive from the experience of others; my want of an outward acquaintance with her being thus amply supplied by the gracious condescension of the Head of the church, who wisely and mysteriously unites together the large and small members of His body, and, by such connection, makes them more useful to each other than they know or can of themselves conceive. Where this union and sense is thus received, I am of the belief that nothing but a departure from the divine life, wherein a christian fellowship stands, can ever alter our inward feelings towards the Lord's anointed. Though I am often dismayed at the sight of things within and without, and since the time alluded to, have been ready to say in mine hafte, "all men are liars;" yet it was matter of renewed confolation and abafement of mind, that on being in company with our beloved friend, C. Phillips, my feelings refpecting her were revived, with fweetnefs and rejoicing. But thefe were mixed with an inexpreffible fympathy, and fenfe of the buffetings and floods of the dragon, yea, and of his temptations as in the wildernefs; where, though fhe hungered, yet, with unconquered fortitude, nobly refifted every importunity, to command the ftones to be made bread. Having fuffered with her Lord and Mafter, and been preferved through many temptations, my fecret belief was that life will again arife abundantly in her, and her garments, even in this ftate of mutability, be wafhed and made white in the blood of the fuffering, yet victorious Lamb. And oh! how did all that was within me bow under this perfuafion, and under a fenfe that the difciples of Jefus have, in proportion to their ftrength and gifts, a meafure of afflictions to fill for their own, and the body's fake, which is His church. Here my reflections on myfelf were exceedingly awful; I confidered that I was juft entering the field, unfkilled in war, with the armour but newly put on, and exceedingly uncertain whether I fhall not fall a prey to mine enemy. But O Lord! teach, I pray thee, mine hands to war, and my fingers to fight, even the good fight of faith, in the fufficiency of thy power, and againft every intrufion of my own; that thou, in all things, mayft be glorified, and if I perifh, it may be at thy footftool!

The yearly meeting at Bristol came on, and lasted three days. It afforded many opportunities for suffering, and deep gloomy exercise, to those who travailed in spirit for the arisings of life, which, nevertheless, for a short season, in divers of them, sensibly circulated; but it seems as if, for want of vessels rightly prepared, the current was often turned backward, and retired again into obscurity, where a baptized number endeavoured patiently to dwell; amongst whom was my beloved companion, who found but little liberty to relieve her burdened mind. The first day after the yearly meeting we were at Claverham meeting, which was a favoured instructive opportunity, and returned to Bristol to their evening meeting; at the conclusion of which, my companion had to revive the message sent to Hezekiah, and, with evident strength and clearness, to apply it to some there. A young man who was then in the vigour of life, was soon seized with an epidemic fever, and in a few weeks removed from this stage of mortality; and several others who took the disorder, narrowly escaped with their lives; to whom the previous admonition, to set their houses in order, was likewise seasonable. Next day we went to Sudbury, to the quarterly meeting for Gloucester and Wilts. Here we found a great want of true zeal, and love to the cause of truth, wherein living members are united in harmonious labour, and cemented together in the covenant of life; which preserves from a disposition that would look only to selfish things, and enlarges the heart in an upright care for the prosperity of others. From

Sudbury we took meetings at Bath, Wesbury, Lavington, Devizes, Marlborough, and Uxbridge, in our way to London, being favoured to get safe there the thirty first of fifth month, which afforded us a few days to rest, before the yearly meeting began. This meeting opened, to those whose spiritual faculties were alive in the truth, a field of exercising labour; wherein a steady, watchful care was necessary for all to keep to their own stations and vocations, with an attentive eye to the great Master; as a busy indiscreet interference of His servants, ever interrupts the beautiful order and prosperity of His work. The select meetings were to me, as they generally are at our yearly meetings, (though not all alike attended with life) seasons of deep instruction, which I was made humblingly sensible could not be the case, by any capacity of my own to render them so, but by being admitted (however undeservedly) for a short time, by the Master of assemblies, into the heavenly treasury, where the saint's provision, the armour of righteousness, and the just balance of the sanctuary, are all to be found; and where, as we deeply and quietly abide, we are furnished with an unerring perception of what, amongst the many offerings in the visible church, proceeds from the divine repository, and what doth not; so that individuals thus gathered, though in an obscure exercise, may say with the apostle, and which I heard revived in one of these meetings, "in every thing I am instructed." And as in the opening of spiritual things, and being favoured in some degree with a sense of truth, respecting the subjects of deliberation which come before these meetings, the natural disposition sometimes prompts us to make public remarks consonant with our feelings; I have, thus far, found it necessary to set a double watch upon this side, lest I should step forward unbidden to put a hand to the ark, (the real state of which Uzza saw as well as I) and so, like him, unavailingly labour, and introduce death upon myself; proving unworthy of an admittance into the treasury, and of being entrusted with divine secrets, which are not to be revealed but in the divine will, and under the sensible direction of the High Priest of our profession; that the bread which we minister, being given us by Him, may also be blessed, and that, however apparently coarse and insufficient, its efficacy and extensive usefulness may abound to those who are fed, and redound to His praise whose will is our sanctificaton. As an attentive care on this hand is necessary, I likewise perceived a danger on the other, when, in the simplicity and nakedness of truth, and consequently unadorned with any thing goodly in my own eyes, a right season has been discovered to express a few words, and through unprofitable diffidence, and undervaluing the smallness of the appearance, I have put by these little openings to duty. This was more than once the case, during the sittings of the select meetings this year, and which contributed to my own increasing weakness. So that, whilst we are desirous to keep our own hearts, and be preserved from prodigality in imparting our religious feelings, we ought also to stand resigned to the secret intimations of truth, in order to approve ourselves good stewards of the manifold grace of God; advancing from one degree of favour, acceptance, and communion with Him, to another, and thus become established before Him as children without rebuke. The meetings for discipline of women friends became exceedingly weighty to me, as the friend who was clerk last year declined the office, and my name was mentioned by divers for that service. I sought to object, under an awful sense of the weightiness of that station, especially in so large and newly established a meeting, and with the feebleness of my qualifications for it; but I soon felt all resistance chained down in me, and a secret, fervent breathing begotten for that holy assistance, which I knew to be superior to every effort of my own without it: for though a degree of exertion is necessary, and the natural faculties of mind called upon to service, yet I saw they are no longer instrumental in helping forward the cause of truth and righteousness, than whilst they are actuated by divine love and life, and abide in the faith, without the government of which, they are no better than sounding brass, and a tinkling cymbal. Under this humbling persuasion, I took my seat, having E. T. and S. D. to assist; and the business of the meeting opened, which proved, in the several succeeding sittings, a profitable service, introducing women friends, more generally than heretofore, into an exercise on their own, their families, and the church's account; for want of which, great declension from the virtue of true religion, and the simplicity it leads into, has long lamentably spread amongst us as a people. And since, in the turnings and overturnings of the great Controller of events, a women's yearly meeting is established, and for these two last years hath been regularly opened in correspondence with the several quarterly meetings, in order more deeply to enter into the state of society, as it is seen in the truth, a necessity was evidently discovered from meeting to meeting, for friends to encrease their acquaintance with the light, which only makes manifest, and without which our judgment is exceedingly imperfect; and when this is obtained, not only to work in it, but to work wisely in it, endeavouring to suppress a disposition which is not purely intent upon reaching the witness in each other, even when under the necessity of humblingly displaying that christian virtue, of rendering good for evil, and of being willing to endure all things. Christian condescension is one of the great wheels whereby the cause of truth is advanced, amongst rightly exercised members, in meetings for discipline. When a burden rests on the mind of any, which in simplicity is removed, it adds greatly to its value, and recommends it to those to whom it is offered, when submitted in the spirit of true meekness, and no inclination discovered to urge that out of the truth, which at first was delivered with the favour of it; even though it may seem to undergo persecution, by that wisdom in others which is from beneath, and is carnal; for a blessing belongs to those who rightly endure persecution, and being reviled, revile not again.

To discriminate between our own spirits, and a right zeal when contending for the faith, requires great singleness of heart, and openness to self-conviction, which I have sorrowfully observed too few arrive at, or dwell in; and hence we are deprived of an encrease in the encrease of God, the fruit-bearing branches not being so effectually purged, as to enable them to bring forth more good fruit.—O the beauty of the living branches, when they abide in the vine, draw their sap from the root, and retain only an holy emulation with each other! a preserving canopy would such form in meetings for discipline, as well as worship, and many who are light in their spirits, resembling the fowls of the air, would be induced to lodge under it. No boasting, no self-seeking, no spirit that would rend or tear the tender feelings of any feeble traveller, could here have any place; because being branches which bring not forth good fruit, they are cut off and cast into the fire. But as, in the present mixed state of things, and especially in these meetings, where friends are untrained to the public exercise of their gifts, and unaccustomed to sit under a diversity of sentiments, occasions cannot fail of being furnished for the trial of christian virtues, I was renewedly convinced, of the necessity which those who act in the station of clerks have to be clear in their views, by dwelling near enough to the spirit of the gospel, so as to receive qualifications therefrom, in pure wisdom, to strengthen or make way for that lowly plant which is righteous, and boasts not itself in the garden of the Lord; but to which the promise and blessing belong, " for all the trees of the field shall know, that I, the Lord, have brought down the high tree, and exalted the low tree, have dried up the green tree, and caused the dry tree to flourish;" yea, the valleys are exalted and the mountains reduced, when the seed of immortal life reigns, and sways its pure sceptre in the assemblies of the people of God. The attention of my mind was, therefore, secretly attracted to the Father of lights, by whose powerful discoveries I saw myself; and notwithstanding the business of the meeting almost constantly employed me, yet I was favoured to feel a frequent abstractedness, and ample opportunities, under a prevailing sense of my own weakness, fervently to petition the Lord to be with my spirit, to keep me patient in my present employ, meek in my demeanour, and truly a servant to His cause and people. And I may with thankfulness acknowledge, to the praise of His grace, which is sufficient for all the wants of His children, that, however deficient in many respects for the station, I comfortably felt divine strength and wisdom underneath; wherein the precious unity of the one spirit, not only with the present, but divers absent friends, consolated my often drooping mind. Notwithstanding the foregoing observations, the meetings, in general, were attended with living virtue, and the humble travailers refreshed and instructed therewith.

After the yearly meeting was over, my husband and I staid a few days about London, as did my beloved companion R. J. to whom I still felt bound in the service which she was engaged in; and therefore set out again with her for the western counties, the seventeenth of the sixth month. We took the meetings of Staines, Basingstoke, Whitchurch, Andover, Salisbury, Rumsey, and Ringwood, in our way to Fordingbridge, where the quarterly meeting for Hampshire was held.

It was a time of some degree of favour and encouragement, to a few honest-hearted friends in that county; some of whom are under a renewed visitation of divine mercy. From hence we went to the quarterly meeting of Dorset, held at Pool; in which my dear companion was enabled to discharge her exercised mind of a load which she found there, in a powerful manner; the state of that county being very low, the living scarcely able to bear the dead. We then proceeded to the meetings of Shaftsbury, Marnhill, Sherborne, and Yeovil, where my dear husband left us, intending for Bristol, and from thence to Ireland. On this occasion, I felt a secret breathing for the continuance of the Lord's protecting providence, both with respect to the safety of the body, and the preservation of our minds in His fear, and an increase in His favour.

From Yeovil we went to Puddemore, Longsutton, Ilminster, Chard, Bridport, and so to Exeter, where we found, as in some of the foregoing places, a few innocent, concerned friends; but the want of that baptism which initiates into the church of Christ, builds up the members into a spiritual house, a holy temple in the Lord, where He presides and ministers, was sensibly felt; and yet the language of encouragement to press forward to this state, appeared to us to be the language of truth. In general, the spirit of the world, though often disguised, so much prevails, that before the right foundation can be discovered, a specious pile of buildings wants pulling down; and therefore for ministers rightly to visit meetings and individuals in this state, requires soundness of judgment, strength in the pure faith, patient perseverance and righteous zeal; all of which, when I see myself, I feel the want of*. We

---

* The following passages are extracted from her letters:————9th of 7th month, 1786. As I trust our alliance to each other in spirit, is stronger than the ties of nature, it is not (we may conclude) inconsistent therewith, to impart to each other without straitness, in the circulation of mutual love and renewed sympathy; for without this quickening experience, all our communications must be lifeless and insipid. How excellent is the life of truth! the want of it in myself, and in others, is a daily burden to my mind; and the burden bearers, in places where we come, being very few, renders it still more heavy.—To say that the state of the society is low in these western parts, is so general, and so just a complaint, that there is a danger of its being taken up without feeling sufficiently the spirit of mourning.

————" Thirteenth of 7th month 1786. We endeavour quietly to get forward; and by the continued sustaining evidence, that the best strength is graciously near to assist in the needful time, and the blessing which makes truly rich sometimes revealed in the midst of our poverty, we are preserved, thus far, in a degree of thankfulness to the great Supplier of all the necessities of His people; though often attended with the spirit of mourning over the scattered remnant of a once flourishing heritage. Though in some places there is but little to visit, yet not being a people wholly given up to reproach, and the pure seed still groaning for deliverance, a little room is left to labour; and here and

staid their first day meeting at Exeter, and then went to Kingsbridge, taking a little meeting at Newton Bushel in our way, and to Plymouth, where we attended their monthly meeting; which is in so weak a state, as to be far short of supporting the dignity of christian discipline in its own spirit; and this is lamentably the case in many other places. It is only as the gathered churches become sensible of their deplorable situation, look beyond their own natural abilities, to the well of life in themselves, and get low enough to draw water thereout, that a restoration of the power will be witnessed, which is Jesus in the midst of them. We also attended their meetings the first day following, which were deeply exercising; but our gracious Helper was near,

there an exercised member dwells, with whom, whenever they were found, our minds could not but dip into near sympathy; so that any little opening to service, in such desolate places, ought not to be declined, but rather cherished in confidence that the good Husbandman will again plough and sow His plantation, and bless the labour of those He puts forth. I cannot say that this is an expectation which hath abundantly attended my mind, in our passing along; but, just as I write, a little hope is renewed, that the vineyard will again prosper by a right and necessary extirpation of the briers, the thorns, and the noxious weeds; and, by an holy cultivation, be prepared for the true plants, wherever scattered, being enclosed within divine protection, and rendered fruitful in holiness, so as to be fitted to receive the heavenly Visitant, and made able to endure the northern and the southern blasts. O that this hope may not perish, but prove true in a future day, when the earth is shaken of her rest!

strengthening to an honest labour; wherein the right way to the kingdom, was proved to be widely different from that wherein many are walking; and under this help, a degree of holy solemnity was felt."

In addition to the preceding journal, which appears to be left short of the visit, the following extracts have been made from her letters; which, though not containing a regular, continued account, may afford further information and instruction.

————" The present journey with my beloved friend, has been a fresh trial of the uprightness of my desire after dedication; for after returning from Ireland, I earnestly sought quietude and obscurity, to settle down amongst my valuable connections and enjoy their society, or the benefits of solitude; but the reward of peace was not the attendant of these prospects; nor did the cloud appear to rest upon my tabernacle: the words, " Time is short," were deeply inscribed upon my heart, so that one thing or other bid me take a few more steps in the tribulated path of gospel obedience."

————" I have felt myself these few days back, as near the end of my present commission, my faith, patience, and every christian virtue, as to the point of land before us; and being so far from home, aggravates the prospect, and gives me very much the feeling of a pelican in the wilderness, out of the reach of almost any other help, save that holy Arm which leads about and inftructs, in what appears to us the moft deferted fituation, and moreover hath promifed to keep as the apple of the eye.'

"Could I believe myfelf to be one thus provided for, and to whom the arm of power will continue to be extended, fome of my fecret cogitations would be lefs painful and gloomy, and with greater pleafantnefs, I could advance forward, though in a tribulated way. From Plymouth we came into Cornwall, taking Germains, Looe, Lifkard, Auftel, and Mevageffey meetings, in our way to Falmouth, where, and in its neighbourhood, we have met with fome valuable friends. In thefe weftern counties through which we have come, viz. Hampfhire, Dorfetfhire, Somerfetfhire, and Devonfhire, the fociety, as to the circulation of that life which we profefs to be feeking the influence of, is indeed lamentably low. A worldly fpirit and a ftate that is neither hot nor cold, greatly prevails; fo that the few living members (for there is here and there one) are fcarcely able to lift the ftandard of truth, or revive the remembrance of the law. But in this county, viz. Cornwall, things are better; a right zeal having fprung up in divers, to fearch into the real ftate of the church, and what is more, a care firft to fearch themfelves; an exercife greatly wanted amongft active members in many places. C. P.'s labours in thefe parts have been, we think, eminently bleffed; and the good effects of fuch a faithful difcharge of duty, and bearing a fteady, uniform teftimony to the truth, and againft error, would, there is no doubt, oftner be found, if that was oftner tried. We get but flowly forward fince we came into this county; for though I have mentioned fome good in it, yet we find it clofe exercifing work, to get clearly down to the good thing alluded to; and have ftaid longer in places hereabouts, than any where before. Yesterday was trying to my almoft worn out mind; my companion got a little relieved in the morning, but I faw no way for myfelf all the day, though under a great weight; but fo it is, we need patience and fubjection in fuch times, left we move before the waters have rifen to their appointed height."

———" We have been favoured to get along without accidents, and have to acknowledge that, many ways, we are helped beyond our frequent expectation; finding, (as we fuppofe others do) difcouragements on the right hand, and on the left; which, if fuffered to prevail, would foon deftroy that little grain of efficacious faith which removes mountains, and without which, however we may labour and wafte our ftrength, fuch mountains of difficulty and unfruitfulnefs, as the chriftian traveller meets with, can never be removed. How neceffary is it then to fight the good fight of faith: that fo, when pure life is circulating, inftead of knowing it not, we may be ftrengthened to lay hold of it, and to experience the inner man fo renewed in us, as to actuate every fervice.—Here we fee our own infufficiency, and how unavailing it is to depend upon our ftrength and judgment, in things belonging to ourfelves or others."

———"I have been at meeting this morning at Collumpton, a small gathering of lukewarm professors, in the general; but a few solid young people afforded a comfortable prospect for the future. Silence was my lot here; but my spirit was deeply humbled, in feeling the baptizing virtue of truth near to purify my vessel, which I esteem more than the fairest qualifications for public service; and am more and more led secretly to supplicate the increase of this solid experience and ability, to endure with christian firmness and patience those dispensations by which it is obtained. Nevertheless, I am often deeply tried in religious meetings, with such exceeding great strippedness of good, and intrusion of thoughts which I by no means approve there, that I mourn under it; and when any thing opens, which appears like a discovery of truth, to give it to others when I am ready to perish with hunger myself, is almost irreconcileable; especially when after giving up to it, I find myself as poor when a meeting breaks up, as when it began. I can hardly describe what I secretly suffer from meeting to meeeting, on this account; so that when I am favoured with a sensible evidence, of the sanctifying power of the Minister of ministers yet dwelling in mine earthen vessel, abundantly doth my soul acknowledge, that the excellency of the power is not of us, but of Him, and that he hath a right to reveal it when and how he pleaseth."

She attended the circular meeting at Gloucester, in the ninth month; from whence she returned pretty directly, into Yorkshire, and was at the quarterly meeting for that county. In the fore-part of the tenth month, she proceeded with G. D. and others to the County of Durham, and attended the quarterly meeting there. Of these services, no remarks can be added, as there does not appear any thing material of her own preserved on these occasions.

CHAP. V.

Family Visit at Sheffield.—Her Illness there.—Consideration of removing into Ireland.—Journey into Lincolnshire.—Removal to Ireland.—Journey into Holland, Germany and France.

IN the first month 1787, she was engaged with Reb. Jones and others, in a religious visit to the families of friends at Sheffield; concerning which she writes as follows:

———— The visit here is got through, and I hope profitably so to many, and especially the youth, of whom here are great numbers; some of the apprentices are very raw, but others seem turning about with desire to find, and make, the right purchase. They are indeed, altogether, a great load of care upon the shepherds and shepherdesses in this place, whose concern I hope is increasing. It is pleasant to find increasing unity and openness amongst rightly concerned friends in this place, and that love which casteth out fear.

At the close of this family visit, she was taken very ill, with a heavy cold and an inflammation of the lungs. This disorder continued for several weeks, during which she was brought very low in body and mind. But the great Physician, on whom appeared to be her sole dependance, saw meet to raise her again, and to renew a considerable portion of health and strength. Of this illness, and the exercise of her mind under it, as well as of her feelings in the review of it, some account will be conveyed, by the following extracts from her letters, written whilst she was on the recovery.

—— I am now favoured with ability to answer your solicitude myself, and say, that the account you had of my illness was, I apprehend, not worse than the reality; having been reduced to the gates of death to all appearance, with an inflammation of my lungs, which had been approaching some weeks, and arrived at an awful crisis: at which time, by the merciful interposition of the good Physician, the disorder took a favourable turn, and opened again my prospects to this mixed state of things. My bodily affliction was great, but the conflicts and gloomy exercises of my mind, were not less, being involved in all the weakness and insufficiency of human nature, in endeavouring to attain to the spring of pure consolation, at the same time that, in unerring wisdom, it was sealed in my view: so that, upon the whole, it was a season of deep proving, and, I humbly trust, lasting instruction; by rendering more single the attention of my mind to divine discoveries, whereby our duty is seen, and strength to perform it acceptably received. To be found faithful in the great work of the present life, is an object of such magnitude, that all things else appear comparatively trifling, when we are looking into a state of eternal duration.

———The ways of wisdom are a great deep, and the designs of removing from, or restoring to, this uncertain and probationary state of being, are often for purposes which require a daily waiting for, and dependance upon the unfoldings of pure instruction, in order profitably to discover them. I consider this to be my own case, and often remember a remark of J. Woolman's to a friend, perhaps similarly circumstanced, " do we (says he) get through with great difficulty, and yet recover; He requires that we should be purged from dross, and our ear opened to discipline."

——— I am favoured to continue recovering, tho' often reminded that in every sense I am a poor weak creature, and under abundant necessity to hold fast the little strength I have, and patiently wait for the renewings of that life which quickens, and gives joy in the spiritual creation. But I am still too carnally minded, too much disposed to look outward, and too little to press through the opposition of nature, to that true weightiness of spirit which I earnestly sought for in a late season of adversity. These things convince us that, in order to win the crown in view, we must fight the good fight, and wrestle for that faith which only gives the victory.

The subject of their removing into Ireland, and settling there, had for a considerable while, engaged her solid consideration ; and the propriety of that undertaking was about this time attended with such clearness to her own mind, and that of her husband, that they apprehended the time was near for their departure from this land. Divers of her letters written on this occasion, shew her sense of the importance of this measure, and how great and exemplary was her concern, that they might be directed wisely and safely concerning it. The following have been selected from them.

———— Our minds have been under frequent, and sometimes, unprofitable concern how to dispose of ourselves. There seems an abundance of places to chuse from, both in Ireland and here; but to know our right lot, is what we are both desiring singly to stand open to the discovery of, if conveyed to us ever so simply; the light which manifests it, be it ever so small, will, I believe, satisfy our fasting minds. We have need to be reduced low, that we may so obtain the knowledge of the divine will, as cheerfully to yield obedience thereto. Though we think we have waited long for instruction, yet as our opinions, of ourselves especially, are often very fallacious, it is not impossible but we are far from that state of self-nothingness and dependance, which I am sometimes ready to hope we are on the brink of. We are at present quite unbound to any place; perhaps to have no place of abode is the lot designed us; a lot that much opposes my inclination, but if right, however trying, it must be submitted to, and its consequences likewise, as the requirings of the day.

———— My mind has of late looked with more clearness than before, towards Ireland. It has been a subject of consideration, attended already with much anxiety; and now that I am apprehensive I have seen a right opening towards it, I wish to be preserved from looking back, or entering into unprofitable considerations about it; but rather to leave the matter at present, only standing open to the discoveries of more light, either for or against it, and respecting the right time of moving, or of not moving at all, which I know to be the situation of my husband's mind respecting it.———I well know, that except we are in our right places, we can have no true enjoyment or expectation of support under, or the blessing upon, our allotted portion of suffering; and we have proved both lands to have in them their share of trials and probations; and know that things which look the most pleasant in either, may soon, as some of them have already at times been, be embittered, and shaded with gloom. I wish however to number my blessings, for they are many, and far beyond my deserts.

——— I often wish that I could learn to be still when I have nothing to do, and instead of straining my eyes in the dark, and watching the breaking of the day, to dwell quietly in the ward all night, believing in the light, and obediently working therein. The outward day breaks gradually upon us, and experience teaches us the certain indication of its approach, a dawning of light, which we are not apt to disbelieve, nor doubt that the meridian of it will come in due time. And as in the outward, we cannot hasten that time, no more can we with respect to divine illuminations. Does it not therefore, remain to be our business, to wait for the light when a little of it appears, to believe in it, and that the fulness of the day will come, though we do not now see it; remembering that, "blessed are they that have not seen, and yet have believed." This is what I apprehend to be right to do, and what I wish to attain; but I would by no means insinuate, that I confidently believe myself to have arrived at it, in the prospect of removing to Ireland; meaning only, that after a state of anxiety, and tossing about with every wind of the sentiments of others, I seemed to get into resignation's harbour. I am however willing to stand open to further conviction; and if the will should be graciously accepted for the deed, my poor bark excused the exposure, and my dear R. G. satisfied, (which I do not doubt if it is right) it will not be an unpleasant release from an engagement to which I now feel myself rather bound: for there are many in this nation, and in our own county, (setting aside my near relatives after the flesh) to whom I am closely attached, and from whom nature will flinch to part; but there are also divers of this class in Ireland, whose friendship will, if my residence there be right, greatly repair the loss, and tend to smooth the otherwise rugged path. This is looking at secondary causes, a view which I don't wish often to take; because to be in the place assigned, (whether I was known of mortals or not) where the great work of sanctification and acceptance in divine favour is going forward, would, I am satisfied, afford a peace superior to all human consolations, and enable the truly abased mind nobly to say,

"Although the fig-tree shall not blossom, neither shall fruit be in the vines; the labour of the olive shall fail, and the fields shall yield no meat; the flock shall be cut off from the fold, and there shall be no herd in the stalls; yet I will rejoice in the Lord, I will joy in the God of my salvation:" a glorious experience worthy our aspiring after! Whatever has a tendency to loosen our affections from mixed streams of refreshment, and centre them in the great source, the well in ourselves springing up unto everlasting life, I apprehend more truly qualifies for service, than a situation replete with opportunities, for the increase of human wisdom and activity in the visible church; which never fail to have in them their snares, by gratifying self, if given way to, in one shape or other.

———— What I have felt at times on the subject of our removal, cannot be easily described; divine support and direction, if singly sought to, under the weight of it, will be found sufficient to sustain, and open the right way; but I apprehend that our small grain of faith, may meet with many trials and buffetings in our future steppings; and oh that we may never make shipwreck thereof!

May the staff of Israel be our support, separately and together, and may we have no other dependance, is the secret petition of my mind; for, in the undertaking before us, we may say, that with our staff only we are passing over this Jordan.

Having come to a conclusion respecting their removal into Ireland, and obtained the concurrence of their monthly meeting, they proceeded to York and attended the quarterly meeting there; from whence, after taking a solemn and affecting leave of their near connections and friends, they set forward for the county of Lincoln; the meetings of which, as well as some others, she felt a desire to attend, in her way to the yearly meeting. Soon after this trying separation, the following letter appears to have been written *. With divers companions in that service,

---

* Last week but one was our quarterly meeting at York, which was favoured with the overshadowings of the heavenly wing. It was a parting time, and almost too affecting for my present weak state; but I endeavoured what I could to look beyond personal enjoyments, to that fellowship which is pure, standing with the Father and with the Son, and which admits of no change by outward separation, if we retain our integrity, and places in the adoption of children. On seventh day morning after, came the dregs of the cup of removal; a heart tendering farewell to my beloved connections at York, with the proprietors of the school, and some of their husbands. It was almost too much for my frame, faith being at a low ebb, and discouragements coming in like a flood; but in the opening of true vision, the spirit of the Lord was lifted up as a standard against them. As to the body, I have now parted with many who seemed interwoven with my existence: with divers of them it was gradual, and I esteem it a favour it was so: but though I am sensible, that in the church I leave both fathers and mothers behind; and as to brethren and sisters in the truth, they seem almost daily added to, and promise, according to their present growth, to be skilful servants in the family; yet the near unity my spirit has felt with some in Ireland, affords me a ray of hope, that should we be spared with life and strength, to enter into

she visited most or all of the meetings and families of friends in Lincolnshire, and attended several other meetings as she proceeded to London. Though but little of the progress of this journey is described in the following extracts; yet the feelings of her mind, and the instructive remarks set forth therein, will, it is apprehended, render it proper to insert them here.

———— We are favoured to get along as well as we might expect, we hope in some degree of sympathy with the state of the best things in this desolate county; but upon the whole, my mind is and hath been favoured with a calm, especially for these few days back, which tends to promote the restoration of health, and strengthens with a good degree of resignedness, to look forward to the prospects before me; and so far from considering the pursuit of them a hardship, I esteem the end proposed thereby, a favour of which I am unworthy; for what is there worth living for, but to be found in the discharge of our duty?

———— We are now in the Isle of Axolm, visiting a few desolate professors, who are like sheep having no shepherd; and yet in a place as much neglected as perhaps any in the society, we are comforted in finding a feed alive, resembling Joseph in Egypt, and may say, for my own part, that I have felt the most solid reward for a little labour here, of any since leaving York. It is not after the sight of the eye, or the hearing of the ear, that we can judge aright.

and rightly stand in our lots at Clonmel, we shall find every want supplied, and true yoke-fellows beyond our deserts.

———— They that suffer with the feed, shall reign with it; but it must not be in our way, nor in our time. Patience is due on our part, and the exercise of that grain of faith which we have received; for, " by faith the elders obtained a good report," I presume of the Lord, rather than of men. Then let us not be afraid of the trial, for its efficacy is proved thereby. O that I was stronger in this spot! for even since we left York, and particularly on leaving it, I have seemed to be reduced to the lowest ebb, and nature hath foreboded discouragements beyond what I thought I was able to bear. But this is not always the case; for sometimes, when every thing else is shaded with gloom, the foundation is most clearly revealed, and its standing sure incontrovertibly known and believed in; so that all things have appeared possible to him that believeth, and the ways of the Most High discovered to be higher than our ways, and his thoughts than our thoughts. Here I love to repose myself, and stand resigned to every dispensation which has the remotest tendency, not only to let me see the work of my day, but to refine and qualify for it.

———— I have recovered so much, that I have now scarce any thing to complain of respecting the body. To be sure it is not very strong, but it has thus far proved able to bear all that was laid upon it; which is encouragement to myself, and also to others, to persevere in yielding ourselves up, under the power of the cross, to every opening of duty, seeing that all things are possible to them that believe. And yet I fainted in my mind many a time, and seemed to be one of those who have no faith: so that, on reflecting upon this little embassy, the prospect and the progress of it, it seems as if it was all done for me by that good Hand, which requires the passiveness rather than the activeness of the creature, in prosecuting His designs. Though I now give a pretty good account of the body, I may also add, that, sometimes, my mind gets encompassed with glooms and discouragements, which nothing can dissipate, save a state of resignation and quiet dependance upon the everlasting Arm of Omnipotence; and this is often so hard to attain, that I am afraid of falling in the struggle, when a hope is again revived, of being under divine protection, and that the day's work is really going forward. This, at times, introduces a quiet serenity, and strengthens to leave the things that are behind, and press forward to those that are before. The sympathy of my friends under my late trials, has been considered a favour of which I am unworthy; and there is undoubtedly no better way of securing it upon the foundation of gospel fellowship, than by learning to live without it, and looking singly to the Rock from whence all good things are hewn, and the hole of the pit, the humbling dispensations of infinite wisdom, from whence they are dug.

Soon after the yearly meeting at London, they proceeded for Clonmel in Ireland, where she was favoured to arrive in safety, in the 6th month 1787, with her health much improved, and under a good degree of peace and satisfaction of mind; which continued for some time after her arrival, as a source of consolation and encouragement she writes as follows:

———— Our removal has altogether been blessed with a good degree of that peace which passeth understanding, and attended with such circumstances, thus far, as we have great cause to be thankful for. An unmixed cup of comfort in human life, is what my short passage through the world, has taught me not to look for, and a small degree of religious experience, not to pray for; and yet to pray for those things which are really good for us, will ever require the renewings of that Spirit which only breathes the will of the Father. Nature shrinks at suffering; sometimes I am ready to anticipate a draught of it, proportionable to the late and present degree of favour; and sometimes I am flattered with a language that tells me, " it is already drunk, and that the bitterness of death is past." An humble, resigned mind is however always our duty and interest to press after. It has a fortification in itself against the varied assaults of Satan, and a sufficient portion of Gilead's Balm for every afflictive dispensation of infinite wisdom; both of which, if my natural life is spared, will, I do believe, be my companions, and prove frequent trials of an abiding and advancement in that gospel Spirit, which loveth, hopeth, and endureth through all.

Her mind had frequently, for a considerable time before this period, been impressed and closely exercised with an apprehension, that it would be required of her to pay a religious visit to some parts of Germany and France: and, a few months after her settlement in Ireland, this concern increased with such weight and evidence, that she was constrained, in resignation, to spread it before the friends of their monthly meeting; who, after solid deliberation and sympathy, concurred therewith, and gave her their certificate of unity and approbation. She received also the near concurrence of their quarterly meeting, and that of the morning meeting of ministers and elders in London, and set forward on this journey in the 3d. month, 1788, in company with her husband, George Dillwyn and his wife, and Mary Dudley; who were also bound to this service, and engaged therein with the unity of friends.

The following parts of her letters on this occasion, describe the previous exercise of her mind, and contain a pretty regular, though short account of the journey, from the commencement of it, to its conclusion.

12th month 1787. My mind after a season of deep trial and exercise, was led to visit, in what appeared to myself an extraordinary degree of gospel love, many in that country, and some parts of Germany contiguous thereto; fully believing, according to my feelings, that there were spiritual worshippers in those parts.

12th month 1787. If the prospect before us be in divine wisdom, we have great cause to acknowledge that it is unfathomable, and past our finding out, because of my incapacity, in every respect, to perform such a journey to the honor of the great Cause. I wish, however, now to leave caring too much about the future, and endeavour after quiet refignation; well knowing, that by taking ever fo much unprofitable thought, I cannot add one cubit to my ftature, nor make one hair of my head, white or black; and alfo hoping, that when it comes to the trial, the will may be accepted for the deed; which I have no doubt will be the cafe, if the province meeting, or my fympathizing friends, advife me againft it; or if no friend of fuperior weight in the miniftry, proves under the like concern, and admits us in their company. Difcouragements of various kinds crowd in at times upon me, but when gofpel love flows from the living fountain, it overpowers all felfifh confiderations, and fhews me my own unworthinefs to be, in the leaft degree, employed in the divine hand.

1ft month 1788. Our fituation at prefent, requires at leaft a grain of that faith which has power to remove mountains; for, truly, vain is the help of man, in cafes where the pure feed is to be exalted. A fenfe of our infufficiency to do any good thing without divine affiftance, will, I truft, whatever our trials or temptations may be, fo humble us, as wholly to prevent a vain dependance upon any thing of our own; but furely there is as much need for watchfulnefs and prayer at this day, as when the difciples were immediately recommended to it.

1ft month 1788. My mind is often under a load of exercife on my own account, and in care left the precious caufe fhould fuffer by me. The prefent is a time of deep trial and fearching of heart, left we fhould be meddling with, or doing, any thing which is not in the clear difcovery of gofpel light. When I confider how little I am experienced in the ftation wherein I may be likely to move, the newnefs and peculiarity of the fervice in profpect, and even the weaknefs of the outward tabernacle, (which to be fure I think leaft of) my feelings fuggeft the applicablenefs of the faying, "I am a worm." This however cheers me, that without fome degree of clearnefs, we need not, neither fhall attempt to move.

2d month 1788. I have been of late confiderably indifpofed, but upon the whole am much better, though every day fenfible of having (by fome means or other) a very broken conftitution. If it do but laft till the portion of work allotted me is finifhed, that is enough, even though it be performed under the preffure of bodily infirmities; all which may be no more than neceffary to keep the mind to its proper centre, and direct its attention, fingly to an inheritance undefiled, and which fadeth not away.

3d month 1788. According to prefent appearances, we, (I mean our little company) ftand in abundant need of the whole armour of light. We are about to embark for a country, the language of which none of us know, and in expectation of a path wherein we can fee no footfteps, and which muft be attended with new and various trials. May our truft be in the Lord alone, who is able, in feafons of the greateft difficulty, to encreafe our faith, and make way for us where we fee no way.

———— Having the concurrence of friends, we left London and proceeded for Harwich, where we were detained feveral days for want of a fair wind;

during which time we had two meetings, and afterwards, (23d of 3d month) the wind turning in favour of our leaving that port, we embarked; but it was fourth day night, the twenty-seventh, before we landed at Helvoetsluys, which was nevertheless a favour, and I hope esteemed so by us all. We got to an agreeable English inn there, and after a pretty good night's rest, set forward towards Rotterdam, by way of the Briel and Delf, and came in safe rather late at night, it being there a great day's work of about twenty-five miles. We travelled in an open waggon the first seven miles, the road being so bad that no other carriage could get along with safety, and the rest of the way went in their boats called Treckschuyts, which are drawn by a horse, at the rate of about three miles an hour. This is a very pleasant and easy way of travelling, and it was through a country made as agreeable by improvements as it is capable of, being very flat and marshy. Many of the inhabitants followed us through some towns, and gazed exceedingly at us; and some of them, as well as they were able, manifested a love which met that in us that drew us hither; but the strangeness of our language to each other, was a continual discouragement; yet as it was not of our own bringing on, we endeavoured to keep quiet under it, and secretly desired that our minds might be so influenced, as to convey to them, in silence, that which is better than words. We have now got into so new a line, that it is no wonder if we should be more than usually blind; and it will be well, if some of us should be also more than usually dependant and patient respecting our steppings; for being separated and remote from our friends, and some of dispositions rather hasty than otherwise, there is, no doubt, a danger of sometimes pressing forward with too much earnestness, and thereby of preventing the completion of those little services, in one way or other, which are intended for the purchase of our own peace at least. Though Holland was not much in the prospect of us who came from Ireland, yet we have been favoured with something more than a hope, that we are thus far in our places, and feel a comfortable and strengthening unity one with another therein. The desire of my mind is at present strong, that, though in ever so much weakness, we may be enabled to pass through the country in that singleness and dedication of heart, which may preserve us from condemnation.

We staid three days in Rotterdam, and had two public meetings at the meeting house belonging to friends; there are a great many English people in that city, and the attenders of our meetings being principally of that class, we had no need of an interpreter. There are some serious people with whom we got acquainted, and to whom our visit seemed acceptable, but no professors with us, except one person, who cannot be expected, in his present state, to throw much light upon the testimony of truth; but he was very willing to render us such services as were in his power, which we took kind.

From Rotterdam, we came forward to Amsterdam, by way of Leyden, Haarlem, &c. and were kindly received by our friend John Vanderwerf. Here our minds, generally, got very low on divers accounts. Several of us were poorly with complaints in the stomach, &c. which strangers are subject to, before their constitutions come to bear the difference of their meat, drink, air, &c. The few under the name of friends in this great city, yielded us little of that strength which is the fruit of sympathy of spirit, and inward acquaintance with divine requirings; and which, if right, would have been truly salutary and cordial to us at that time, as we looked upon ourselves to be then embarking upon the most arduous and discouraging part of our journey; having a great distance to travel, entirely unacquainted with the country, strangers to all their different languages, except a little French, and no interpreter to accompany us. Under these complicated trials, our faith got into the furnace afresh. This was much the case with me, and my dear companions felt no less. However, as we endeavoured after resignation, and were sometimes replenished with strength patiently to wait for renewed manifestations of duty, way opened, by degrees, to get clear of that place. We attended their little monthly meeting, the business whereof was transacted in the Dutch language; so that we had not an opportunity of judging much about them; except that their appearance, and the feelings of our minds, convinced us that true religion is at a low ebb amongst them; and yet there is something tender which loves truth, and with which, a family visit amongst them, made us better acquainted *. We had also three public meetings there,

* We were comforted in the belief that their solita-

which were attended by many of the inhabitants of different descriptions; but there are a few with whose company, both in and out of meetings, we were comforted. They are a serious religious people, not connected with any society, and believing in the spirituality of all true worship. We paid a visit to one of their families, which consists of a widow, her son, and two daughters, none of them young. They are people of considerable property, which they devote very much to the service of the poor. They were affectionately kind, and demonstrated their unity with, and attachment to our principles, as far as they had heard them in the meetings which they attended, and were fully convinced of the necessity of an inward work, and that all true worship must be performed in spirit and in truth. In a religious opportunity which we had with them before we parted, the cementing influence of gospel love flowed amongst us like a stream. From this family, we were furnished with letters of recommendation

ry situations are divinely regarded, and hope that divers of their deficiencies in some points wherein we have been otherwise taught, are counterbalanced in the sight of holy compassion and justice, by the sincerity of their intentions, and the discouragements in many respects peculiar to them, which we, by experience, know little about. The keeping up of a meeting for worship every first day, in their weak state, is an act of faithfulness, which we might be often ready to faint under, were we in their situation, separated from the strengthening communications which religious society affords, (not having received a visit of this kind for four years) and being despised amongst the worldly minded.

to such as themselves in Germany, some of whom we have seen to our satisfaction. During our stay in Amsterdam, we were interpreted for, by John Vanderwerf, or one of his sons, both in public and private. It seemed strange, and rather hard to us women, especially at first; but we soon got over it, and had reason to hope that our religious communications were not materially affected; our friend seemed to have an awe upon his mind when he stood up, took off his hat, and delivered, sentence by sentence, what was expressed. Thus after spending eight days at Amsterdam, and being deeply tried in that place, our minds were strengthened to leave it, (the 9th of the 4th month,) with a renewed trust, that the great Shepherd of Israel, who knows his own sheep in every trial and situation, however remote from the knowledge and consolation of their friends, would superintend us, and graciously reveal himself for our help, in the needful time. We essayed to proceed by way of Utrecht, (where a few books were distributed, and much love felt for the inhabitants) Nimeguen, and thro' part of the king of Prussia's dominions, into the Elector of Bavaria's, to a place called Duffeldorff, where we again made a little stop, finding a few who could speak English, and most of them French. Here we commenced acquaintance with a solid, religious man, named Michael Wetterboar, to whom we were recommended by the people whom I have mentioned at Amsterdam. Being gathered to the principle of truth, and engaged to conform to it, as revealed in the line of his own experience, he walks much alone in a dark and diſſipated place. He was a kind friend to Claude Gay, when paying a ſimilar viſit to our's in this country, many years ago, and was rejoiced to ſee us. He lamented the loneſomeneſs of his ſituation, and ſaid that his mind was ſtrengthened by the viſit. From hence we went eighteen miles and back, out of our road, to Elberfeld, where, as at many other places, for want of an interpreter, we ſuffered what often appears to us an unavailing baptiſm for the teſtimony's ſake. But perhaps it is not ſo much ſo as we are apt to think: the ways of the Moſt High are not our ways, nor his thoughts our thoughts; we know not but this deeply humbling path, and the ſecret exerciſes we have daily to paſs through without any viſible relief, may have a uſe beyond our finite conceptions; ſo that it is ſafeſt to leave theſe things, and outward conſiderations about them, in the hand which can bleſs, and render fruitful, the things which are not, by cauſing them to bring to nought the things which are. However, we found an opening to ſome ſolid converſation with a few in this place, and underſtood that there are many religious people there; but we were diſcouraged by the difficulties we found in getting an acquaintance with them; ſo we returned, after ſtaying one night, to Duſſeldorff. We left that place, and paſſing through a dark country, arrived in two days at Newvied, the 18th of the 4th month. We have had very little rain ſince we came upon the continent, conſequently the roads are dry, but being for the moſt part a deep ſand, we have not been able to travel over it ſo quickly as is deſirable. Thirty miles a day, is I think nearly the average of our expedition, though we moſtly travel poſt. The vehicles are heavy, being generally covered waggons or clumſy coaches. We moſtly prefer the former, as ourſelves and luggage meet the beſt accommodation in them. The inns are pretty good, and the people reſpectfully kind to us, and in that line but little difficulty occurs in making ourſelves underſtood. Our road has lain upon the banks of the Rhine, and furniſhed us with proſpects of a country extremely beautiful, and, in ſome places, for miles together covered with vineyards. But the pleaſure which we might innocently have derived from thoſe ſcenes, has met with continual damps, by the groſs proſtitution of ſacred things which, in the croſſes and images thickly ſcattered upon the road, give pain to every feeling whereby ſpiritual worſhip is promoted. The Roman Catholics are very numerous in many parts which we have paſſed through; but, in moſt places, the Proteſtants enjoy the privileges they deſire without interruption; and amongſt them there is undoubtedly an awakened, ſincere hearted people. On our arrival at Newvied, we found a great change in the face of things, it being a new and pleaſant town, inhabited by ſerious Proteſtants, and principally by the Moravians; though there are about twenty families of the Menoniſts, and as many of a people who call themſelves Inſpirants, but by others are often called Quakers. We were directed to a Moravian inn, which proved very agreeable, feeling ourſelves in that family very much as if we were at home. Here we were soon visited by several of the Moravian brethren and sisters, some of whose minds appeared unprejudiced, and intent upon spiritual improvement; which drew them often to our apartments, and opened a door for the communication of such gospel truths, as, from time to time, occurred; and we had a comfortable hope, that they dropped into some of their minds as seed into good ground. We had the advantage in that place of an interpreter, a young man of the Moravian œconomy, who cheerfully befriended us on many occasions; and though, at the first, he appeared under difficulty in communicating religious matter which was new to him, yet before we went away, his understanding seemed more opened, and his feelings much more cordially disposed to the principle of truth as we profess it, and to the several branches thereof. We had a public meeting in that place the evening before we left it, after a week's deep exercise and secret suffering; but this opportunity furnished us with renewed cause, to put our trust in the gentle puttings forth of the Shepherd of Israel, and in the revelation of His power, which we humblingly find is sometimes withheld, till the seasons of our greatest extremity. The young man, our interpreter, readily accepted his office in the meeting, without any previous request, and performed it with great solidity. Our visit to that place was closed by a season of divine favour, in a family which cheerfully received the testimony we had unitedly to bear, to the efficacy of spiritual worship, and the necessity of preparation for it; and in much love and tenderness of spirit we left Newvied. "O the depth and extent of the riches, both of the knowledge and wisdom of God! how unsearchable are his judgments, and his ways past finding out!" We had abundant cause in our travels through Germany, to say, that we were led in paths which we knew not, and frequently reduced to a state of extremity. We were sensible, according to our measures, of the mist of superstition and idolatry which overspreads a great part of the country; and also had, at times, revealed that most sure word of prophecy, which penetrates the obscurest recesses of Sion's travellers, draws them into hidden fellowship one with another, and unites them in the sufferings of the precious seed, though differently situated in the world, and their profession in it various. Thus were we led in paths which we knew not, and ways we had not seen, and were often incapable of finding out those whom we thus felt, and when we did discover such, we were unable, for want of a knowledge of their language, fully to communicate to them: but trusting in the all-sufficiency of almighty help, for the supply of all their needs, we were favoured, when dedication of heart had been attained, and the green pastures of life opened, to lie down beside the still waters, and leave the event of our travel to Him who blesseth, or blasteth, at his pleasure. From Newvied we came to Wisbaden, a place in great request for warm bathing, there being several boiling hot springs in the town, from which the water is conveyed to private cisterns, where it cools for use. There seemed something rather attractive in this place to our minds, and yet, as was often the cafe, difcouragements prevailed over our beft feelings, and we proceeded to Frankfort, a day's journey. There we ftaid two nights; but though we had letters of recommendation to religious characters, yet for want of being able to make ourfelves underftood, we had no converfation with any but a Pietift who fpoke Englifh but poorly, and who, after fome difcourfe on religious fubjects, left us with profeffions of love. From Frankfort we proceeded to Bafle, a large proteftant town, where we arrived the 3d of the 5th month. Here our minds feemed arrefted, and all efforts towards purfuing our journey were painful, till we had fettled a few days under our exercife, and embraced, though in the crofs, fuch opportunities as opened for relief. Having fome letters of recommendation to ferious people, they were prefented to them; in confequence of which, feveral vifits were paid us, and we obferved in fome rather a critical inveftigation of our principles. They were cautious of embracing us till they perceived the doctrines we held; after which there was great opennefs in fome of their minds, candidly to receive fuch communications on religious fubjects as from time to time opened. One of them underftanding the Englifh language well, was, in feveral inftances, a very friendly interpreter to us; and his mind being acquainted with divine illuminations, he often difcovered fymptoms of conviction and fenfibility, when, as a channel, the openings of truth were paffing through him. In a large company to which we were invited, this person, observing our disposition to silence, kindly and feelingly proposed and requested a compliance of the company. We were favoured, to our thankful admiration, with the humbling influence of divine love, and strength renewedly to bear testimony to the necessity of an inward preparation for the solemn act of true worship, which requires neither forms nor ceremonies, to render it acceptable to the Father of Spirits. The opportunity was concluded in solemn supplication, which our friendly interpreter rendered, sentence by sentence, into the Dutch language, with a reverential awe, whereby the liveliness of it was preserved. We had also a comfortable season of retirement in the family of another of our friends there, whose wife and daughters profess not to see the necessity of a religious circumspect life, as he, and his eldest son do; but they were affectionate and attentive to us, and we had reason to hope, received no unprofitable impressions by this little act of dedication. This person conducted with true brotherly kindness towards us, discovering great simplicity of heart, and an openness to receive the truth, wherever, or however he might find it; being experienced in that great work of repentance unto life, and ceasing from many entanglements in the world, which he believed had a tendency to enslave his mind, and to keep him in a state of separation from divine favour: so that to meet with fellow pilgrims who could tell him a little of their knowledge of the right way, seemed like marrow to his bones. We have several times fallen in with persons who kindly entertained Claude Gay, in his lonesome travel through these parts; and in Basle we have found two agreeable religious old men, with whom he was hospitably sustained for three weeks. They are of a people called Inspirants, and often by others Quakers; but upon an acquaintance with them, especially at Newvied, we found them no less active than other professors in singing, praying, preaching, &c. in their congregations. They appear to be descendants of the French prophets; and amongst them there is an honest hearted number to whom the love and language of the gospel flowed with more openness, and appeared to be received with more simplicity, than amongst some others. To these two elderly men we paid several visits, which were not unattended with instructive conversation; but this did not afford that relief which our exercised mind seemed to want, nor could we comfortably see our way from the town, till we had, in their family and amongst such as they might invite, borne testimony, by our example also, to the necessity of silent waiting *. It was a season obtained with difficulty, and passed through in tribulation of spirit. The candle was not easily put into the candlestick, and when there, evidently suf-

* To put the light into the candlestick, so as to bear, even in private, a testimony to the truth, and spiritual anointing in silence, is here a greater trial of our love and faithfulness to the cause, than any can readily believe, who have not been led amongst those who are ignorant of a cessation from their own works.

pected by these people, not to be in its right place. But before the meeting closed, public testimony was borne to it, and to the resurrection of that life which is the light of men, being the only qualification of spirit, to come forth from that state of darkness and death in which we are by nature, and to perform any religious duties, or acceptable service to the Lord. At the close of this opportunity, we parted with these two men in love, though not a perfect unity of sentiment, which appeared more fully by an affectionate letter which one of them sent after us. There was also in this place, and in most others where we stopped, a prejudice against women's preaching, which encreased the difficulty our minds often felt in obtaining relief amongst a people of a strange language; but though our efforts were few and feeble, yet as far as dedication clothed us, and we were careful not to cast away our confidence, we had ever cause gratefully to acknowledge, that great recompence of reward was vouchsafed, and the soul strengthened to return to its rest, under a renewed sense that the Lord had dealt bountifully with it. The kindness we have met with in many places, exceeds what we might have expected, having several times experienced so much of the promise fulfilled, that we have met with brethren and sisters, who, though not altogether of the same profession, are fellow travellers in the christian path. Sometimes a wisdom appears in our being stripped of that outward help, so desirable, of an interpreter; as in our present circumstance, if any good is done, there is no part of it wherein the creature can glory. There is one thing which exposes us, that does not often suit the disposition of our minds, which is, that at the best inns (where we generally go) we must always dine and sup at the ordinaries, where there is often a great resort of company. If there is any use in this mortification, it will amply make up; the only testimonies which are publicly borne this way, are by our men friends keeping on their hats, and refusing to pay for the music which sometimes accompanies our meals. We took a coach from Basle * to Bern, where we staid over a first

* The following letter was written at Basle the 9th of 5th month 1788.
As it is probable we may leave Basle without taking leave of thee, and acknowledging thy kindness with a gratitude due to it, and feeling in my heart a christian salutation, I take the liberty, this way, of expressing my desire for thy increasing knowledge of the mysteries of the kingdom of God; which our blessed Lord thanked his Father for concealing from the wise and prudent, and revealing unto babes. The sacred influences of divine light upon our understandings, are cheering to the mind, and animate its efforts to obtain the liberty of the children of God: and as we wait in this light, and believe in its manifestations, we are favoured to see more light, the means appointed to procure it are revealed to us, and strength given to follow. But as it was prophetically spoken of the Saviour of the world, that there was no form or comeliness in him, that when we should see him, we should desire him, so the simplicity of his gospel is found to be. Nothing more strongly opposes the will, wisdom, and activity of the creature, than in all abasement, singly, to depend

day pretty much in private, save that an agreeable solid man, an Inspirant, paid us some visits, I believe to mutual satisfaction. We heard of a religious exercised coachman for whom was left a book or two, he not being at home. And thus, after secretly suffering, as in many other places, we took our departure for Geneva, travelling through a very beautiful country the last twenty miles, by the lake of Geneva, and in prospect of the Alps;

upon the promised Comforter, the Spirit of Truth, the anointing which an Apostle said the true believers received and had abiding in them, the unspeakable gift purchased by the precious blood of the Lamb, and dispensed in infinite mercy for our salvation, which, through its converting, purifying power is effected; for he gave himself for us, that he might redeem us from all iniquity, &c. Nevertheless the glorious end for which this sacrifice was made, ought to be advanced to, and our dependance increase upon the smallest discoveries of the spirit of Christ, though to the natural mind there may be no form nor comeliness in them: but it may sorrowfully be said, with respect to His inward appearance the second time without sin unto salvation, that he came to his own, but his own received him not; yet let us remember for our encouragement, that to as many as did receive him, he gave power to become the sons of God. So that if we surrender ourselves as clay into the hands of the potter, and our wills to the refiners fire, we shall, this way, be made living partakers of the sufferings of Christ, being fools for his sake, and, according to our measures, conformable to his death. This is an experience which closes the lips in awful silence, and restrains the imagination from feeding upon the Tree of knowledge; without which restraint, there is a danger of our not sufficiently embracing the excellent example of Him, who was led as

which were covered with snow in the latter end of the fifth month, although the weather was very hot with us. These, with the steep and craggy rocks of Switzerland, and pines of various kinds growing spontaneously upon them, and forming shades and wildernesses, compose a scene in nature truly magnificent; indeed for six hundred miles back, the prospect of mountains spread over with vineyards, with the grandeur of the Rhine, flowing below them, and its banks adorned with variety and abundance of fruit trees in full blossom, would have afforded a scene of pleasure to spirits at liberty for such enjoyment. But our hearts were on the whole too sad to be captivated thereby; a seed attracted us in sympathy, which was not so visible, nor had carried with it these sensible delights; and for it, in part, we travailled in spirit. We spent one day and two nights in Geneva, where being informed that John Eliot and Ady Bellamy were

a lamb to the slaughter, and as a sheep dumb before her shearers. The spirit of this world, in any of its false refinements, cannot preside here, neither can any righteousness of our own; because we humblingly see with the apostle, that it is not for any of these works which we have done, but of the mercy of Christ, that he saveth us, and by those means which he died to obtain, even the washing of regeneration, and the renewings of the Holy Ghost. Fervently desiring that thy sincere mind may, through the humbling processes of true spiritual baptism, be led, in the faith and patience, to the rest which is prepared for the children of God. I remain in gospel love,

Thy Friend
S. G.

waiting for us at Lyons, we hasted to them, and found their patience tried by a week's detention in that town. We joined them, and became comfortable; and spending one day to rest and be refreshed there, took a boat, and rapidly poured down the Rhine, one hundred and thirty two miles in seventeen hours, to a place called Pont St. Esprit, from which we came to Nismes and Congenies, the 22d and 23d of the 5th month, having travelled nine hundred and fifty miles from Amsterdam. It now looks pleasant to think of being soon amongst our friends, and a people to whom we may speak without an interpreter; for in that respect our situation is a sort of exile, but greatly made up, by a secret sense, more often renewed to us than we might have expected, that we are here in the appointment of Him who graciously regards the sparrows, so that not one of them falls to the ground without His permission: and truly these innocent open hearted people are of more value than many sparrows. We entered Nismes, with such a peaceful serenity upon our spirits, as portended the acquaintance we have since commenced with minds panting after the waters of Shiloh, and the strengthening effects of true gospel labours. We went next day to Congenies, about four leagues. Our arrival drew out of their habitations the people in general; some looked at us with astonishment, and other's with countenances which put me in mind of Mary's salutation to Elizabeth. These soon acknowledged us, and drew us into the house of a steady, valuable widow, where we were solemnly saluted and received, and our minds melted together; and such a stream of gospel love flowed, as some of us thought exceeded what we had before experienced, though no words were used to express it. We obtained lodgings at the house of a person not professing with them, with a view not unnecessarily to interrupt them in their useful employments, and to be at liberty ourselves to go amongst them as there appeared a service; but we only lodged there one night, and that with difficulty, their desire to have us amongst them, and to render us their services in their own way, was so strong, that, after contending the point, we gave way, and returned to the widow's, where we were entertained with every thing of the best they could supply. Our friends are most of them poor, industrious people; but we were favoured with all that was needful, though those things we call so are scarce, the country being generally overspread with vineyards, oliveyards, and mulberry-trees. It can hardly be thought how comfortable we were: peace of mind sweetens every inconvenience. We found these people different from our society in their outward appearance, and in their want of settlement, and sufficient quietude in their religious assemblies; but the humility and simplicity of their meetings, attended with a lively consciousness of their own weakness, make them ready to embrace every offer of help, that is suited to their capacity and progress in the truth. There are a few of them, amongst the younger sort particularly, who furnish a hope that there will be a society in this dark part of the world, established upon the right foundation. We soon found, that to be useful to them, the visitors must be weak with the visited, and in christian condescension bear with them, till truth opened a door of utterance to shew them a more excellent way. Their monthly meeting was held on first day, wherein, of their own accord, they laid open their discipline, by reading their minutes or agreements acceded to on their first setting up these meetings; which, for consistency with their profession, are, in general, superior to our expectations. But it extends no farther than to a care over their poor, and one another's moral conduct; they have no other tenets, nor any testimonies, recorded, by which they may be distinguished; and our little band were not without a guard, with respect to proposing, or urging any thing to them, which they have not, at present, a capacity rightly to adopt and support. At Congenies, and in its neighbourhood, we spent two weeks; visited all their families; attended their monthly meeting; had a meeting for conference with the elder rank; a youths meeting, and a very satisfactory public meeting with the inhabitants; and divers solemn opportunities unforeseen: all which brought us into near sympathy with them, and often deeply humbled and baptized our spirits on their account, as well as our own. Our parting was a very affecting one, but under a comfortable sense that the Shepherd of Israel has them under His gracious care. From Congenies we went to Giles's, about twenty one miles, where there are between twenty and thirty who profess with us, as they do at Congenies: but they do not appear so much awakened in their minds, nor so earnest to be visited. They received us, however, with great kindness, and were pleased with the visit, which perhaps may be profitable to some beyond what we can now see. As without faith it is impossible to please our all-wise Director, so it is impossible to persevere and hold to the end in His service, and in the humiliations which the creature meets with in it, without this precious ingredient, which is his own peculiar gift, and silences all fleshly reasonings. After having three meetings at Giles's, we came to Nismes, and there took coach for Lyons, one hundred and fifty miles. From that we travelled post, by way of Roane, Fontainbleau, Paris, and Versailles, to Alençon, where we arrived the 2d of the 7th month, several of us being weak and weary, after having travelled near six hundred miles from Nismes. In our way to Lyons, we passed through Dauphine, where some of our minds were not insensible of an attractive influence: but having no certain information of some we had heard of there, and several of our company strongly bending homewards, it did not seem the time easily to find them out.

Truly there is a hidden, precious seed scattered up and down, not only in these parts, but in Holland and Germany, measureably gathered, both from the superstitious, and the vain world; and seeking a foundation whereon they may rest the sole of their feet. This appeared beyond all doubt, both from a little knowledge which we obtained in those countries of some, and from that most sure word of prophecy, which penetrates the obscure recesses of Sion's travellers, and unites them all together in the ocean of gospel love. At Alençon, we were affectionately received by John De Marsillac, and courteously by his wife, who, through the whole of our visit there, which was three days, appeared to enjoy the company of their visitors. Here we endeavoured to take fresh counsel about the way of proceeding to England, which ended in the conclusion, of George and Sarah Dillwyn and John De Marsillac going to the Island of Guernsey, to visit the few friends there; and T. E. A. B. M. Dudley, my husband, and myself, to London directly, by way of Dieppe, which we pursued accordingly, and arrived in London the 13th of 7th month 1788.

We have had a solitary and exercising travel; but through infinite kindness, are again restored to our friends, and some of us to our native country. We attended the quarterly meeting of London: the sight of so many friends was new and reviving to us; and the renewed evidence, that the Lord had been mercifully with us, that he had led us about, and instructed us, and tenderly preserved us when, in child-like simplicity, we depended upon his counsel, afforded, and still affords, abundant cause to praise him for his mercies past, and humbly hope for more.

Thus, after a journey of more than two thousand five hundred miles, attended with many difficulties, and close exercises of body and mind, she was enabled to return to her home at Clonmel, in the 8th month 1788, under the comfortable sense of divine favour and protection. Some parts of her letters written after her return, on a retrospect of this visit, appear to be worthy of insertion.

———— We have had, since leaving York, many new scenes of trial, and new demonstration of providential care; especially in the course of the long and deeply proving journey which we undertook, in hope that the Hand of Omnipotence led forth to the Continent. The state of mind in which I was involved previous to it, the inexpressible humiliations and besetments which attended the accomplishment of it, and since that, the commemoration of unmerited support, with the renewed discovery of human frailty, seem to change, in many respects, the face of this world to me. Not that I am redeemed from the love of it; but that I have learned to expect less from it; seeing more and more, that this is indeed a probationary state of being, and that our sufferings and joys in it are no otherwise important, than as they affect our attachment to the one great object of eternal good, and our communion with it in the silence of all that is fleshly.

———— It is a joyous consideration, that the glorious light of the gospel is emitted from the Sun of Righteousness; and that, though instruments may be used to bear testimony to it, yet that he, before whom all nations are but as the drop of a bucket, the small dust of the balance, and who takes up the isles as a very little thing, can, when they fail, do his work without them, and " glorify the house of his glory." I humblingly reflect upon our late journey on the Continent, and am bound to acknowledge (however as an individual I have failed in truly saying, " thy will be done") that the word of the Lord is faithfulness and truth. My mind is settled in a comfortable belief, that, through the creating and converting word of Omnipotence, the pure seed of divine life was visited with greater efficacy, than the discouragements which we were under, allowed us to know at that time. But ah, poor Amsterdam! yea, poor Rotterdam! and many, many places on that side the Continent, touching whose inhabitants my soul, at times, sings mournfully to its well-beloved!

CHAP. VI.

Her Concern respecting a Boarding School for female Youth.—Visit to Friends Families in Cork.—Journey to London.—Visit to Dunkirk, Holland, Pyrmont, &c.—Her Return—and Decease.—Testimonies concerning her.

IT may now be proper to take some notice of a concern which had weightily engaged her attention, respecting the propriety of opening a boarding-school at Clonmel, for the religious care and education of female youth. This subject had, for some time, been deeply pondered, both by herself and her husband; and had, at length, so matured in their minds, as to afford an evidence that it would be right to set forward the work.

Their motives for this undertaking appear to be purely disinterested, and with the single view of promoting a guarded and religious education of children; being themselves in easy circumstances, and under no necessity to pursue this employment, for family support.

When we consider the susceptibility of youth to early impressions, with the general permanency thereof on their minds; and reflect that they are soon to participate in the concerns of life, and will, in a few years, be the principals on this stage of being; we cannot but perceive the extensive importance, both to individuals and the community, of an early moral and religious education; nor be surprised that this earnest labourer for the good of mankind, should feel it her duty to cultivate this sure ground of general reformation, and to encourage others, upon pure principles, to engage in an employment so truly honorable and productive of good.

Though under doubts and discouragements of mind, arising chiefly from the humble sense of her own weakness, and want of qualifications for so arduous and important a service, she was enabled to open the proposed institution, the month after her return from the Continent.

She was much concerned that the children committed to their care, might be preserved in innocence, and trained in the paths of piety and virtue; and when not called from home on religious service, laboured faithfully in advancing such measures as tended to promote the solid advantages of this institution.

On the subject of this school, there does not appear to be much remaining written by herself: a few of her letters have, however, been collected, expressive of her tenderness left she might interfere with other institutions; and of her cautious steppings in this concern; with divers other instructive sentiments; most of which have been extracted, and are as follows:

——— 'The prospect of removing to Ireland in any line, continues to my mind very awful; and undertaking a matter of so much consequence as the proposed school, is not less so: but if our friends whose judgments we esteem, feel uneasy with it, and freely express themselves, it will rather be a relief than a disappointment; especially as we have no intention of getting, or saving money by it to ourselves. If we are but favoured to see the work of our day, and found faithful in the performance of it, though ever so humbling to flesh and blood, I sometimes think, it is all that I desire.

——— I don't like the thoughts of crowding new institutions upon friends, imposing objects, or doing any thing which has the remotest appearance of opposing our own, or others' prospects, by dividing or scattering the little strength, which, if put together, might prove no more than sufficient for one undertaking at first; though afterwards, it might encrease for whatever further openings might be perceived in the truth.

——— I have, at times, been much depressed with a fear of interfering with the school at Mountmellick, and discouraging the valuable friends engaged therein. I felt most easy to write them a few lines, with a view, as I tell them, " to open a door for a free communication of sentiments, respecting what we both have in view;" expressing my love and esteem for them, and belief, that as both they and we are disinterested in our views, desirous of promoting the same cause, and rightly directed, we shall move, either separately or together, with a comfortable degree of unity and sympathy; and requesting their openness with me, in saying whether any thing has occurred to them, on hearing of our plan, which would be any strength or encouragement to them, and which is in our power to afford; whether they wish us to be united in our undertakings, or think that two schools will answer; and lastly, whether they do not think it will be better for them steadily to pursue their own prospects, till our house is opened, (if ever it should be) and then to stand resigned, either to unite or keep separate, as at that time appears best. So much seemed a little relief to myself to say, feeling great affection and tenderness towards them; at the same time that my own faith is nearly tried. I, however, feel a hope as I am writing, that if our offering is not accepted, but proves like David's proposing to build the house, that, nevertheless, we shall feel that secret supporting language, " thou didst well, in that it was in thine heart, &c."

———— Dost thou not wonder at the undertaking we have in view? my dear R. G. has kindly condescended to make ample preparations for a boarding school for girls, and has built a considerable addition to our present dwelling; which stands upon an island, in a navigable river called the Suir. It is about a hundred yards across, and near a quarter of a mile long; has on one side of it, the quay and town, and on the other, cultivated mountains, which seem almost to hang over it. The prospect from the front of the house, is through the garden and a pasture, to the river and valley, and is terminated by a very high and rugged mountain, several miles distant. The place is altogether very commodious, and pleasant for the intended purpofe; but how we fhall meet with fuitable, difinterefted perfons for undertaking the immediate care of the children, &c. is not clear; a hope however cheers us, that if our views are right, and deferving a blefling, all things needful will be afforded us in the needful time. I fhould like to have fuch, for almoft every ftation in the family, as poffefs a fincere concern for the profperity of the work, and find a dedication in their own hearts to it; being afraid of drawing any, merely to gratify ourfelves, that have not fome fuch foundation to fupport them in feafons of trial, which, generally, more or lefs, attend the moft upright and difinterefted defigns.

—— I have had a very low dull time of late about this undertaking, from a fear that we fhall not be found equal to it. I don't mean, in the fight of men, for probably we could not pleafe all, let us do ever fo well; but I mean in the fight of Him whofe blefling is more craved and panted after, than the moft fpecious appearances it can wear.

—— Having formerly mentioned the difcouragements of my mind in the fetting out of the fchool we are engaged in, it is but juft alfo to fay, that things refpecting it now wear a pleafanter afpect; with a hope that that which was fown in weaknefs, feems, through divine help, (for to that only it can be attributed) rifing into greater ftrength. The minds of fome of our precious charge are evidently encreafing in verdure, by the dew of heaven; and, in the general, innocence is to be felt from the influence of their spirits. Our helpers also grow (we hope) in the root of true religion. Indeed, did the world, or our religious and civil concerns with its inhabitants, speak no more trouble to us than what we find upon our little island, it would be too great a state of prosperity for human nature profitably to be indulged with; for even that calls for a watchfulness and industry, which the flesh is at enmity with, and which I fear being found wanting in. To feel an evidence that we are under the care and blessing of the Shepherd and Bishop of souls, after conflicting doubtings respecting it, is such a cordial as reanimates the soul to fight the good fight of faith, and to lay hold on eternal life. In seasons of favour this has been the case; but it is hard to lay down all these precious gifts, still to walk as the master walked, to testify, by our dedication, that we believe he came to save sinners, and, as to the means whereby his glorious work is promoted, to say, " not my will, but thine be done."

In the 12th month 1788, she engaged, with other friends, in a visit to the meetings and families of friends in the city of Cork: and during her employment in that service, the following letters appear to have been written. Though they do not express much account of the visit, yet they may be acceptable, from the instructive remarks they contain, and the weighty and concerned spirit which they manifest under this engagement.

———— We have been steadily engaged with fitting in four families a day; and though we often seem ready to give up, and feel like imprisoned spirits, yet, upon the whole, we have no just cause to be discouraged; best help being near to strengthen us with might in our inner man, or such a proportion of it as is necessary for the performance of, and perseverance in, the work of the present day. As doing the will of our heavenly Father, is the only thing really worth living for, I wish to consider it as an unmerited favour, to know what that will is, and to be furnished with any degree of capacity to do it.

———— The season of the year, the closeness of the city, and the complicated occasions of heaviness and depression, in the view of the state of things here, all contribute to suffering both of body and mind; so that were we clear of unprofitably adding thereto, we do not lack a pretty full cup thereof. Indeed we have no business to seek for a portion or baptism, differing in nature from that which the great Pattern himself submitted to, and which the true seed here and elsewhere, have still, for wise purposes to experience.

———— Whether any good may come of our labour and travel here, must be left: it is the blessing only which can render this, and every other endeavour of the poor servants, effectual to the building up of any drooping member in the most holy faith. My soul has in the course of our visit to the families of friends in this city, passed by the gates of death. But the deceitfulness of my own heart is such, that it cannot be removed by pleasant things ; nor does fitness for the little services we are engaged in, spring out of the most sensible and gratifying operations of the spirit ; but out of these unsearchable baptisms, which, nevertheless, demonstrate they are of the Holy Ghost and fire, because they leave an empty temple, a temple ready to be filled with the presence wherein there is life. According to my small knowledge of good, I may assert that, after all, the joy of the Lord is our strength ; and were it not that, in the beginning of this visit, my spirit had been sweetly consolated therewith, I very much doubt whether, from many of my feelings and deep provings since, I should have held out till now: peradventure it possessed some of that sacred efficacy, which Elijah's forty days sustenance is distinguished for, and thereby, to the praise of that grace, by which I am what I am, my confidence has not wholly failed me in the deeps.—All that is within me prays, that as we have been mercifully strengthened to drink, in this place, a bitter cup, we may not, in our own wills, refuse any dregs which in infinite wisdom are intended, in part, to constitute the cup of salvation. But the flesh is weak ! A few have refused us, and whether their hearts will relent, is yet to try. We cannot however but sympathize with a tried, afflicted remnant in this meeting, whose hands I do believe, will grow stronger and stronger, be more and more instructed to war, and their fingers to fight ; for however the boasters over the pure lowly feed may exalt themselves, yet they cannot stand in the day of judgment, nor prevent the fulfilling of the promife, that the law fhall be magnified and made honourable. I concluded to ftay third day meeting; and though, as is often my lot, fpeaking to men did not relieve my inward oppreffion, yet in proftration before the almighty Helper, who in abundant mercy is touched with a feeling of our infirmities, there was a fecret fuftaining evidence, of living again in His prefence, whereby thofe bones that were broken did rejoice. Thus are the poor of the flock helped in their extremities, and encouraged to maintain their confidence in the omnipotent gathering arm of Ifrael's Shepherd.

———— May we not be afraid of fuffering; for in this land however, they that dwell with the feed, muft dwell in a low fpot, and give up their names to reproach. " If ye were of the world, the world would love you, but becaufe ye are not of the world, the world hates you : it hated me before it hated you." To be of this happy, though afflicted number, is more to be defired than to join ourfelves in affinity with a fpirit which, inftead of fuffering with the feed, wars againft it, in the wrath and cruelty of the king of the locufts which came out of the pit; a fpirit that cannot ftand in the day of judgment, but which being airy and unfettled, leads from the quiet habitation, and leaves the mind without a ftay. How excellent, yea how much to be defired, is that ftate wherein, through holy chaftifement and fuffering for the feed's fake, that precious feal of adoption, the language of Abba Father, is feelingly obtained and breathed! This is indeed a

Something in ourselves wherein we can rejoice, an unmerited gift which excludes all boasting, a preservative from moving in the line of others' experience, further than it is made our own, or from having our rejoicing in them. Were the active members of our society, more generally and individually gathered to this deep inward feeling of the life of truth, and the evidence of its operations in themselves, how much more effectual would their labours be, in building up one another in the most holy faith? I am afraid for myself; I long to be more truly weighty in my own spirit; not to assume a consequence amongst men, or to plume myself with borrowed feathers; but really to be preserved in company with the seed, and through its operations, to live, move, and have my being, in the church especially. A series of deep exercises has fallen to my lot, on account of the law and testimony of truth in this province, and near sympathy with some who dare not let it fall to the ground, without discovering themselves, and on whose side they are. These find it to be a day of trial, of perplexity, and of treading down; and there are so few, even amongst the well minded, who are skilful either in lamentation, or in war, that the work lies heavy on a few; and sometimes I am afraid, that the ointment made after the art of the apothecary, gets unpleasantly tinctured by the dead flies (the unquickened efforts for the cause) being cast into it.

———— Though I often find it my duty to wash and anoint, rather than appear to men to fast, yet the secret travail of my soul is sorrowful, and beset with many discouragements unknown but to itself, and its almighty Helper; and I find, that the more deep and hidden my exercises are, and the more I seek for strength to unite myself, in a covenant never to be broken, with the Beloved of my soul; the more I am capable to distinguish the consolations of the Spirit, the pure unerring Spirit, from every inferior or corrupt source of gratification to the natural senses. I know my experience of this is but very small, and yet, as far as I have attained, I have abundant cause to admire the wisdom there is in the paths of true abasedness and self-denial; yea, the fortress they lead to, and the safety there is in them.

Never are we favoured with a clearer perception of our religious duty, in little as well as greater things, than when our spiritual eye has been purged, by the ministration of some baptism that has afflictingly removed every film of self-love; which discovers itself by an over-attention to our own reputation, to the ease of the flesh, and a desire for pleasant things in spirituals as well as temporals. Ah! may we think nothing too near or too dear to part with, for the secret acceptance of the Beloved! The very putting forth of his hand, as through the hole of the door, little as the intimation may seem, is a powerful call to admit him in the way of his coming, however it may oppose our own way.

She attended the half year's national meeting at Dublin in the 5th month 1789; and from thence went to York, where she made her relations and friends a short visit, and proceeded pretty directly for the yearly meeting at London; which she attended, and returned home with an evidence, that, in this journey, she had been occupied in her proper place. This is agreeably testified by the following letter, which is the only one that has appeared on this occasion.

——— Our little flock looks pleasant and healthy. Our joy was mutual at meeting yesterday, and home is felt by us to be a peaceful retreat. In a little sitting which we had at home in the evening, there seemed some ability to lie down as beside the still waters; a consoling experience: and on looking back upon our late journey, though there was no great professed draft to it, a hope arises, that, consistent with our religious duty, we were going on with the work of the day.

In the latter part of the year 1789, she felt her mind drawn to have some public meetings in divers places, where none of our society dwell, particularly at the town and garrison of Kinsale; where, as well as at other places, these services tended to open, and spread the knowledge of the truth. Concerning her visit to the abovementioned place, she writes thus:

—In much fear, and I trust humiliation of spirit, I have been to the town of Kinsale, and suffered to have appointed, through an apprehension of duty, a public meeting there. It was large, nearly as much fo as the houfe belonging to the fociety would admit. There appeared to be about two hundred people, who generally behaved with decency and folidity, and the meeting was owned with the gathering influence of Ifrael's Shepherd; which, in time of filence, was I thought comfortably experienced. We alfo paid a vifit to the fort, and particularly to a large company of deferters, who are collected there for tranfportation, many of them good looking young men; and I alfo ventured to remind fome of the officers, of their religious and civil duties. It was altogether a fervice much in the crofs, and deferving of no reward, for want of timely refignation to it: but, in unmerited mercy, I was favoured with a peaceful calm, which my beloved companions alfo enjoyed, and earned with honeft labour.

She was, indeed, much concerned, and laboured in her meafure, for the propagation of that holy principle, which is the light, and life of men; and fhe counted nothing too dear to give up, or part with, for the promotion of this pure word in their hearts. A renewed evidence of this appears, in a frefh inftance of dedication to a very trying and arduous fervice. During her late travels on the Continent, her mind had often fympathized in fecret, and been united in gofpel love, with a precious feed fcattered up and down in thofe parts; but which, it feemed not then the appointed feafon, to vifit in perfon. This time now approached, and, as fhe apprehended, in the openings of divine wifdom; so that she believed it her indispensable duty, to give herself up, in pure resignation, to this service; which appeared in her view, to comprehend a visit to Dunkirk, Holland, Pyrmont, and some other parts of Germany. Under the weight of this important concern, she experienced the near sympathy of friends of the monthly and quarterly meetings to which she belonged, with those of the national meeting in Dublin, and yearly select meeting in London; who concurred in testimonials of their unity and approbation. Thus strengthened by the feelings and concurrence of the church, and by a similar concern of her friend George Dillwyn, she set forward to engage in the work before them, in the 6th month 1790; accompanied also by her husband and Sarah Dillwyn, who felt their minds engaged to enter with them on this journey.

Her letters written under the prospect of this visit, during the progress of it, and upon its conclusion, appear to form, in general, so regular and connected an account of it, that nothing further appears necessary, than to lay the extracts from them before the reader.

2d month 1790. I seem very like one who hath no resting place on earth, or any consolations here in which I dare to trust; but if I am found worthy, in the smallest degree, to resemble the great and holy High Priest of our profession, it is enough. As to the performance of great works, I look not for it; my mind is taught to believe that I have no right thereto, or reason to expect that an instrument so feeble, and so little a time in use, is likely to be owned, in any extraordinary degree, in the discharge of my small part of the great work. But my spirit hath often been dipt into sympathy inexpressible, with a seed in those parts, of which I have not yet attained the outward discovery, and peradventure, this second visit may prove like fishing, and catching nothing. This I desire to leave, and to attain to a daily and simple reliance upon unerring direction, which the creature knows must be attended with a dying daily.

2d month 1790. We stand in need of care, both of our own, and that of our friends; our endeavours for peace being, in many respects, in a line rather new and important, and in which we desire to be preserved from moving further, than the good Shepherd leads and goes before.—It has not been without a portion of deep exercise, and frequent baptisms, known only to the Searcher of hearts, that I have obtained so much strength as to cast my burden for a time upon the church; and since they have taken it, and I believe some of them felt it, my relief has, beyond my expectation, been effected.—But this is temporary. I know, in a spiritual sense at least, that bonds and afflictions await me; yet with thankfulness may acknowledge that, feeling the everlasting arms to be underneath, none of these things at present move me.—My capacity to promote the work of righteousness on the earth, is very small; but according to that capacity, I long to be found faithful, not counting my life dear unto myself.—I have not heard of any companion in the little services before me, nor do I feel any anxiety on that head; believing that, if the concern is right, suitable fellow labourers will be provided, without any toiling interference of mine.

3d month 1790. May my mind be preserved in stability to the end: for that I both watch and pray, well knowing that when I lose that, it must be distinguished mercy indeed, that preserves my poor little vessel from total wreck. As a very hard gale of even fair wind may occasion great danger, so I perceive that the urgency I feel, at times, in my spirit, to do the Master's apprehended will, may render frustrate the gracious design, if ballast be not on board. I never felt my mind so sensibly sustained in the prospect of any journey before. I esteem it an unmerited mark of the great Shepherd's condescending care, who hath, blessed be his Name, richly replenished my soul with faith, and so abundantly ministered its sister virtue, patience, that my frail tabernacle being at times overcome, the language of my heart is similar to that of the Spouse; " Stay me with flaggons, comfort me with apples, for I am sick of love."

This is a dispensation which I do not expect to continue; for when a testimony of this love is called for, when difficulties are to be encountered, both within and without, when we are to be offered up a sacrifice in the service of the christian faith, oh how inconstant is the human heart! how many substitutes for obedience, how many subterfuges does it find! Remembering these things, the wormwood and the gall, yea the anguishing exercises attendant on our late journey, my heart is humbled within me, and preserved from expecting the journey in prospect to be unmixed with similar trials; or even to see in it, gratifying demonstrations of that glorious work, which, in gospel vision, is beheld to be begun in the German Empire, and many other parts of the globe less known to us. On any presumption of this sort, I have not dared to take one step; but have much desired that my spirit may be deep enough, according to my measure, to suffer and rejoice only with the pure seed, whether obviously the fig-tree blossom, and fruit be on the vine, or not.

———— On second day morning, at the yearly meeting of ministers and elders held in London the 17th of the 5th month, our certificates were read; which, far beyond what I durst have looked for, created expressions of gospel unity and church encouragement, that were not entirely unseasonable to my mind; feeling myself as poor as seemed possible for spiritual existence. But what also greatly contributed to lift up my head above the overflowing billows, and say to the winds and the waves, " Be still," was the indisputable evidence, that the Master had separated for a similar work, my beloved friend, George Dillwyn; under which his oppressed mind was constrained publicly to acknowledge, to his own and others relief, that he believed it to be his duty to go with us. How precious is that help, which is dispensed in better wisdom than our own! and being the fruit of mercy, it is often reſerved for the moment of extremity. It was a very ſolemn uniting ſeaſon; the ſpirit and the bride (the church) appeared cordially to unite in the ſame language of encouragement. I greatly deſire a heart capable of humbly and reverently returning acceptable obedience for theſe favours, in the few feeble ſteppings through my future pilgrimage. Trials I have learned to expect, having a diſpoſition that will not ſuffer me to be exempt, till it becomes loſt in the ocean of goſpel love. In ourſelves, as in the world, there is trouble; oh that our acquaintance may become more and more intimate with Him, in whom is the fulneſs of undefiled peace! Then may we rejoice in every tribulation, which has urged us to lay hold on eternal ſubſtance. No female companion appearing, our former valuable fellow traveller, Sarah Dillwyn, was naturally looked to, and no obſtructions occurring, Ratcliff monthly meeting (of which ſhe is a member) cordially teſtified its approbation therewith, and granted her a certificate. Thus we four being banded, left London (Joſhua Beale accompanying us) on the ſeventh day after the yearly meeting. There we met with many friends like bone of our bone, and fleſh of our fleſh; yea, ſo cemented have ſome of us at times felt, as fully to convince us that it was the work of both grace and nature; the latter of which, in our many ſeparations, is learning I truſt to be more and more ſubject, and to ſurrender its will to the divine will, which indeed ſweetens many bitter cups, and ſtrengthens us to ſay amen to every requiring of truth. Without this experience, how are we like bullocks unaccuftomed to the yoke! The yearly meeting was large, and fatisfactory in a good degree; but fuch affemblies, compofed of minds fo various, have generally a confiderable portion of exercife and weight for the feeling part of its members; and it is an unfpeakable favour that there are fuch preferved in the church, whofe fpiritual faculties are fo alive, that, like watchers on the walls of Zion, they can give an alarm at the new and various attacks, which our common and unwearied enemy is making upon truth's ramparts: and it is alfo a diftinguifhable mercy in our poor fociety, that there are, amongft the younger part of it, fuch as, by the livelinefs and faithfulnefs of their fpirits, promife a fucceffion of ftandard bearers.

We were at Rochefter on firft day, at the monthly meeting at Canterbury on third, and got to Dover that evening; from whence we failed next day for Dunkirk, and had a fine, but flow paffage, being on the water fixteen hours. Here we found John De Marfillac waiting for us; and Jofhua Beale, alfo uniting himfelf to us, we became fix in number. The day we arrived, was their week day meeting; and it may with thankfulnefs be acknowledged, that it was mercifully owned with divine refrefhment, and the communication of counfel from the living fpring thereof. And what tended to heighten our joy, on fitting down with the friends here, was the fcene which we had beheld juft before. What they call the hoft was carried about, with such a procession of the army, corporation, clergy, and little children, as I never saw before, or could have supposed; there being many thousands both of people, and images of silver, pewter, and wood; hundreds of candles near six feet long; abundance of rich silk and other vestments; barefooted and shaven headed friars; music, drums, &c. cannon firing, and bells ringing. So that, after all this stir, to sit down with our friends, under our own vines and fig-trees, and measurably to partake of substantial food, was truly joyous; and more especially so, under the belief that the one shall decrease, and the other encrease. We spent a full week at Dunkirk, to a good degree of satisfaction, perceiving the blessing that those new settlers may be in that land, and at this important juncture, if they wisely keep to, and are graciously kept by, the preserving, unchangeable principle of truth. They are at present worth visiting, and their number is likely soon to be encreased from Nantucket.

After having four public meetings in Dunkirk; (at all which divers not of our society attended) and several private ones, we proceeded to Ostend, (B. R. going with us) here we spent a day to satisfaction, finding a man and his wife from London belonging to the society, who had not seen any reputable friends for seven or eight years. Though they had the marks of being, in some degree, robbed and spoiled, yet there was also something in them to visit, and which accepted the testimony of truth, as far as related to themselves. Divers books were also scattered, and not without a hope that the blessing accompanied some of them; for even in this little service, there is a great difference in our feelings. It is often like casting bread upon the waters, and, sometimes, without hope of return in any day or age. From Ostend we continued our course along the coast, by way of Bruges, Flushing, and Middleburgh; at the two latter of which, we solemnly paused, and also exposed ourselves to the observation and acquaintance of the people; intimating to some our errand, and making enquiry for such as were seeking the truth. With some small exception, they appeared to be in their strong holds, and fenced cities, intent upon this world's gain, which is, with too much propriety, called their god. However, a few books were left among them; and finding the son of a friend at Middleburgh, we had an opportunity of religious retirement with him, and of dropping such counsel as opened therein. He appeared, by his acknowledgement and attention to us, to accept the visit kindly; but his situation is exceedingly unsafe. From Middleburgh we went to a little port, called Campveer, and there hired a vessel to take us to Rotterdam. We had a very pleasant passage, our minds being favoured with much tranquillity; and after a thirty hours sail, arrived at our port, the 18th of the 6th month; where, as we expected, we entered into a fresh trial of fidelity to the precious cause. Here we staid three days, visited some former acquaintances, who were very kind; and commenced new ones with such as seemed to understand how to receive disciples, in the name of disciples. To one or two of this class, our minds were particularly united. Being there on a first day, we had two public meetings, both considerably attended, but especially the latter, which was also a truly solemn and profitable opportunity. Between Dunkirk and Rotterdam, we had divers opportunities of disseminating the knowledge of the principle of truth, by the distribution of books, and some conferences in a private way; but had no public meeting, though our minds were, in several places, brought under a considerable weight of exercise; which seemed to answer no more end, than the people's walking round the walls of Jericho; and were it not that we are convinced, even from outward observation, that the Lord is at work in the kingdoms of men, and making a way for his own seed, we might conclude, that the fortifications which this world's spirit hath erected, particularly in Holland, will hardly ever be taken down. We went pretty directly from Rotterdam to Amsterdam, where we had our share of secret dippings and discouragements; but not expecting great things in our setting out, or desiring to be borne up above a feeling of what we are, and the oppression and obscurity of the true seed, we are the less exposed to a spirit of dismay; and engaged at times, in simplicity, to sit down together, profeffedly to wait for the guidance of truth, or a difcovery that the cloud refts upon the tabernacle. In thefe feafons, we have been ftrengthened, and cemented in beft unity, and alfo encouraged to hold on in a path to be trodden more by faith, than fight.

In the public meetings, of which we have attended three, we experienced painful exercife; and yet I thought on firft day, that both the fittings were, upon the whole, folid and lively. We received accounts of our brother, Jofeph Grubb being in a very declining ftate of health, which had made its appearance before we left home; and being in partnerfhip with my Robert Grubb, and the care of bufinefs forbidden to my brother, my hufband thought it his duty to offer him all the relief he could; a tranquil mind refpecting outward things, being of unfpeakable confequence to the latter part of a man's life: this, without any anxiety about our own property, and a prefentiment before we left home, that he would hardly go through the journey, induced us, though much in the crofs, to feparate. We were detained at Amfterdam longer than we expected; one occafion of which was the printing of fome extracts from Hugh Turford's writings, with an addition from Mary Brook on filent waiting, which fome of our company tranflated into French. It contains very fuitable matter for the prefent age, and is an acceptable publication to J. M. and B. R. to diftribute in France, and alfo convenient to us in this journey, as many underſtand French. We have a large ſtock of other books, very eligible for our purpoſe, which the meeting for ſufferings has given us for diſtribution. The 6th of the 7th month, we came to Utrecht, where J. M. being tender took cold, and was confined next day to the houſe; and as he did not ail a great deal, it ſuited our plan of ſpending one day quietly together, before we parted, he and B. R. having concluded to go from hence to Dunkirk, and J. M. from that place to his home. This has been a trial to us, but knowing J. M's attention to beſt direction, and alſo his deſire, if right, of keeping with us, we dared not to perſuade him to ſuit our inclinations and convenience; and therefore, after enjoying each others company, in ſweet fellowſhip and tenderneſs of ſpirit, we parted; our little band then confiſting of George and Sarah Dillwyn, J. B. and myſelf, with the moſt arduous part of the journey in proſpect. Perhaps this ſtripping of outward help is wiſely difpenſed to us: in that light we view it, and dare not diſpute divine ſufficiency. Soon after our friends were gone, we concluded to pay a viſit to a family of Amſterdam, (with which we were acquainted when there before) who now reſide at their country houſe about half way from that city to Utrecht; and accordingly ſet off, and arrived about five, and were received more like near relations united on the beſt ground, than as people of another nation and profeſſion. We alſo met here two women of considerable account on a visit; to one of them particularly, our minds were nearly drawn, and the little instruction which was in our power to communicate, from the exercise of our minds, broken French, and the use of the scriptures, to particular passages of which we directed them as they occurred, was received with a religious sensibility, which greatly united us together, and which words cannot fully set forth *. Though we often

* Some time afterwards, she wrote the following letter to one of the women of that family. Remembering thy request to hear from our little company when we returned from Germany, and being now so near you, I felt an inclination to tell thee, and thy valuable brother and sister, that, through the merciful direction and care of providence, we have got along to a good degree of satisfaction, and been favoured, upon the whole, with a moderate share of health. We pursued our journey from Utrecht, by way of Arnheim and Munster, to Pyrmont; there we staid two weeks, and then went to Rinteln, Minden, Osnabruck, and Bisefeld, and so, by way of Munster, to Crevelt, Duffeldorf, Mulheim on the Rhine, Elberfelt, and from thence to Cleves. We found a few in many of these places, who, being weary of the ceremonial part of religion, are desiring its living substance, and to be true worshippers in spirit. These have many difficulties from within and without; but if they depend, singly, upon divine help, and cease to recommend themselves by their own dead works, we have a hope, that they will gradually retire from the confusion of the carnal mind, to the true sheepfold. Were the professors of christianity more generally acquainted with the undefiled rest, which the redeemed mind is strengthened to gather to, they would detect the fallacy of unsanctified forms and ministry, and rejoicingly receive the eternal Witness for God

lament our ignorance of the language of this people, and its attendant inconveniencies, yet I was never more convinced of the influence of truth qualifying to fpeak to one another in our own tongues, though utterly incapable in any other language, than that of the fpirit; for in the prefent cafe, we were not fenfible of either us, or the caufe, fuffering under our apparent difadvantages. We cannot always judge why we are fo led, and why fo deftitute of fome outward accommodations to the fervice, which human prudence would naturally point out; but I may acknowledge that, on this account, I never was more contented and fupported in an humble truft, that the good and Almighty Hand is with us in " thefe mortifying labours." We left Utrecht on feventh day morning, and came to Wageninge, which is an agreeable little town. The inhabitants were greatly furprifed at feeing us, but became uncommonly civil and courteous; in part owing to a man who drove us from Utrecht, who by fome means, unknown to us, conceived fo favourable an

in themfelves, for their Lawgiver, Friend, and Comforter.

We reflect with fatisfaction upon our vifit to Middlewaart; not only in remembrance of your affectionate hofpitality, but alfo of the uniting virtue of truth upon our minds, which left a pleafant favour after we feparated; and now reviving, with renewed defire for all our prefervation, and increafing intimacy with the good Shepherd of his fheep, I falute thee, my dear friend, in fifterly affection.

S. G.

opinion of us, and seemed furnished with such materials for description, that wherever we stopt, he was sure to influence the people in our favour, and they united in testimonies of affection and kindness. We spent all first day in Wageninge; had a little, but solemn and refreshing meeting of our own company, and had also the company of a young Priest of good character. He and George Dillwyn conversed (I believe intelligibly) upon some important subjects in French, though perhaps neither of them were fully acquainted with the language; but the best sense being present, that defect was made up thereby.

We left a few suitable books with them, which were very kindly accepted; and our parting was with apparent sentiments of affectionate esteem. We also gave books to divers others, and had a satisfaction in spending this little time amongst a kind, simple hearted people. The people of the inn are particularly of this description, their conduct manifesting a pleasure which they had in entertaining us. These comfortable spots and feelings, somewhat resemble Elijah's food, on the strength of which he had to travel many days. As neither the great work, nor the capacity to do it, is ours, so we may be emboldened to hope, that our acceptance will stand in proportion to our obedience to that we have, rather than to that we have not. From Wageninge we came to Arnheim, where we spent one day agreeably, were at the house of very civil people; and though we did not commence much acquaintance, yet were satisfied with our little detention there, and to one or other left several books. Here we met with a kind man who speaks English well, says he was seasonably, and effectually served by a friend in England, when he was a stranger there; and this is (no doubt) an additional inducement to lay himself out to oblige us, which he does with the appearance of much sincerity. These journies, I sometimes hope, will in future open my heart with more cordiality to strangers; for " knowing the heart of a stranger," a deficiency herein would be doubly culpable. The next place we went to was Doesburgh, where our feelings were rather unusually pleasant; but we did not find any stop thereby in our progress. The landlady at the inn where we stopped, appeared and approved herself to be far from the common sort, for dignity of manners and solidity, if not religious weightiness of mind. Her conduct to us was truly friendly, manifesting an affection and liberality becoming other parts of her character. We gave her a Barclay's Apology in Dutch, and several books in French, which she appeared fully qualified to read, and in a good degree to understand: she wanted much to pay for them, but on any terms was glad to receive them; and after looking over the summary, promised to lend them among some of her neighbours. Germany is a country very unlike the Netherlands, both in the face of it, and in the manners of its inhabitants; the people being kept in a state of greater servility under princes of small territories. Our difficulties in the way of travelling commenced when we left Holland; for after gliding along in Treckſchutes, upon their quiet waters, we got into waggons, the beſt public conveyances the country afforded, and the roads being extremely bad, we were jolted to a degree not eaſy to ſuppoſe; and for want of knowing the language, were impoſed upon, and induced to take our paſſage in the poſt waggon, underſtanding that we ſhould have it to ourſelves, arrive ſeaſonably at our lodgings the two nights in proſpect, and have time enough for reſt. But inſtead of theſe fine things, after they got our money, a Capuchin Friar, and a very ill looking man, were put in with us, and we kept in this ſituation, with two meals wanting, through a dark rainy night (the wet coming in upon us) till three o'clock the next morning; when, after two hours reſt, we were ſummoned again, and without ſtopping to take any meals, ſave our dinners, travelled on till we arrived, about one o'clock next morning, at the gates of Munſter, a fortified city; where we had to wait for an entrance more than half an hour; and then had to find our lodgings among a people of a ſtrange language, whoſe principal object was to get from us all they could. This is a hint of the manner in which we got along, and I mention it to ſhew the inconvenience ſtrangers are ſubject to, and how different the fare of theſe countries is from that of England; at the ſame time an acknowledgement of providential care is abundantly due from us. Our minds, during this extraordinary trial of body and ſpirits, were remarkably ſuſtained with cheerful tranquility, and an abounding defire to comfort one another in this painful imprifonment. We were alfo preferved at the time from fuffering in our health, and found that part of two days reft in Munfter, recruited us finely.

Our ftay in that city was very fatisfactory, finding it to be a place of confiderable opennefs. One man in particular, a profeffor of languages in the univerfity, who was fick, received our men with brotherly affection and joy, had very fatisfactory converfation with them, and was glad to receive divers of our books, fome of which he intended to put into their public library. He told them of a relation of his, in a part of Germany where we have not been, who is fully convinced of our principles, but who has not dared openly to avow them; and faid, that in fome other parts, there are many fuch, which we have fince found to be the cafe. A ferious young nobleman, a pupil of his, intending to take a tour to England, was defirous of being recommended to fome friend in London, in which George Dillwyn gratified him. Many other opportunities occurred of cafting books into the hands of ferious people, and in an imperfect way intimating to them fuch truths, as at that time we were furnifhed with. From Munfter we came, by way of Warrendorf, Padderborn, &c. through Weftphalia, to Pyrmont, which we reached the 23d of the 7th month. Here our minds were foon comforted in the belief, that there is a feed in thefe parts, which, however hidden from the world, and the many churches profeffing the chriftian name, are preffing after an eftablifhment on the right foundation. Our minds were greatly favoured with peaceful serenity, and a steady reliance on providential care; so that instead of difficulties depressing, they rather animated our spirits to press forward, toward the fulfilling of our allotted portion of travail and exercise, and to bear up one another, according to our ability, through all. Nevertheless, there have been seasons when Satan did not fail to suggest to the weakness of my mind, that we were running in vain. But to all our humbling encouragement, after we arrived at Pyrmont, and particularly in the second meeting there, among a simple hearted, seeking people, we were convinced that it was not so, and that infinite kindness would also preserve us from labouring in vain. It was an opportunity wherein (to the praise of the grace which we depend upon) we may say, that, for a time, " the seed reigned over all." Visitors and visited experienced it to be a season of uncommon contrition, and during the extension of the holy Wing, our spirits seemed gathered into perfect unity; so efficacious is divine life and love! It appears that two years ago, there were about twenty in Pyrmont, who being uneasy with the dead formality of many professors, met together in their own houses, sometimes reading, singing, or praying, as they apprehended most right. They underwent considerable persecution on this account from the avaricious priests, who persuaded people not to do business with them; and being generally low in the world, they suffered in this respect; but it appears that they were not hindered thereby from meeting together: yet their rest, not being a pure one, was broken up; some of them finding their reformation from what they saw to be wrong, was very small, concluded there was something more substantial than what they had yet experienced; and this being suggested to the rest, occasioned a division amongst them. A few returned to the profession they had left, and the others ceased to meet together; yet it is wonderful to see the brotherly kindness which distinguishes them from others. They call themselves friends, and with much propriety, to each other. We spent about two weeks in Pyrmont, with satisfaction of mind. For three rooms, three beds, fire, candles, and the use of the kitchen, we paid 15s. per week, found our own provisions, cooked them ourselves, with the assistance of a girl, and an elderly man, one of the friends who spoke English pretty well. He marketed for us, interpreted on more important occasions, and served us with great solidity and cheerfulness. In many respects, we felt as if we were at home, though amongst a people, few of whom knew what we said; but they told us by signs, that they felt that which was better than words, and which required none to set it forth: O! that we may be preserved in, and feel more and more bound to, our own line and measure of duty; that as the work is the Lord's, the management of it may also be in his wisdom, and tend to his glory; and then no matter how low and abased the creature becomes. During our stay at Pyrmont, we had many meetings, some of which were uncommonly contriting opportunities, wherein their doubts seemed to subside, and the virtue of truth to sweeten and refresh their weary spirits *. In many respects they are weak, and yet so sincerely desirous to obtain " the one thing needful," that we entertain a hope, that some of them will encrease in stedfastness to what they know to be right. Our minds are often involved in discouragement and conflict: the weakness of our frames, and perhaps the prospect of the unfinished part of the work, may be the occasion of these. But let us remember, that till they are overcome by the power of victorious faith, it is our seed time rather than harvest, and therefore we are called upon, by merciful and heart-solacing intimations, to sow in hope. Whether any apparent fruits ever appear from this journey, we seem comfortably satisfied at times, that it will not be lost in the unlimited family of the one universal Parent; and if we are but favoured to keep the word of his patience, so as to hold out to the end, and return without condemnation, it will not be lost to us. We set off from Pyrmont for Rinteln upon a different plan from that on which we had travelled before; for having a man to do little services for us when there, who is one of their friends, and speaks English well, we saw an extraordinary convenience would attend our taking him with us; and there-

---

* At one meeting we had the company of four men, who walked the day before near twenty miles, to sit with us; and that of another man, who came about forty, also on foot.

fore have taken a light waggon, and a pair of horses, which saves us imposition and trouble in procuring carriages, &c.

Our man conducts himself with great propriety and simplicity, as our friend, guide, interpreter, and servant; being charioteer, and doing a great deal for us besides. We spent a week at Rinteln, and had several meetings amongst them, besides private religious opportunities, in several of their families, and left some of our books for a university in that town. In our way here, we came through a skirt of Hanover, where we beheld, in the improvements of the country, and the appearance of the people, a cheering resemblance of England. About Rinteln, there are near twenty of those who call themselves friends, and some of them we believe to be lively spirited people, and considerably experienced in the inward work of religion; of whom we have a comfortable hope, whether they are ever known to our gathered, visible church, or not. We are now in this country under a frequent sense of inward poverty, and with many confirmations that, of ourselves, we can do nothing; yet trusting that best wisdom has turned us into this little field of labour, we dare not, with our present feelings, desert it; but we go on from spot to spot, as we apprehend is most in the line of our duty. From Rinteln we proceeded to Minden, where we found a little company of sincere hearted, and exercised christian travellers, who appeared glad of our visit, and expressed a belief that it was in divine appointment for their good. They seemed more desirous for a right opening to sit down together in silent waiting, than to enter into conversation about what they had already experienced. We had several solid, and I hope edifying, meetings among them, to which several came from the country many miles on foot, which demonstrated their earnestness to be helped on in the right way; amongst these was a blind woman who gets her living by spinning, and who walked seventeen miles to meet us. She is an example of christian fortitude, and true nobility; for on our asking her, if she was not under difficulties in procuring herself a living, she gratefully answered, that her friends sometimes helped her, that she knew she was poor, but when she reflected upon her supplies, and the query revived in her mind, " if she lacked any thing," the acknowledgment always succeeded, " nothing, Lord." She told us, with great humility and tenderness, that her knowledge of the truth was not obtained by books or outward means, but by the operation of the divine principle in her own heart. I hope we have been preserved, thus far, from drawing the inward attention of those whom we have visited, to ourselves, or attaching them in the affectionate part to any representation of good. The secret, sympathetic exercise which we have felt on their account, and in company with them, hath, I do believe, brought us all at times, to the renewed discovery of the everlasting foundation; and we have a hope that some of these will acceptably build thereon. We here met with great civility, and tenderness of spirit, from a counsellor and director of this place; but the cross is a mighty stumbling block; he often makes me think of Nicodemus: when we left the town, he kindly went before us to an Inn on the road, where he had provided coffee, and convened several of the friends to take their last leave; a parting which I hope was attended with true solemnity, as well as brokenness of spirit. With tears, he expressed his desire, that He who said he would be with his disciples to the end of the world, would go with us, and bless his own work. Next day we travelled towards Buer, and dined sweetly in a field, on provision which we took with us, whilst our horses were eating corn. We then turned a little out of the road, to visit a man and his wife, whom the Priest is persecuting for absenting themselves from his place of worship. He has got the Magistrate to fine them near twenty shillings, (which is a great deal for them) and they refusing to pay it, from an apprehension of duty, have suffered distress of their goods, with christian simplicity and firmness. After spending near two hours with them (I hope to our and their edification) we came on to Buer. In the neighbourhood of this town live a little company of Zion's travellers, with whom we had a meeting; and our gracious Helper being near, by his good spirit, rendered it an humbling and refreshing opportunity. We have many encampments, and when we shall get through this wilderness, is very uncertain; for my part, I see no way yet! This blindness is, probably, to try my patience, of which I seem, at times, to have a reducing stock; but am secretly supported, in knowing Him in whom I have, through holy help, believed. We have great cause to be humbly thankful, for that portion of sure direction and ability, which, for our instruction as well as comfort, have been revealed in the midst of our weakness, and become as a table in the wilderness, furnished with food wisely adapted to the necessities of weary and hungry travellers. It seems very singular, when I recollect myself, that we are keeping house in Prussia, and considerably united to some of it's inhabitants, who were lately entire strangers; and, in degree, feel as if we were at home, though so far from that which is called home. It is a little like being in a new world, yet so near the old one, as to be distinguished for similar evils, and that *fashion* which passeth away, when truth, which is strongest of all, takes its possessions. It is very pleasant in these journeys to feel this sentiment lively upon our spirits, " the earth is the Lord's," &c. We went from Buer to Osnabruck the 26th of the 8th month, where we spent several days under considerable exercise of mind, and not finding that our visit was likely to be attended with any use, and being also fatigued various ways, we were so discouraged, that we were about concluding to leave the town next day, though we thought the way to it had opened as clearly as to most places we had been at; but on feeling further about it, we thought it safest to try a little longer, and not move in the dark. Our situation was unfavourable, being at a Roman Catholic Inn, where the Protestants are afraid to come, and our Friend and interpreter having no acquaintance in the place. Thus we continued 'till seventh day evening, without any thing satisfactory occurring, except giving a few summaries * to some shopkeepers on whom we had called, and having the company of a young woman who had enquired concerning us, and discovered a serious desire to be with us, and to have some of our books: she appeared to us to be possessed of much sweetness, and valuable sensibility. On seventh day evening, our men called upon the merchant, on whom they had a letter of credit, who speaks English well, behaved with great kindness, and soon apprehending their errand, (having some knowledge of the society in England) went with them to an overseer of part of his business, who was a religious man, and discontented with the ceremonious part of the world's worship. They found this person a little shy at first, but he soon opened to them with simplicity, and discovered himself to be a man who was awakened to a profitable sense of his own state, and to a sincere desire to be led in divine counsel, to greater acceptance than the shadows of things could yield him. He came with them to the inn, and we spent the evening agreeably together. He

---

* These were books containing a summary account of our principles.

told us of a few more in the town of his sentiments, who met together every firſt day evening, to read, &c; and on being aſked, if they would be willing to ſit with us after our manner, he expreſſed his own inclination ſo to do; and after inquiring of others, told us next morning, that it was agreeable to them all. In the morning, we were ſurprized and comforted with the ſight of a very ſolid, feeling young woman from Buer, in the capacity of a ſervant, who had walked fifteen miles to meet us, in conſequence of a ſecret draft in her own mind, without having any reaſon to expect, from what had paſſed, that we ſhould be at Oſnabruck ſo long. After getting her ſome refreſhment, we ſix ſat down together, and had a ſtrengthening opportunity, wherein dear George Dillwyn miniſtered to us. At four in the afternoon, we had a meeting with about eight more, amongſt whom was an officer, who behaved ſolidly. It was a time of favour, and I believe deep inſtruction to ſome there, who had not before ſeen the neceſſity of ceaſing from their own works, and depending only upon the renewal of divine life in the ſoul, for qualifications rightly to worſhip. After meeting, we paid a viſit to one of their friends who was ſick, with whom we were led into ſympathy and ſilence, and to whom we imparted ſuch counſel as truth unfolded at that time. Theſe were relieving circumſtances to us, and ſet us at liberty, comfortably to depart on ſecond day morning for Hertford or Herwerden. We therefore ſet off with the proſpect of a pretty eaſy day's journey, but found the road very rough, and in many places dangerous, and more of it than we expected; so that we were grievously jolted, and out till near ten at night, very contrary to our inclination; for we tried much to get lodgings in a town a few miles off, but the people would not take us in. We appear very strange to many here, but so different to a few who are acquainted with the truth, that the distinction of countries seems almost lost, and proves the cementing virtue of religion. At Hertford we were visited by two religious men, who come under the description of those called friends in these parts; and they were encouraged to faithfulness. Our men also visited a lawyer, who being discontented with the usual ceremonies of religion, &c, keeps much to himself. Next morning as we were at breakfast, proposing to depart, there came two men from different parts, who had walked many miles through the rain to meet us. One of these men, some time ago, refused to be married by the Priest, in which, and in other things, he bore a steady testimony, under persecution, against an hireling ministry. The openness, kindness, and solidity of his manners and countenance, were pleasant to us; and being evidently acquainted with silent waiting, we had a solemn instructive opportunity together. From Hertford, we proceeded to Bilefeld, a town where, and in its neighbourhood, there are many religious people, and particularly agreeable as to the outward; but it was a visit attended with as deep baptism, and continual travail of spirit, as we have experienced in any place that we have been in;

which, with the providential openings, and strength to visit the precious seed in the needful time, tended to convince us that we were in the way of our duty; a most cheering evidence, in this dreary wilderness, and a full reward for all our little toils. At this place there are some who live separate from all public profession, who under an apprehension of being turned out of the way, were afraid, for a while, to give us any of their company: but being also afraid to let the opportunity slip, we were invited to one of their houses, to confer with several of them on such subjects as might occur, in order to know a little of each other. Both sides were somewhat surprized to find so much similarity of sentiment, respecting the ground and testimonies of truth. They told us, that if there were a people there, who ceased from all forms or activity of their own, and sat down in simple dependance upon the operation of the heavenly gift, they would embrace them with brotherly affection, and rejoice to unite with them herein; but they were loath to believe, that they two or three might be required to bear such a public testimony; nor were they willing to unite with us in so doing, for fear of the people whose eyes are much upon them. They are people of considerable account, and are very fearful of drawing the lower class of their neighbours to themselves; and being of Nicodemus's class, like better to obtain and enjoy, their religious knowledge in private. We had, nevertheless, several opportunities of solid conference together; which were attended with great unanimity and cordiality; the laſt of which was particularly owned with the circulation of divine virtue, and with ſtrength fully to relieve our minds towards them. We were very kindly invited to the houſe of a merchant, who appears to be a very ſincere man. We paid him and his daughter a morning viſit; but they were not content with that, and therefore preſſed us to ſpend firſt day evening with them. In the morning of that day, we ſat together in the inn, where we had the company of an honeſt man, who came on foot ſixteen miles to be at meeting with us, and alſo of four others, of the town. In the afternoon, as J. B. was taking a ſolitary walk, he was met by a ſerious man, who deſired his company to a houſe a little way out of the town; he complied with his invitation, and when they got there, they found fourteen people met together, for the ſake of religious improvement, who ſoon made their requeſt that we would all go and ſit with them. I was laid down, in a tried ſituation of mind, when J. B. brought the invitation which had in it ſo much of the right favour, that we embraced it, and immediately ſet off, having above an Engliſh mile to walk. By the time we got there, they were about twenty in number. We ſoon ſettled down into a ſilence truly ſolemn, which laſted a conſiderable time without interruption of any kind; and when the channel of inſtrumental miniſtry opened, the precious life mercifully continued, and our parting was under its tendering impreſſions. This circumſtance, of dropping in with a people of whom we had had no intelligence, and with whom we contracted no further acquaintance, with the senfible feeling of divine care over thofe who are as fheep having no fhepherd, affords altogether a fweet and pleafant reflection; accompanied by this encouraging truth, that " the Lord can make a way, where there feems to be no way:" O that He may gracioufly continue thus to favour us! After this opportunity, we went to the aforementioned merchant's, and were treated with genuine hofpitality. After fupper, there came in eight or ten perfons with the expectation of a meeting, in which they were not difappointed; and I hope it was edifying to them, George Dillwyn having fuitable and lively matter to communicate. We had alfo a religious fitting with a family from Elberfelt, a lively fpirited couple, and another perfon with them. After fpending five days here, and bearing the crofs as faithfully, perhaps, as in fome places where a more open door was miniftered, we departed in much peace, and under the belief, that the power of truth is making its own way in that neighbourhood. In our way from Bilefeld, we ftopped at a large village called Guterflots, where there are many well difpofed people. We ftaid one day there, and fat with a few people who met us at one of their houfes; after which, and diftributing a few books to others in the town, we went forward to Munfter. We are often very weary, and the accommodations we meet with but indifferent, compared with thofe of England: the roads are alfo bad where we have already been, which, with the conftruction of the carriages, occafion us fometimes to be grievously jolted; and yet we have no cause to complain, having our consolations as well as toils; as it seldom happens that Zion's travellers are qualified to salute each other, even in a thorny difficult way, but the immortal birth, in some degree, leaps for joy. This experience, with the belief that the Lord is at work in the kingdoms of men, and even graciously rewarding such feeble endeavours as ours, with a morsel of the bread that the world knows not of, render any little services of ours as objects unworthy the notice of ourselves, or our friends. From Munster we went to Crevelt. We found, our discouragements on entering it, being refused admission at one inn we went to, and at the next, we had such a crowd gathered about us, with such shoutings and rudeness, as greatly frighted our horses, after we were out of the carriage, and our driver had alighted, so that they ran away, and he following, and taking hold of a chain behind, was thrown down, and his head, to appearance, much hurt against the wheel. Some of our feelings were low enough on this occasion. But through the continued kindness of providence, our man soon recovered, being able to move about next day; and the people of the house conceived such an affectionate respect for us, and treated us with such true civility, as made our situation so far comfortable. We also gradually made so much acquaintance, as afforded a degree of hope that our going to Crevelt was right, and that our secret and known exercises there, will not be in vain. About the time of our concluding to come away, our company began to be more fought; which opened the way for the difpofal of fome of our books, and I feel a fecret hope that they will be bleffed to fome there. We came to Duffeldorf where we ftaid one day, and had the enjoyment of M. Wetterboar's company. He feems aged, but is alive in the truth. We proceeded to Mulheim, where we arrived the 23d of the 9th month. It is a town about two miles from Cologne, like a Gofhen on the confines of Egypt, where many awakened, and fome truly religious people refide. We commenced an acquaintance with a few, who have got a clear infight, from the work of truth in themfelves, into the gofpel difpenfation, and the fpirituality of the chriftian religion; concerning thefe we have encouraging profpects; yet not without a mixture, knowing fomething of Satan's devices. They received us in the name of difciples. We had divers religious opportunities with them, and parted under the precious fenfe of divine love and life. We paid a vifit to a merchant's wife, a woman of amiable character, who through religious concern, has got into a defpairing condition. It was attended with great fatisfaction to ourfelves, from the fweetnefs which attended our own minds in her company, and in that of her hufband's, who feems bending under the affliction, and likely to profit by it. She often expreffed an earneft wifh, that fhe had feen us at a time when fuch a vifit might have been bleffed to her; but faid, that now it was too late for any thing that was good to be offered to her. This was, however, very far from our fenfe. Now, through the renewal of unutterable mercy, and never failing help, my soul acknowledges a relief and answer of peace (as far as relates to this service) which I am sure my little endeavours, and compelled dedication are unworthy of. We have had many discouragements since we came to the continent, and many baptisms into death: we have also partaken largely of providential care, and been favoured, from time to time, when resignation was attained to, with that direction whose effects have often proved its rectitude, and strengthened our faith; and my soul, at times, has been put into the capacity of lying down as beside the still waters. Some of the last openings, or sense of duty, have been the most trying and in the cross; but being yielded to, and the work performed, a comfortable retreat hath been clearly and sweetly founded from this large field of arduous labour; and at a time, when an openness amongst the people was manifestly encreasing. This I esteem an inexpressible favour, and such a one as they only can be sensible of, who have gone under the weight of similar mountains, and been involved in the fear of being misled.

At Mulheim, she drew up and signed a letter to Leopold the Second, King of Hungary, &c. since Emperor of Germany, in which her companions united. For some time before her arrival at this place, her mind had been very weightily exercised with the important subjects expressed in this letter; insomuch that, at one period, she was under an apprehension that it would be required of her to go in perfon, and relieve her mind to the king. But from this very trying fervice, fhe felt herfelf comfortably releafed, and the mode of addreffing him by letter, was fatisfactorily fubftituted. The addrefs was intrufted to the care of a reputable merchant of Cologne, who engaged to forward it without delay. The following is a copy of it.

To LEOPOLD the Second, King of Hungary, Bohemia, &c. &c.

Amongft the numerous congratulations awaiting thy acceffion to the imperial crown, accept, O King! our chriftian good wifhes and folicitude for thy prefent and eternal well-being. We are confcious that we have no claim to the liberty of addreffing thee, but from a belief that the Lord Almighty, who ruleth in the kingdoms of men, and giveth them to whomfoever he will, hath inclined us to leave our habitations to vifit fome parts of this country, and now engages us, in gofpel love, to exprefs our fecret and united prayer, that thou mayft be an inftrument in his holy hand, for the advancement of that glorious day, fpoken of by the prophet, " when fwords fhall be beaten into plow fhares, and fpears into pruning hooks, when nation fhall not lift up fword againft nation; neither fhall they learn war any more." The great defign of our univerfal Parent, in fending his beloved Son a light into the world, is for his own glory in the falvation of mankind ; and for this gracious end, he hath given to all men a meafure of his own eternal fpirit. To co-operate with Him herein, dignifies human nature, and is particularly deserving the most scrupulous attention of princes. The smallest revelation of this heavenly gift in the believing soul, having a degree of omnipotence in it, brings into subjection the natural will and wisdom of man, and discovers to us the noble purposes of our creation; it diffuses that true benevolence which characterizes genuine christianity, and renders dear to a prince, the happiness of all, even the meanest of his subjects; imprinting upon his mind the superior value of an immortal soul, to all worldly acquisitions. Through the neglect of a principle so pure and important, how hath the rational part of God's creation been sacrificed to the irregular passions of sovereigns; and many unprepared souls precipitated into an awful futurity! That the gospel dispensation is intended to remedy these evils, and promote the government of the Prince of Peace; that the Gentiles are to come to its light, and kings to the brightness of its arising, are truths to which the sacred records abundantly testify. May this be thy happy experience, O king! that so the power thou art providentially intrusted with, being subservient to divine wisdom, thy example may influence the minds of other princes, who also beholding its excellency, may unite in encouraging their subjects to decline, in mutual charity and forbearance, whatever is contrary to the purity and simplicity of the religion of Jesus. And may'st thou be enriched with all spiritual blessings; that these added to thy temporal ones, may not only perfect thy happiness, but perpetuate it beyond the narrow limits of time, and qualify thee, acceptably, to caſt down thy crown at the feet of Him who is King of kings, and Lord of lords, who lives and reigns for ever and ever.

George and Sarah Dillwyn, of Burlington, New Jerſey, North America.
Sarah Grubb, Clonmel,
Joſhua Beale, Cork,
} Ireland.
} Members of the religious ſociety of friends in thoſe countries and Great Britain, commonly called Quakers.

Mulheim on the Rhine,
29th of 9th month called Sept. 1790.

A ſhort time before her return home, on a review of ſome parts of this journey, ſhe wrote as follows·

In many places, we found a people who were diſcontented and weary with the mere profeſſion of chriſtianity, and the deadneſs of thoſe forms and ceremonies with which it is encumbered; and who were convinced of the ſufficiency of the heavenly principle. Theſe, having been mercifully viſited with a lively ſenſe of the ſpirituality of true religion, received us in the name of diſciples, and rejoiced in being directed to the chriſtian's reſt. This true ſabbath, was, however, imperfectly underſtood by many of them, for want of ceaſing, when they met together in little companies, from all activity of their own, and depending ſingly on the quickening virtue of truth, to qualify them for, and lead them into, ſuch ſervices as are moſt acceptable, and moſt conſiſtent with the duty of true, ſpiritual believers. Some of this people appeared to be ſo near this great point, as soon to discover and acknowledge it; but their encreasing testimony thereto, will, if rightly borne, prove the closest trial which they have yet met with. We are indeed convinced, beyond all shadow of doubt, that there is a choice heritage in Germany, and in other parts of the Continent, who are gradually retiring to the true sheepfold; but, at present, they are, like the disciples, secreted in an inner chamber for fear of the Jews. Our visit to this people, though attended with a degree of suffering, hath been productive of solid peace.

Her mind being thus comfortably released from this field of labour, she proceeded from Mulheim to Cleves, and from thence, through Flanders, to Dunkirk, and arrived at London the 27th of 10th month 1790; and feeling a desire to visit her relations at York, &c. before her return home, she went pretty directly for that city; where she staid a few days, very much to the comfort and satisfaction of her relatives and friends there. At this time, she laboured under evident indisposition of body; but the sweetness of her spirit, and the cheering effects of meeting again her beloved connections, with the prospect of soon returning to those at Clonmel, supported her in a great measure above it, and encouraged her to set forward and proceed towards home; which she did by way of Ackworth, Sheffield, Manchester, &c. At these places, she was again refreshed by the company of divers near and dear friends: it appeared, indeed, by thus encompassing, in this short visit, so many of her beloved connections, that, as the time of her sojourning here was soon to close, she was enabled and permitted to wind up the labours of her day, with the mutual consolation of seeing again many of those with whom she was closely united, and bidding them a final farewell in mutability. At Ackworth, she spent the night with a near and beloved relative, to whom, in much brokenness of spirit, she thus expressed herself: Oh! my dear, I think sometimes that I shall soon be gone; it seems, as if my day's work was nearly done, and on looking towards home, as if I might not be long there."

She reached Dublin in time for the half year's meeting, and in the select meeting there, gave an account of her late journey, with great meekness and humility of spirit; ascribing nothing to the creature, but rendering to the Lord the praise of His own works. From hence, she proceeded directly for Clonmel, (having account of the small pox being in the family) where she was favoured to arrive the 12th of the 11th month, much relieved from a severe cough which had lately attended her, though greatly exhausted in her strength and spirits. On her way from Dublin, she writes thus to a friend:

To be strengthened rightly to fill up our appointed measure of sufferings for the body's sake, whether at home or abroad, is a mark of divine favour, and will be succeeded by undefiled rest.—I am now returning home, under a grateful sense of Providential care, and in peaceful poverty of spirit.

The following is extracted from a letter which she wrote at Clonmel, a few days after her return.

I can now once more salute you from home, in renewed and endeared affection, and gratefully acknowledge the multiplied preservations of our never-failing Helper, in thus far bringing through a variety of exercises, from which the natural mind cannot relieve itself. I reflect with solid satisfaction upon my visit at York, &c. and am glad I paid it, though I feel myself a poor worn-out creature. The 24th of the 11th month she set off from Clonmel to attend their quarterly meeting at Cork; previous to which she wrote the following letter to a friend:

My present affliction hath gained great ascendency over my mind, so that I seem fast losing my hold, and sense of Him that is invisible; and remembering some past exercise, when I was in danger of losing the best life, I am ready to say, with mournful Jeremiah, "cause me not to return to Jonathan's house, lest I die there." I know that nothing hath yet occurred, which needs to scatter a well regulated mind from the source of good; but I am left to such a sense of my own wretchedness, that even the grasshopper or things comparable to it, are become a burden. To attend a quarterly meeting under such impressions, is a prospect which I need not describe; but I fear to make a prey of thy sympathetic mind. May I be preserved from a murmuring disposition, by which the holy Spirit is grieved!

At the quarterly meeting, she delivered, in an humble account of her late mission, appeared in divers acceptable testimonies, and at the close of the meeting was taken ill. This last conflict of nature, which was at times very severe, continued about ten days, when it pleased infinite wisdom to remove her from the toils and troubles of mortality, to a mansion of everlasting rest, on the 8th of the 12th month 1790 and on the 12th, her remains were attended to the burying-ground, by many friends. It was a solemn, memorable time; and living testimonies were there borne to the sufficiency of that power, (which had so eminently qualified her, for his service,) to raise up and abilitate others to follow her footsteps. During her illness, which was at the house of her beloved friends Samuel and Sarah Neale, she dropped a few expressions, worthy of preservation, which have been collected, and are as follow: In a message to a young woman who presided in the school at Clonmel, she said; Salute her very affectionately. I desire the sympathy of her spirit, and that she may be endued with additional qualifications to bear her own, and our joint trials, under these complicated circumstances. Tell her, I have been much favoured with quietness of mind from the first, though a stranger to how the present afflictions or trials may terminate; but the grain of faith and hope which is mercifully vouchsafed, I esteem preferable to all knowledge. She further said; give my dear love to all our young women; I hope that each will be preserved in their respective lines of duty. I know their tenderness for me, but would be sorry they should let down their spirits too low; for I believe that truth would rather increase, than lessen our strength, at such times as these. The children are all affectionately remembered by me: I hope they will each endeavour to lighten the general burden, by their sobriety, and doing that which they know to be right. I am trying to get my mind to a settlement, that all things work together for good; but it is hard to get at it. She several times said: "I must go. You must let me go." And nearly tho last words she spoke were, repeating that passage of scripture, " my peace I give unto you."

Four days before her decease, she dictated the following weighty, instructive letter, to a particular friend. Thy salutation met me, though apparently out of course, in the right time; being under impressions, which make time and circumstances of little account, compared with the unlimited consolations of the Spirit, or a preparation to receive them at the Divine Hand. My soul, though encompassed with the manifold infirmities of a very afflicted tabernacle, can feelingly worship, and rejoice in nothing more than this, that the Lamb immaculate is still redeeming, by his precious blood, out of every nation, kindred, tongue, and people; and making a glorious addition to the church triumphant, whose names will stand eternally recorded in the book of life. I express not these things from a redundancy of heavenly virtue, but from the soul-sustaining evidence, that, amidst all our weakness and conflicts of flesh or spirit, an interest is mercifully granted in Him, who giveth victory over death, hell, and the grave.

Thus hath the setting sun of this humble follower of the Lamb, gone down in brightness; and though she hath been called away as in younger life, (being only in the 35th year of her age) yet her day's work appears to have been compleat, and, with respect to herself, every measure worth living for, filled up. Honourable age is not that which standeth in length of time, or that which is measured by number of years; but wisdom is the grey hair to man, and an unspotted life is old age. May we who remain behind, whilst we deplore the church's loss in the removal of so useful and dignified a servant, be encouraged to imitate her example, and to surrender ourselves in faithfulness and dedication to all the Lord's requirings: that so, when the residue of our days is accomplished, we also may be favoured to receive that blessed declaration; " well done, good and faithful servant, enter thou into the joy of thy Lord, and into thy master's rest."

A Testimony from our monthly Meeting for the County of Tipperary, concerning Sarah Grubb deceased.

Our minds being deeply affected by the recent great loss which the church hath sustained, in the removal of our beloved friend, Sarah Grubb, daughter of our friends William Tuke and his late wife Elizabeth of York, we feel it incumbent on us to give forth a testimony concerning her; for as the memory of the just is blessed, so the remembrance of this dignified and eminently useful member in the church militant, is precious to many; to whom she was a nursing mother, raised up, by a thorough submission to the operation of the divine hand, to the stature of an elder in the truth, though, as to years, she had scarcely attained the meridian of life. She was a woman of extraordinary natural abilities, strength of judgment, and clearness of discernment; and being favoured with the visitation of heavenly love in the morning of her day, and submitting to be brought into that passive nothingness, wherein the vessels in the Lord's house are formed and fitted for usefulness, she witnessed an early preparation for service, coming forth in public ministry about the 23d year of her age. After exercising some years the precious gift committed to her, to the consolation of many, she joined in marriage with our friend Robert Grubb, and very soon after manifested the fruit of entire dedication, by visiting the meetings of friends in Scotland, where her service was truly acceptable, and continued in such a line of devotedness, that in the course of about five years she visited most, or all the meetings in Great Britain and Ireland. About three years since, she removed with her husband to reside within the compass of this monthly meeting; wherein she was deeply exercised in spirit, for the arising and spreading of life, and frequently and earnestly engaged in exciting her brethren and sisters to diligent labour after it. In ministry, she was sound and edifying, not only like the scribe instructed to the kingdom, bringing forth out of her treasure things new and old, but qualified by pure wisdom, to bring them forth in the demonstration of the spirit and with power, in the authority and becoming gravity of the gospel, being in her delivery an example to all concerned in bearing a public testimony for the Lord's cause. The view of coming to settle in this nation, was accompanied with a sense of divine requiring to establish a school, for the education of the daughters of friends in useful learning, simplicity, and that unaffected piety into which truth leads its followers; which she was enabled to accomplish, we trust, to the lasting advantage of some of the rising generation. Soon after her coming to reside amongst us, she, in consequence of a concern which had for a considerable time rested on her mind, engaged in a religious visit to Holland, some parts of Germany and the south of France; in which she was joined by several friends, and wherein she was eminently gifted for the service to which she was called; her ministry, private admonitions, and exemplary deportment, reaching the witness in many minds; so that her fervent labour, and the sweet favour of her exercised spirit, we believe is still felt, and will be long profitably remembered in those parts. After her return, she paid an acceptable visit to several parts of this province, and had meetings where none of our society dwelt, much tending to spread the knowledge of the truth. And lastly, under the prevalence of gospel love, and earnest solicitude that the sheep not yet of this fold might be gathered to the teachings of the great Shepherd, she again left her own habitation, and engaged, with some of her former companions, in a very arduous and exercising visit, to Dunkirk, Holland, and some of the northern parts of Germany; wherein, we have reason to believe, she had eminent service, to the confirming of many visited minds in the faith, and promoting the blessed cause of truth and righteousness; in which glorious work, her intrepid spirit shrunk not from suffering: the extending of the government of her dear Lord and Master in the hearts of the children of men, and the promotion and increase of His spiritual kingdom over sea and land, being nearer to her than her natural life, or any other consideration, she was brought to a willingness to be spent therein. In her return, she attended our national meeting, and in the meeting of ministers and elders, giving an account of her late journey, under the influence of that humility which was so conspicuously the covering of her spirit, she ascribed all to Him, whom she knew to be the Author of every good work, in these expressions: "we have done but little, but the Lord is doing much;" concluding with, "return unto thy rest, O my soul! for the Lord hath dealt bountifully with thee;" as though prophetic of that everlasting rest, into which she was so near being gathered: for her bodily strength being considerably impaired, by almost constant exercise and fatigue, it proved unequal to the force of a distemper, which soon after seized her frame, and, by a rapid progress, terminated those afflictions of which she had so largely filled up her measure, for the body's sake, which is the church.

She attended our quarterly meeting at Cork, returned a lively account of her journey, and was acceptably exercised in the meetings there; after which, she was confined by sickness at the house of our dear friend Samuel Neale, near that city, where, amongst other weighty expressions, she uttered the following, "I have been much favoured with quietness of mind from the first, though a stranger to how the present afflictions or trials may terminate; but the grain of faith and hope which is mercifully vouchsafed, I esteem preferable to all knowledge." In a letter which she dictated to a near friend four days before her decease, she said; "My soul, though encompassed with the manifold infirmities of a very afflicted tabernacle, can feelingly worship and rejoice in nothing more than

M

this, that the Lamb immaculate is still redeeming, by his precious blood, out of every nation, kindred, tongue and people, and making a glorious addition to the church triumphant, whose names will stand eternally recorded in the book of life. I express not these things from a redundancy of heavenly virtue, but from the soul sustaining evidence, that, amidst all our weakness and conflicts of flesh and spirit, an interest is mercifully granted in Him, who giveth victory over death, hell and the grave." Which, with other corroborating circumstances, clearly evinced, where her hope and dependance were, and that her refined spirit was prepared for its glorious mansion, into which we have no doubt it was admitted. She departed this life the 8th of 12th month 1790; and after a solemn meeting being previously held at the meeting house, wherein, and at the grave yard, several living testimonies were borne, her body was interred in friends burying ground, in Cork, the 12th of the same; aged about 34 years.

Her conversation was innocently cheerful, which endeared her to the youth of both sexes, and gave her much place and influence with them. To her beloved husband, she was a truly affectionate wife; to her friends, a near sympathizer in affliction; and being clothed with that charity which seeketh not her own, and breatheth peace and good will to all, was ready to reach forth the hand of help, so that the whole of her conduct was an uniform consistency with her holy profession, and the purity of those doctrines which she surely believed and was engaged so extensively to publish. May she, being dead, yet speak with a prevailing language to us all who are left behind; " follow me as I followed Christ;" that so we may die the death of the righteous, and our latter end be like theirs.

Given forth at a monthly meeting for the county of Tipperary, held at Clonmel by adjournment, the 13th day of the 2d month 1791.

Signed in and on behalf thereof, by many friends.

The annexed testimony concerning our beloved friend, Sarah Grubb, has been read in our quarterly men's and women's meeting for Munster Province, held in Cork the 21st of the 2d month 1791, with which we have near unity.

Signed on behalf of our men's meeting by
                    RICHARD ABELL, Clerk.

And on behalf of our women's meeting by
                    MARGARET GRUBB, Clerk.

Read, and approved, in our half years' meeting for Ireland, held in Dublin, from the 1st of the 5th month 1791, to the 5th of the same inclusive, and on behalf thereof signed by

    JOHN DAVIS, Clerk to the meeting this time.

A Testimony of York quarterly Meeting concerning Sarah Grubb, late Wife of our Friend Robert Grubb, of Clonmel, in Ireland.

This our valuable friend, having been a member of this meeting 'till within the four last years of her life, and the remembrance of her being precious to many of us, we feel our minds engaged to unite in a short testimony concerning her, with desires that many, from her pious and excellent example, may be stirred up, according to their different measures, to follow her, as she followed Christ.

She was born in the city of York, in the year 1756, and was favoured with a guarded and religious education, which, with the divine blessing upon it, preserved her from many dangers and follies to which youth are often exposed, and prepared her heart for that open reception of the truth, and entire surrender to its dictates, which remarkably distinguished her through the more advanced periods of life. But though she was early under the visitations of divine love, yet being of a quick and lively disposition, joined to great natural abilities, she found it hard work to submit to the lowliness and simplicity of the cross of Christ; and endured many sore conflicts before she surrendered her will to the government of the Prince of Peace. Whilst under the Lord's preparing hand for the work of the ministry, she experienced many deep baptisms of spirit; but He who knew her sincerity, and earnest desires for His holy help and direction, graciously sustained her in this proving season, and in due time brought forth living offerings, to His own praise, and the comfort of many minds. In the exercise of her ministry, she was careful not to move in her own time and will, nor to exceed her gift; but to be attentive to the arisings and continuance of life, with patient resignation and dedication of heart.

Her love and gratitude to the Father of mercies, and her fervent concern for the prosperity of his cause on earth, made her unwearied in her labours to promote it, and to be willing to spend and be spent for his great Name's sake. She was an example of true humility and abasedness of self, feeling that all her springs were in the Lord, and that though the creature may at seasons be honoured, yet every good and perfect gift came from above, and called for unfeigned acknowledgement. To the necessity and powerful efficacy of the pure principle of light and grace in the soul, she bore many living testimonies, and recommended, above all things, the closest attention and obedience to its holy manifestations, as that alone which can preserve from the spots of the world, redeem the mind from its spirit and enjoyments, and confer that peace which the world can neither give nor take away. She beheld and mourned over the breaches and waste places of Zion, and we believe laboured honestly, according to the strength received, for the repairing thereof, and the restoration of ancient beauty and simplicity. Her superior abilities, sanctified by the humbling operations of the holy spirit, qualified her for extensive service in the administration of the discipline of the church; wherein she was concerned to act, under a degree of that covering, which ought to influence every religious movement. Of a solid and weighty spirit, she was engaged to dig deeply for the hidden treasure, and laboured to dwell near the spring of divine life: yet infinite wisdom saw meet to suffer her at seasons to experience great inward poverty: but under these proving dispensations, she murmured not, being resigned to the will of her Lord and Master, and made willing "to suffer with him, that she might also reign with him." And having partaken of the sufferings and consolations of the gospel, she knew how to sympathize with the exercised and mourning spirit, dealing her bread, when qualified, to the hungry soul, and pouring in the wine and oil to the help and refreshment of many. And as this devoted faithful servant of the Lord, was thus instrumental in glorifying His name amongst mankind, and promoting the divine government in their hearts, so she became more and more refined, and redeemed from all visible enjoyments; 'till, in unsearchable wisdom, He who put her forth and went before her, was pleased to " cut short the work in righteousness," and to remove her, we doubt not, from His church militant on earth, to his church triumphant in heaven.

Read, approved, and signed, in, by order, and on behalf of our quarterly meeting held in York, by adjournments, on the 30th and 31st of the 3d month 1791 by

MORDECAI CASSON, Clerk to the meeting this time.
ELIZABETH TUKE, Clerk this time.

APPENDIX:

CONTAINING

AN

ACCOUNT

OF

ACKWORTH SCHOOL,

OBSERVATIONS

ON

CHRISTIAN DISCIPLINE,

AND VALUABLE

EXTRACTS

FROM MANY OF HER

LETTERS.

SOME ACCOUNT

OF

ACKWORTH SCHOOL,

ADDRESSED TO A

FRIEND IN AMERICA.

Dear Friend,

THE following imperfect account of Ackworth school is presented to thee, in confidence that thou wilt not expose it, and yet with a hope that it may privately aid thy endeavours to establish a school, for the religious education of youth, in another part of the world; an engagement worthy of thyself, but requiring something better to render it truly succefsful.

As religious concerns cannot, any more than those of a civil nature, be rightly carried forward without order and method, it becomes a very important inquiry, what rules and adjuſtments of things pertaining thereto, are conſiſtent with the ſpirituality of their origin, and when theſe are found, they call for great care in officers and their ſuperintendents, to keep them in their proper places, leſt that which is begun in the ſpirit, ſhould be ſought to be made perfect in the fleſh.

There is a moral rectitude, fabricated in human wiſdom, which is beautiful to the natural eye, ſeizes on the paſſions, and draws from a ſuperficial judgment, an inconſiderate approbation of what, perhaps, when it is ſcrutinized into, has ſprung from a love of popular applauſe, and tends to ſettle thoſe who are active in it, in a reſt and enjoyment of the work of their own hands.

To know the firſt ſpring of action, is a noble attainment; and if it prove pure, then carefully to keep it ſo, is a work (thou well knoweſt) of far greater magnitude; and which will tend more to the regulation of a ſchool, than a fine-ſpun ſyſtem of poſitive rules, untinctured with faith in the ſufficiency of divine aid, immediately communicated.

To obtain a right form is ſurely of abſolute neceſſity, becauſe regularity is one of the wheels whereby the intended work is to be effected; and perhaps ſome uſeful order may be gathered from the following pages, which I hope will not be implicitly adopted. Indeed, I have been thoughtful, in the courſe of my penning them, whether ſuch as are rightly influenced to promote an education confiftent with our holy profeffion, would not be better furnifhed with qualifications to fettle even civil concerns, without a model of the experience of others; feeing that the fountain of divine wifdom is inexhauftible; that for the conducting of temporal things, there can be no order like that which immediately flows from it; and that a very fmall digreffion of our attention from this fource, is often fucceeded by many erroneous fteps.

To thy prudence, therefore, I commit this little work, believing thou wilt not ufe it improperly. If it afford thee any ufeful reflections, in times of relaxation from the weight of gofpel fervice, be the means of opening for me a door of accefs into thy clofet, make me a partaker of thy treafure, and fometimes revive me in thy remembrance for good, I fhall be fully fatisfied. One obfervation further occurs to my mind, for which, as this is all a piece of freedom, I fhall not apologize. As nothing can be faid to be truly religious, (whatever the firft defign may be,) but what is religioufly conducted, a very fpecial care ought to be maintained to the pointings of truth, in choofing inftructors and fervants for a fchool; who fhould be more directed to the fchool of Chrift themfelves, than loaded with injunctions about trivial matters, and their conformity to them confidered as their qualifications. No law or rule ought to be fo framed, as to interfere with their religious duties; and when any make a wrong ufe of the liberty truth allows, great care should be exercised, left alterations take place, which have a tendency to circumscribe the righteous with the transgressor; for where this is the case, people of an outward, steady conduct, a cringing temper, and who know but little about revealed religion, seem to be most adapted to such an institution. These may, to the utmost of their natural abilities, preserve order, and prefer the works which most recommend them to those in superior power, being as earnest in their endeavours, as any, to promote the establishment of civil authority, and of a great many specious forms: but the vitals of the institution being oppressed, and the spirit and life of every act of duty to the children, and of christian discipline amongst them, disregarded, the whole body must gradually grow diseased and corrupted.

Education is a subject so copious, when unfolded to the inward attention of those to whom the care of children is rightly committed, as to require a better assisted pen than mine, to do it justice; but this I believe, that simplicity, godly sincerity, and a righteous zeal and tenderness, with an improving and imparting knowledge of useful things, can hardly fail of rendering a person who is under a secret sense of duty, qualified to undertake it.

To be sensible of the divine influence, to propagate the knowledge of it, and so to prefer it to all other considerations, as to walk worthy of its blessing being shed upon our endeavours, is the Alpha, and the Omega, of our profession. That "the blessing of heaven above, and of the deep that lieth under," may rest upon thee, dear friend! crown all thy labours, sweeten all thy bitter cups, and render invincible the habitation of thy spirit, when storms may assail it, and discouragements wait at the threshold of its door, is the present fervent breathing of thy truly affectionate friend,

SARAH GRUBB.

Foston, 1st month 5th 1786.

SECT. I.

Ackworth school is an institution intended for the religious education of children, members of our society, between the age of nine * and fourteen, and particularly of those whose parents are not in affluent circumstances. It admits of three hundred, viz. one hundred and eighty boys, and one hundred and twenty girls. They are paid for, at their entrance, by a bill of admittance of eight guineas value; for which they are provided with board, learning, clothing, and other necessaries, for one year; four shillings and four pence are also then deposited, as an allowance of one penny per week for pocket money. This school is under the immediate care of two committees, in each of which there are twenty-eight members; one is constituted of friends of London, and held there; the other of friends in the neighbourhood of Ackworth; divers

* The present limitation of age is between eight and fourteen.

of whom are twenty, thirty, and some forty miles distant from the place.

Each committee meets once a month; when the general state of the institution is considered, particular regulations proposed, complaints received, the intended resignation of services reported, and friends appointed to enquire for a supply of assistants, &c. &c.

As it often happens that divers friends are at Ackworth the night before the sitting of the committee, or early in the morning, three of them inspect all bills of parcels, and the treasurer's accounts; and report to the committee the state thereof, the number of the children admitted and returned since last month, and those that are upon the list for admittance: others examine the improvement of such as are likely to depart the ensuing month; and, generally, religious opportunities are taken with them, and an account given thereof to the committee. Copies of the minutes of each committee are transmitted to one another, and neither of them conclude upon any thing new, of importance, without mutual approbation. Several friends, once a year, give up to an appointment to spend some time in the house, in order to value the stock, to settle all accounts, and to take a more general and minute survey of the state of the family, than could be done at any other time with so much propriety: and generally, on visits to the family, at other times, the company of women friends has been desired, a number having their names down on the committee's books for such services. Agents are appointed in each county, who undertake to negociate the business between those who send the children, and the institution, by providing bills of admittance and certificates, and giving notice of their readiness, &c.

A general meeting is held at Ackworth once a year, constituted of friends appointed to attend it from the several quarterly meetings. Here the state of the institution is intended to be laid open; all subjects of doubt, and especially such as the two committees could not agree upon, to be refered for candid discussion and determination, and new regulations or rules established.

A large number of friends from distant parts, is appointed to inspect the children's advances in learning, &c. and to obtain a knowledge of their teachers' abilities, a free and honest representation whereof is thought absolutely necessary. This general meeting adjourns to a suitable time in the yearly meeting week, when their minutes are read, and a report made from thence to the yearly meeting at large.

N. B. The inspection of the female side of the house is committed to the women friends, assembled at the general meeting at Ackworth; who appoint different committees to examine the different departments, have free conferences with the officers, inspect the girls' improvements, take religious opportunities with them, and report the substance of their observations, and the propriety of such amendments as occur to them thereupon;

after which, minutes are formed, and a copy of them sent into the mens' meeting.

SECT. II.

There are stationed in the family, a treasurer and his wife, to whom is committed the superintendence of the whole *.

The boys have generally four or five masters, whose salaries are from 25 to 100l ‡. per annum, intended as proportionate to their services, and abilities; and there are also some apprentices. The number of the schools is four, and the masters keep much to the distinct branches of learning for which they are best qualified; as one, reading, another writing, a third arithmetic, &c. and the children pass in classes from school to school, except the little ones, who are principally kept under the care of one master.

The apartments for teaching are so commodious as to render all crowding unnecessary, especially at writing; the desks, though in one continued length, have nevertheless such divisions, by openings for each boy's books, &c. that there need not be any interference, if they keep their places.

Ten or twelve of the eldest and most solid boys, are chosen monitors, who lend some assistance in the

* These serve the institution without a salary, which greatly adds to their authority.
‡ 100l. was the salary of the principal master; but this office being discontinued, no salary is now so high.

schools, particularly in settling the children to their places, and taking care that each has his own.

About ten minutes before every meal, a bell is rung, at which the children are quickly collected in ranks, either on the open ground, or under a colonnade which shelters from wet and heat. The masters stand in the front in their own divisions, whilst the monitors survey them behind and before, taking care that their buckles are in order, their hair combed, and if any be dirty, to send them to wash.

Here the masters have a frequent opportunity of making useful observations, giving general directions, administering counsel, and selecting out offenders for the table of disgrace; which is no otherwise distinguished, than by being detached from the rest, and having no cloth upon it.

When the second bell rings for meals, they advance in couples with great regularity to the dining-room, (the least going first) and divide at the foot of the table, one going up on one side, and the other on the other; by which means they are seated with dexterity and expedition.

A general silence immediately ensues, which, by an intimation from one of the masters, is soon broke, and all begin their meal; but no conversation louder than a whisper is allowed, during the time of eating, and no more in that manner than is necessary for transfering their victuals from one to another, when some have too much, and others too little, the latter of which are freely supplied by the masters, if they ask.

When all appetites appear fatisfied, and a meal is ended, filence again takes place, after which, with an intimation of quietude, and fedatenefs, they are beckoned to depart. They unite again in couples at the foot of the table where they parted, and walk fteadily out of the room into the places appointed for play, where they difperfe. It is thought neceffary, that one of the mafters fhould beftow a general overfight on them in thefe times of relaxation, with no more interference than is abfolutely neceffary.

SECT. III.

The fame order is obferved amongft the girls, as with the boys, at fchool and meals; they have feldom lefs than four miftreffes, whofe falaries are from 12 to 25l. per annum; thefe teach fewing, knitting, fpinning flax, reading, and the Englifh grammar. Writing and arithmetic are alfo taught by one of the mafters, who is particularly fet at liberty, part of every day, for that purpofe, and has a certain divifion of girls each time; but the committees are defirous, that fome of the female teachers fhould be qualified to inftruct in thefe branches of learning *.

A wife attention is paid in the girls fchools to quietude and regularity; each is to know her own bufinefs, and the time for applying for inftruction about her work, &c. There are two or three apprentices for

* Thefe branches are now taught by female inftructors.

whom there is a confiderable fphere of action, in affift-
ing the miftreffes, as there are many more articles
of care amongft the girls than the boys; fuch as large
ftocks of goods to be made up into wearing apparel,
cutting up work, teaching various branches of the exe-
cutive part, and dealing out haberdafheries to the
children. A difcreet allotment of care and employ
to thefe, preferves the miftreffes from too oppreffive
a load of anxiety about fmaller matters, and gives
them an opportunity, in their refpective fchools, to
cherifh a neceffary recollection of mind, enabling
them more fenfibly to partake of a meafure of divine
ftrength, by which alone they can govern with right
authority and tendernefs. They have alfo monitors,
who have fimilar offices to the boys. The reading
miftrefs has feldom more than one clafs in her fchool
at a time, which confifts of fix or eight, and they
read paragraph by paragraph, all ftanding fo remote
from her, as to render a proper exertion of their
voices neceffary, by which they are inured to read
audibly. The miftrefs or affiftant teacher, to whom
is committed the care of fpinning, attends to that
employ only a few hours each day; the reft of her
time being taken up with mending the children's
linen, efpecially that of the little ones, and inftructing five or fix girls at a time in that art, having them,
and that kind of work, in a room wholly fet at liberty for the purpofe. The eldeft girls take it in turns,
one or two at a time, to affift the mantua-maker,
who is fupplied with plenty of work. They alfo
take it in turns to work with the laundrefs every
week, in wafhing, and getting up fmall linen, and

in waiting at meal-times at the houfe-keeper's table; and one in turn is under the peculiar direction of the treafurer's wife, who keeps her pretty much to her own parlour, and employed in her work. Two of the girls are weekly appointed to fweep the lodging rooms every day, and all the girls make their own beds, (as they fleep in couples,) which are curled hair mattreffes laid upon rails; they have a bolfter, an under blanket, a pair of fheets, two upper blankets, and a counterpane of fingle furniture check, but no curtains. A cheft with partitions ftands at the head of every bed, and furnifhes two girls with conveniencies for the keeping of their clothes, having two drawers at the bottom for their fmall linen.

Their apparel in general, and efpecially fuch as paffes through the wafhings, is marked with the initials of their names, and the number of their bill of admittance.

The girls are provided with work by the inftitution, and for their improvement, finer needle-work is taken in for hire than the family can furnifh them with; and when that falls fhort, child-bed linen is fometimes made to fell, in which fuperfluous work is guarded againft.

The girls and boys go to bed in the fame order; and all their clothing is fo folded up, and laid upon their chefts, that though there are twenty or thirty beds in a room, yet after they are fettled in bed, there is fcarcely one article of clothing out of its proper place, and confequently no interference in putting them on. The lodging rooms have feveral ventilators in the ceiling. One or more of the mistresses, or steady apprentices, sleep in each, and a healthy cheerfulness and decorum are preserved through the whole.

SECT. IV.

At meeting the boys and girls enter in the same method, the boys first, a master leading the way; the least children immediately follow, and are seated on the uppermost cross forms, the rest regularly succeeding according to their height; and coming in by couples, they fill two benches at a time, and very soon get all settled. The monitors are placed on a side bench, which gives them an opportunity of inspecting the behaviour of the other children, and of instructing them by their example, the masters and mistresses are placed at little distances, on a seat one step higher, by which they can oversee the whole. They depart with no less regularity than they come in, the children joining again in couples; and in suitable weather, they take a circular walk round the area in the front of the house; after which, they are advised to retire to reading, a considerable library of friends books being provided, part whereof is produced on a first day.—The children every evening settle to read, the boys and girls separate; and they all, with the family, are collected once a week for that purpose, previous to which, they quietly settle down in silence for a little while, then one of the masters reads a chapter, and about six boys, and as many girls, read six or eight verses each; after which, they paufe again, till it is judged a fuitable time for the children to withdraw, which they do, not in couples as on other occafions, but fingly, going immediately to bed, and at fuch a diftance from each other, as to admit of no converfation by the way, the teachers paffing with them in certain divifions, preferves the quietude without interruption. They generally rife at fix in fummer, and feven in winter, and go to bed at nine in fummer, and eight in winter. It is a rule that every child, on admittance, fhall have a certificate figned by a medical perfon, expreffive of his or her being in health, and having no infectious diforders, or apparent fores; and if a child has not had the fmall-pox, the parent or guardian fignifies, whether, if the contagion fhould break out in the family, they choofe inoculation. Whenever an illnefs of any kind appears, the fubject is configned to a fteady matron in the ftation of a nurfe, who has convenient apartments for the reception of fuch; and an apothecary in the neighbourhood has a falary for attending at ftated periods, whether he is wanted or not, and as much oftener as occafion requires; the drugs are kept in the houfe at the expence of the inftitution, and the nurfe has the care of them.

N. B. The children's drefs, if not fo when they come, is modelled to a certain fimplicity, which meets with the general approbation of the moft confiftent part of the fociety; and fuch apparel as is provided by the inftitution, is of a fubftantial, and rather coarfe texture, but neat in its colour and make, and a care is exercifed over it, which preferves it fo to the laſt. An exact uniform in colour, &c. has not been adopted.

SECT V.

The houſe-keeper has the general care and command of the kitchen, the keeping, giving out, and providing the houſe linen, ſhe gives an account what victuals and ſtores are wanted, ſees to the proper uſe of them, and delivers an account to the treaſurer of her diſburſements, once a month.

There are two chamber-maids, whoſe buſineſs it is to make the boys' and family's beds, to ſweep their lodging rooms and the ſtairs, every day except meeting days, to aſſiſt in getting up linen, mending ſheets, the boys' ſhirts and ſtockings, and alſo to help in waſhing and combing the boys. The nurſe likewiſe aſſiſts in mending linen, but nothing is to interfere with her ſervice to diſeaſed children.

Two cooks are found ſufficient; they contrive their buſineſs ſo as to have little hurry at meal times, and on the evening preceding meeting days, the victuals are ſo prepared for next day, that little more is neceſſary, having in ſummer, cold meat, or fruit-pies, and in winter, boiled plumb puddings, which only require one perſon to ſtay at home, to keep the coppers boiling.

They have one ſervant whoſe buſineſs is principally waſhing diſhes, &c. A ſteady, and rather elderly man, is generally kept for renewing the fires, and jobbing about. There is one dairy-maid, who has the care of the milk of upwards of twenty cows, assists in milking them, and makes the butter, &c. The laundress's work is only to inspect and assist in the washings. A mill, something like the bleachers, is used for large cloaths; it is in a building detached from the house, and is wrought by a horse; the linen is washed in bags, being first sorted and soaped; two washer-women are provided for one day, who, with a man that is kept in the capacity of a carpenter, can, with industry and the laundress's assistance, accomplish all that is suitable for that engine. These washings come every week. One man has the care of baking and brewing, in which is included the children's dinners, when they have baked meat or pies, and making the bread, &c. There are 80 acres of land, and two men in the capacity of farmers, who, with a labourer occasionally, find sufficient employ in raising a little grain, taking care of the cattle, assisting in milking, going to market about three miles distance, and fetching coals from the pits a few miles. The treasurer, his wife, the house-keeper, with all the masters, (except those who have families) mistresses, nurse, and mantua-maker, eat together at the house-keeper's table; and the other servants sit down regularly together in the kitchen, where order and solidity are made incumbent for every servant to observe. A tailor and shoe-maker, who have families, are stationed in cottages adjoining the house, and have salaries sufficient for their support. Single men lodge and board in the house, being found necessary to sleep in the boys' rooms. The family is supplied with vegetables from a large garden on the premises, and the care of it committed to a man in the station of gardener, and his assistants.

N. B. Admitting into the family such as are not in profession with friends, is guarded against.

SECT. VI.

Inconveniencies have been found by recommending persons with too partial an eye to their private interest, and obtaining for them a comfortable asylum; so that some who were not objectionable in their own spheres, and within the compass of their own abilities, have obstructed the right order of the institution, and have necessarily become objects of disapprobation; being defective in those faculties which were peculiarly requisite for the stations to which they were introduced: whereas some others, from a secret apprehension of duty, and an upright desire for the good of the institution, have, under discouragements and much diffidence, before their qualifications were ripened to public view, been put into offices; and yet these have in due time, been wonderfully opened in religious and civil usefulness, and have become as pillars in the support of right government in the family. It has been found expedient, from which great advantages have arisen to the family, that friends who travel in truth's service, and those that come disinterestedly on the business of the institution, should be freely accommodated in the house; any expense occasioned thereby, being more than compensated by their religious concern and endeavours for the prosperity of the whole household. Nevertheless, inconveniencies and unnecessary expense have evidently arisen by the children's connections, and those who only come from curiosity, having free access to the accommodations provided by the institution; and therefore an inn has been opened in the neighbourhood *, where people may be agreeably entertained, and enjoy, as if they were in the house, every privilege of seeing the children, observing the order of the family, and attending religious opportunities. As a library of suitable books is provided by the institution for the children's use, and as others of a very different tendency have unwisely been sent by their connexions, it has been found expedient to forbid the introduction of any publications but what first undergo the teacher's inspection.

Divers advantages have arisen by the school's not being limited to the children of friends in straitened circumstances; as those who had their outward affairs in good order, might be expected so to have extended their care to their offspring, as that their example amongst the more ignorant and less guarded youth, might promote solidity and good order in the family: and in cases where that care had not been sufficiently extended, the good of such children, not less than others, appears to be the object of the society's concern: and as their

---

* As the premises belong to the institution, the committee has some control on the tenant.

parents were not prevented from contributing to the support of the institution, so as amply to allow for the additional expense above the stated sum, and even to exceed it if they thought proper, no reasonable objection could arise on that account.

By this means the house was more easily supported, and that distinction in the spirit of the world, which is the bane of religious society, was in some degree removed. Thus children intended to fill different stations in life, being set upon an equality, with which nothing interfered but their merit or demerit, has proved a great encouragement to friends in low circumstances to send their offspring, when they found there was no design publicly to mark them as objects of charity; which, no doubt, from diffidence in some, and an unwillingness to be denominated *poor* in others, would have been generally so disagreeable, as that the number of three hundred children could scarcely have been found, whose parents would have submitted to receive a national benefit, if thereto the badge of poverty had been affixed. As the poor in civil, much more in religious society, are entitled to necessary and comfortable accommodations, and those who are in easy circumstances, upon the principle of loving our neighbours as ourselves, have not a right to more, such an education as is suited to the one, may not be inconsistent with the other, if instead of training them for children of this world, the cultivation of their minds, as followers of Christ, be the principal object in view. A friend may, for procuring the necessaries of life, be in easy circumstances, support an honourable appearance amongst men, and a generous hospitality towards his friends, being of those who rather desire to give than receive; and yet, if out of a large family, he wishes to send three or four to school, and thinks it his duty to provide the most guarded education, it may be quite inconsistent with his abilities, and the education he wishes them to have, to place them in a more expensive situation than what, upon an average, they cost the institution at Ackworth: to prevent such a friend from the benefit of so generous a design, is incompatible with the avowed concern of the society for the welfare of its youth. Our judgment of one another's circumstances in life is often erroneous, and it hath sorrowfully appeared, that many have been strangers to their own; and some who might be unkindly judged for sending their children to Ackworth school, because of the appearance of affluence, which they unwisely supported for a time, have proved unable even to bear the expense of keeping them there without the assistance of their friends. There have been objections in the minds of some friends to an open door for *all* children whose parents approved the plan of education, from a supposition that the house would be crowded with such as might be otherwise as well provided for, and that the poor would be excluded the benefit and preference they ought to receive from such an institution; and also, that the annual subscriptions expected from all the monthly meetings in the nation, would be too much appropriated to the use of those who might afford to pay for their children elsewhere; from whence, discouragements being thrown out to friends in easy circumstances sending their children, the school has much fewer candidates, and the design of it not so fully answered. These objections would be removed, if friends were more liberal and unconfined in their views, as to numbers or stations in life, and were so far from excluding, either the rich or the poor, as to be concerned for, and feel after, the propriety of extending their accommodations, and diffusing their endeavours for the admission of all who offered, and by opening a door for those of ability to pay sufficiently for their children, they might also provide a means for the relief of such as require the help of others in bearing their burdens, remembring that, " the liberal deviseth liberal things, and by liberal things shall they stand."

Upon the whole, it is evident that all children ought to be confidered as proper objects of such an institution; for, in general, even the situation of the rich, as to their prosperity in the truth, is as much to be compassionated as the poor; being often educated with ideas and impressions more repugnant to gospel simplicity, and less inured to the self-denial of a christian, than the offspring of some who labour under difficulties in temporal things. When parents are wife enough to feel difpofed to place their children in a fituation, fo favourable for the growth of virtue, and fo oppofing the ambitious views, and prefumptuous endeavours after felf-exaltation, it would be greatly to be lamented, if fuch were excluded from a feminary, which under the peculiar care of the fociety, is better infpected, regulated, and furnifhed with religious officers, than private fchools can often experience. And as, by this inftitution, a religious education and improvement in ufeful knowledge, is offered to the acceptance of friends for their children, upon moderate terms, and a place large enough for the prefent prepared, there is no doubt but that by an indifcriminate mixture of children belonging to our fociety, divers advantages to their future fteppings in life may arife.

There is in one quarterly meeting, a fund for the affiftance of thofe, whofe parents and monthly meetings may be unequal to bear the expenfes of their children's education, &c. This fund has been extenfively beneficial; the intereft is appropriated to pay one half the eight Guineas for each object; and the reft left to be raifed either by the children's connexions, or their monthly meetings.

For the further information of thofe who may be, in fome meafure, ftrangers to this inftitution, a ftate of the accounts refpecting the fame for the year 1791 is fubjoined.

A Report of the State of Ackworth School, the 31st of the 12th Month, 1791.

An Inventory of the Estate and Effects belonging to, and of Debts owing by, this Institution, the 1st of the 1st Month, 1792.

A Report of the State of ACKWORTH SCHOOL, the 31st of the 12th Month, 1791.

The Income and Expenditure this Year have been as under, viz.

INCOME.

	£.	s.	d.
Donations and Legacies, as per List	392	7	0
Annuitants deceased	250	0	0
Annual Subscriptions, as per List	871	6	10
Bills of Admission; 287 with Children educated, at 8l. 8s. per Annum	2410	16	0
Ditto, Over-time, 66 Weeks, at 5s. per Week	16	10	0
Interest of 3 and 4 per Cent. Annuities	226	0	0
John Fothergill's Annuity, 1 year's dividend	50	0	0
Rent of New Inn, and Land, 1 Year — 24l. Ditto, of a Cottage and 5 Acres of Land, 1 Year — 11l.	35	0	0
Balance of Farm Account	356	16	11½
Total Income this Year	4608	16	9¼
Total expended this Year	3971	4	2½
Increase in Favour of the Institution	637	12	7
Balance of Stock the 1st of the 1st Month, 1791,	8712	5	6¼

Improvements on the Estates since they were purchased, estimated at 1000 0 0

The following articles reckoned in last year's Inventory are discontinued, viz.

Improvements at N. Inn	34	0	4½	
Trees in the Garden	40	0	0	
Cart-house, &c.	90	0	0	
Washing Mill	100	0	0	
	264	0	4½	
	£.735	19	7½	

Errors in Bills of Admission — 42 5 0
D° in stating the cost Prices of 3 & 4 per Cent. Stocks 487 15 0
——— 530 0 0

205 19 7½

Balance of present Stock, the 31st of 12th Month, 1791, as per the following Inventory 9555 17 9

EXPENDITURE.	£.	s.	d.
House Expenses; in Provisions, Coals, &c.	1880	0	9¼
Clothing for Children - - - - - -	831	16	7½
Salaries and Servants Wages - - - -	545	4	10
Interest paid to Annuitants, at 5 per Cent.	212	1	0
Repairs, including the new-making and enlarging of the principal Drain from the building - - - - - -	124	14	6½
Conveyance of Children at 2d. per Mile, exceeding 50 Miles - - - -	130	10	8
Stationary - - - - - - -	60	19	4
Furniture, Bedding, Linen, &c. for Wear and Tear - - - - - -	100	12	11½
Apothecary Account; Salary, Drugs, &c.	42	4	4
Contingencies - - - - - - -	17	17	5
Garden - - - - - - -	25	1	8

An INVENTORY of the ESTATE and EFFECTS belonging to, and of DEBTS owing by, this INSTITUTION, the 1st of the 1st Month, 1792.

BELONGING TO THE INSTITUTION.   £.   s.   d.

	£	s	d
The Estates at Ackworth, cost	8952	11	0
*Improvements on said Estates	1000	0	0
New Office for the Secretary, built this Year, cost	83	18	10
Consolid. 4 per Cent. Annuities 5500l. cost	4328	15	0
Three Months Interest due thereon	55	0	0
Consolid. 3 per Cent. Annuities 200l. cost	143	5	0
Six Months Interest due thereon	3	0	0
John Fothergill's Ann. ½ year's Interest due	25	0	0
New Inn and Land, half Year's Rent due	12	0	0
Cottage and 5 Acres of Land, 3 Quarters due	8	5	0
Furniture; Linen, Bedding, &c. on hand	1673	4	8
Farm; Cattle, Hay, Oats, &c. ditto	678	19	0
House Expenses; Provisions, Coals, &c. ditto	473	9	9½
Clothing for Children, ditto	312	13	7
Stationary; Books, Paper, Quills, &c. ditto	151	15	4
Contingencies; Money lent on leaving School, to be returned	5	16	0
Ditto due for 45 Children who have had the Small Pox	47	5	0
Garden; Dial, Utensils, &c. therein	16	12	9
Bills of Admission; due for 4½, and Forty-Seven Weeks	51	13	0
Drugs, Medicines, &c. on Hand	45	7	11
Materials for Repairs, ditto	24	15	8
Balance in the Treasurer's Hands	107	14	8¼
	18201	12	3¼

* The Money expended under the Head Repairs, (which includes Improvements since the Estate was purchased) in the course of more than twelve Years, amounts to near Four Thousand Pounds.

OWING BY THE INSTITUTION. £.   s.   d.

Annuities at 5 per Cent. on the Life of a Subscriber and Nominee   --   4150   0   0

American Committee, due to them   -   2679   16   10¼

Childrens Account, due to 299 now in the House, being for Time unexpired   1357   6   0

Barclays and Tritton, due to them when outstanding Drafts are paid   429   3   8

Bills of Admission, for 3½ for 1792   -   29   8   0

Balance of Stock in favour of the Institution, the 1st of the 1st Month, 1792   9555   17   9

18201	12	3¼

AN

ACCOUNT

OF

YORK SCHOOL.

The following account of an inſtitution at York, written by Sarah Grubb, was alſo found amongſt her papers; and as ſhe was one of its ſupporters, and it appears to be connected with the preceding ſubject, it is judged proper to introduce it in this place.

AS the ſchool at Ackworth did not receive children but within certain limitations as to age, &c. ſomething further, by way of appendix, was found neceſſary; viz. a ſchool ſomewhat ſimilar to Ackworth, which could receive girls of any age or deſcription, whoſe parents or guardians inclined to ſubmit them to the rules of the houſe; where a ſteady religious care might be exerciſed, uninfluenced by any pecuniary conſiderations, and inſtructions afforded in uſeful learning and houſewifery.

One friend having felt her mind under a ſolid concern for the eſtabliſhment of ſomething of this kind, imparted it to divers others, as truth opened the way; and they finding a concurrent engagement, were willing to unite a little property and attention, for the opening and carrying of it forward; in expectation that others would be concerned to succeed them, for its future continuance and support.

As an oversight superior to what might be expected from such as should be placed in the station of mistresses, appeared to be proper, one friend, (her husband uniting therein) offered herself to the service; and several religious young women of improving abilities, were engaged to step in, for a time, as teachers, &c. without expectation of any pay or reward, save that peace which is the consequence of disinterested faithful labour.

A sum was accordingly raised, a suitable house provided to accommodate about thirty girls, and furnished in a plain, useful manner, at the expense of the proprietors; except the parlour and a lodging room, which the superintendents were intended more particularly to occupy, and which are furnished at their own expense.

They also pay to the institution an ample sufficiency for their own living in the family.

Simplicity of manners, and a religious improvement of the minds of youth, were the principal objects in view of the friends who established this school; and therefore, whatever has a tendency to obstruct this work, is cautioned against, and such apparel as the children bring with them, if deemed inconsistent with the plainness which truth leads into, is not allowed during their residence here; nor such literary publications as unprofitably elate the mind, and give a disrelish for the purity of gospel truths; but a knowledge of useful history and geography, as additional branches of learning to those of reading, writing, arithmetic, and the English grammar, are by no means disapproved. And whilst a careful attention is paid to the improvement of the children in necessary needle-work and knitting, all that is thought merely ornamental, is uniformly discouraged.

The girls make their own beds, sweep their own rooms, and take it in turns, by couples for a week, to wait at the superintendents' and girls' tables; and such as are set apart for that service, are subject to be called upon in extraordinary cases, to assist in preparing victuals, and other necessary employments in the family.

N. B. Each girl pays at entrance fourteen guineas for learning, board and washing.

SOME

REMARKS

ON

CHRISTIAN DISCIPLINE,

AS IT RESPECTS THE

EDUCATION OF YOUTH.

THE Author of the Christian religion came to redeem and save from that spirit which opposed the coming of his kingdom. He has wonderfully displayed the efficacy of that good, by which evil is overcome, proving through the whole of his dispensations a coincidence of mercy with justice. And the operation of this benign principle appears to be in no case more necessary and profitable, than in the true support and discharge of the duties which we owe to those who are placed under our superintendence and care. As there are dispositions manifest in children, after the knowledge of good and evil is contracted, which degrade the mind from that innocency wherein they were first created, and which like an evil tree (if suffered to grow,) will produce unwholesome fruit; so there is also in the power of those who have rightly the care of them, a means which may, by the concurring operations of truth, be rendered effectual to the reduction thereof: and as both the disorder and the remedy lie deep in the heart, they must be sought for there, without the love of superiority, a carnal judgment of good and evil, or the influence of self-will.

To bring children to a true and profitable sense of their own states, and direct them to the spiritual warfare in themselves, is the main end of all religious labour on their account; and herein a single eye ought to be kept to the witness of truth in their minds, for that must be visited and raised, before they can so see, as to repent and convert from evil. When this is the principal object in the view of those, who consider themselves as delegated shepherds, accountable for the preservation of their flock, they are religiously engaged to promote it by such means as are put into their power, under the influence of a christian spirit; which preserves from a desire of occasioning suffering, or more of it than is absolutely necessary for the obtaining of that end, gives patience to persevere in labour without fainting, strength to bear and forbear in their waitings for the springing up of the good seed, and opens an eye of faith to look for, and depend only upon, the blessing on their endeavours. Hereby the conduct of such is deeply instructive to children; and may seal upon their minds the pious concern of their preceptors, and affectionately endear them in a friendship lastingly profitable, when they prove, through the influence of divine love upon their own understandings, the justice, mercy, and nobility of that christian discipline which has been exercised towards them, and whereby they have obtained sweet communion with, and an opening to, the fountain of good in themselves.

If in our passage through life, we are often brought to acknowledge that of ourselves, without divine assistance, we can do nothing, is it not abundantly obvious in the work of bestowing a religious education on youth? and should any wisdom preside over that " which cometh down from above, and is first pure, then peaceable, gentle, and easy to be intreated, full of mercy, and full of good fruits, without partiality, and without hypocrisy?" It is lamentable to see how people in general, and even some who seek the sense of truth on other occasions, seem to consider themselves, at any time, or in any disposition, qualified to instruct and correct children, without perceiving that their own wills require to be first subdued, before they can acceptably be instrumental in subduing the will of others. Though acts of indiscretion, or severities, may have a tendency to humble those who receive them (through whose sincerity all things work together for good, even as persecution has been blessed to thousands) yet the instruments are by no means acquitted thereby, their conduct not being the produce of that faith, which worketh by love, to the purifying of the heart. It is not to be expected but that there is reserved for such, a proportionate degree of suffering, to that which, in their own wills, they have occasioned to others: though, by their natural understanding only, their perception of divine recompense may not be clear enough to distinguish it, yet a righteous retribution, or receiving that measure themselves which they have meted to others, may await them.

"Provoke not your children to wrath," said the apostle. A conduct may be exercised towards youth, which being under the influence of the passions, has a natural tendency to raise a similar return. To punish a child because it has offended us, without the discovery of an evil design, is to act under an unchristian spirit, which revenges injuries. This is a disposition which is apt to receive its gratifications from a flattering, cringing spirit, and from such marks of respect as originate in an impure spring of action; and hence, teachers of children may, from a superficial judgment, approve and strengthen the little pharisees under their care; whilst the pure life that is struggling in the hearts of some who resemble the publican, is crushed and disregarded. Many and deep are the sorrows of the childhood of some, which proceed from different causes: and doubtless that incapacity wherein they are placed for obtaining redress from real grievances, and the abuse of power being strengthened in those from whom they receive them, may be numbered amongst these affecting occasions. Many children, even in our society, have a loose unguarded education, and grow up as degenerate plants of a strange vine, having very little care exercised towards them, except to indulge their unruly appetites, and paffionate defires; thefe require the yoke to be laid upon them with caution and true judgment, left more fhould be commanded than they poffefs abilities to perform, and fo their deficiency be unjuftly laid to their charge: yet the cultivation of their minds fhould be fteadily purfued, under that holy affiftance without which we can do nothing acceptably. Paft experience does not appear to be a fufficient qualification for this, any more than for other religious fervices, even where it has been right, and much lefs fo, when it has not been ftrictly under the influence of that wifdom, which is pure and without partiality.

Wifdom and ftrength muft be waited for, day by day, for the right performance of our duties, before Him who weighs our actions in the balance of pure juftice, and only approves thofe which are wrought in the fpirit. To educate children religioufly, requires a quietude of mind, and fympathy in their guardians, with the ftate of the good feed in them, which will lead rightly to difcriminate between good and evil; to difcover the corrupt fource of many feeming good actions; and to perceive that a real innocency is the root of others, which cuftom, and a fuperficial inveftigation, have rendered reprehenfible. Here we fee the neceffity of true wifdom being renewed, and the infufficiency of that which is carnal, and boafts its own experience and ftrength. It is the humbled mind to which is unfolded fuch myfteries of true godlinefs, for its own edification, and that of thofe under its care, as could not have been received in the support of a false consequence, and the love of superiority. If children are to be instructed in the ground work of true religion, ought they not to discover in those placed over them, a lively example thereof? or ought they to see any thing in the conduct of others, which would be condemnable in them, were they in similar circumstances? Of what importance then is it for guardians of children, to rule their own spirits; for when their tempers are irritable, their language impetuous, their voices exerted above what is necessary, their threatenings unguarded, or the execution of them rash, however children may for a time suffer under these things, they are not instructed thereby in the ground work of true religion; nor will the witness of truth, as their judgments mature, approve a conduct like this; tho' thro' the bias of self-will, it may be adopted in similar cases, in a succeeding generation, by those who, instead of having gathered good seed, have, from the mixture of their education, preferred the bad, which meeting with a soil suitable to its nature, grows and becomes fruitful, to the corrupting of many more.

The love of power is so deeply implanted in the natural mind, that without we discover it, and its evil tendency, in the true light, we are not likely to consider it as an enemy of our own house, against which we are called to war with as much righteous zeal, as against the evil in others; yea with more, because it is declared such are our greatest foes. Where this corrupt part is cherished, it stains our actions; and having gained the ascendency over the pure, lowly seed, bribes and influences the judgment respecting good and evil, and establishes the mind in a self complacence, which, however productive of reproof, has seldom an ear open to that instruction by which itself stands condemned. The prodigal display and use of power is the very destruction of christian discipline. Power is necessary; not to be assumed in the will of the creature, but to stand subservient to the judgment of truth, under which it ought to be exerted; lying in ambush as a waiting, assisting force, ready to be called in cases of difficulty; when, if it step forth in true dignity, the appearance, rather than the use of it, may generally prove sufficient, and its wise retreat render it still more useful and reverenced. True love, clearness of judgment, and the meekness of wisdom, are the supporters of true dignity; and where these prevail in a mind under divine government and control, they give authority, firmness, and benevolence, in thought, word, and deed; which have a profitable and comfortable effect upon those who are placed under their influence, and open a door for undisguised familiarity, and affectionate intercourse, wherein children receive instruction more suitably and cordially, than under the arbitrary sway of a continually assumed power. Should we lay hold of christian discipline in all its branches, and return with it to its root, either amongst children or in the church, we shall always find it originates in a christian spirit, and that every plausible appearance which is defective in this ground, is so far no better than sounding brass, or a tinkling cymbal.

The right education of children, especially in boarding-schools, is no doubt a close and arduous work; those, however, who are rightly engaged therein, and endeavour after their own refinement, and an encreasing acquaintance with the Fountain of Purity in themselves, need not have their eye outward for the establishment of power and authority; for He who feeds the ravens and clothes the lilies, knows what they stand in need of, and is able, out of his own treasury, to supply all their wants; to be " mouth and wisdom, tongue and utterance ;" and will not fail to help under their greatest difficulties, if they support a patient dependence upon Him alone, and profitably live under the persuasion, that when He shuts, no one should attempt to open, and when He opens, none can shut.

EXTRACTS

FROM

LETTERS

WRITTEN BY

SARAH GRUBB.

SHEFFIELD 5th month 1772*—I cannot but wish to spend a few weeks with thee, either here or at York; but as I am sensible it is not good for any of us to have our inclinations gratified at all times, I am desirous to be easy, and resigned to every thing that may cross my natural propensities; that so, when affliction and probation may present themselves, which certainly will attend our pilgrimage through this uncertain stage of life, I may be the more strengthened to undergo these trying seasons with patience and fortitude. But I may conclude with the words which thou hast repeated before; " to will, is present with me, but to do, I know not:" for though this fortitude and resignation are things much to be desired, yet to be entirely given up to

* In the 16th year of her age.

the will and difpofal of a kind providence, is no eafy atttainment. Thou mentioned the difference of our fituations; and it would be ungrateful if I did not confider, and look upon my privileges, as favours from indulgent heaven, if I make a proper ufe of them. But it is the ftate of the mind that limits our happinefs; and alas! it is the want of a fuffi- cient care in the cultivation of my mind, that is a means of obftructing that peace which it would be fweet to enjoy.

YORK, 7th month 1773—I often think our troubles are much augmented, by looking on thofe who are in a more advantageous ftation, according to our opinion; when, if we could but content ourfelves with putting their many mortifications, to balance the adverfe conditions of fome on whom external circumftances feem never to have fmiled, and whofe life has been a feries of affliction, it would amply compenfate for the labour. Due confider- ation would make our forrows appear greatly fhort of what providence might have allotted for us, and would frequently prove them to be the refult of paffion, or imaginary ills.

YORK, 4th month 1774—Thy Letter was falu- tary and grateful, arriving when my mind was anxioufly concerned on many accounts. The care of fo large a family, thou wilt readily own, muft engrofs a large fhare of my attention; it is a tafk to which I often think myfelf unequal, efpecially amongft children; but that I am wil- ling to make the beft of, if I may but be enabled fo to conduct, as to give no real caufe of offence, nor to example in any thing that is contrary to the simplicity of truth. Under these considerations, I see my own insufficiency, and how unable I am to act the part of an elder sister, without a daily support from the Fountain of every good. What should we do, were there nothing to fly to but the instruments, the publishers of the gospel? what aid can they lend us? what strength in weakness, in comparison of that inward stay, which, if enough looked unto, would be the staff of our lives? And with this gracious privilege, how mournful is it to consider the preference that is given to the foibles of this transitory life, before that true peace which flows from the Divine monitor, the teacher within?

York, 8th month 1775—And now permit me to tell thee how welcome a part of thine was; it led me, when I read it, to conclude, that after looking on all the frailties of human nature, and perplexing ourselves with a view of the various and intricate scenes of this life, the necessary result should be, " to be quiet, and mind our own business;" or, as thou sayest, to endeavour to feel ourselves approved by Him who sees not as man sees. If we make welcome every obstacle that is presented in the way to peace, we may justly conclude that we shall never arrive at the peaceful Jerusalem, the quiet habitation which cometh down from God out of heaven. The consideration of this enjoyment, sometimes prompts the mind to soar, or to ascend gradually to the holy mountain, where we may be taught the ways of righteousness, and be instructed in the paths of true peace: but how fast we descend to the place from whence we came! how precipitately do we drop into some region of darkness! for surely there are many degrees; but happy are they who are redeemed from its power. May we not justly deem ourselves, when under any entanglement, any fetter that prevents our deeds being brought to the true light, the light of the Lamb, as alienated, in part, from the Father of mercies, and estranged from His celestial spring! how necessary therefore is it for us to watch at all seasons, in times of peace, as well as in the spiritual warfare; for we know not when the hour of temptation cometh, and our fortification may prevent the engagement. How preserving is that language; "I will get me to my watch tower;" and what a favour it is, our not being ignorant, that the name of the Lord is a tower to the righteous.

10th month 1777—I expect this will find thee at ———, where I wish thy visit to be attended with more solid satisfaction than thou looked for; if not, it may be no less profitable. My very small experience has taught me, that endeavouring to keep near to the Fountain of life, in company where its arisings are evidently suppressed, often tends more to our real growth in the root of true religion, than the easy enjoyment of valuable friends company, with whom we are not driven to our refuge.

12th month 1777—I doubt not but thou haſt thought, with myſelf, the conduct of the generality of young men to be painful; for what numbers do we ſee of theſe, who, prompted by the irregularity of youthful fervour, ſuffer their minds to be entangled with every fluttering object of vanity; little conſidering that they are expoſing themſelves to innumerable ſorrows, and inconſiderately and rapidly purſuing an Ignis-fatuus, which will lead them into a labyrinth of perplexities. Oh! could they, inſtead of this, centre and retire to that reverent fear in themſelves, which would prove a fountain of life, preſerving from the ſnares of death, there is no reaſon to doubt that the inexhauſtible Fountain, would not only turn their feet into the path of peace, but ſo far eſtabliſh their goings therein, that every important concern of their lives would be favoured with divine direction; and in that very momentous one of marriage, the language of truth would be ſo intelligible as to direct them to the right object; and then, with what holy confidence might they propoſe theſe connexions, while our ſex, with an humble awful diffidence, wait alſo for counſel from on high, and to feel the ſame aſſurance of divine approbation: thus all would be conſummated to the praiſe of Him whoſe favour they had ſought and implored. Much do I wiſh that my heart may ever be favoured to poſſeſs a degree of this primitive purity, though no matrimonial conſiderations require it; the ſaying of the Apoſtle often occurs to my mind; " that godliness *is* profitable unto all things."

7th month 1778—We are now again left with the care of a family that requires some attention and circumspection. I never felt more unfit for the task, nor more ready to query, who is equal to it, and to conclude, surely not I. A discreet conduct, an affectionate behaviour, attempered with just so much steady authority as to excite respect united to an unavoidable love, and these not to fluctuate with the situation of the mind, is an attainment which I fear will never be mine, and which indeed will be unnecessary in a very few years with respect to my sisters; but yet it does appear, at least in my eyes, absolutely requisite for those on whom the education of children devolves. Where people are thus qualified, and discharge their duty, they will find a pleasure with the important charge; " for in it there is a happiness, as well as care." There is certainly something in the affectionate part of us, which tends rather to defeat, than promote the growth of true religion, except it be sanctified under the operation of the divine hand; when that is happily experienced, some of the natural propensities become blessings, and very laudably heighten the enjoyment of spiritual ones.

11th month 1778—Thou hast, I doubt not, already heard of the unsettled state we have lately been in, occasioned by a sorrowful and affecting event, the death of our dear friend ———. She seemed but just arrived at the summit of earthly happiness, and to have conferred the same enjoyment upon her beloved partner; yet alas! how transient was the duration of this state; and indeed, how unfit is it for minds who are too apt to rejoice in prosperity without trembling, and whose affections are centred only in social comforts! We cannot but conclude that, by these instructive lessons of mortality, the divine intention is to refine and purify, and to shew all who behold them the necessity, the great necessity, of having our minds centred where fluctuating things can never come. This was, beyond a doubt, the happy situation that her mind was in sometime before her departure; for about a week before her death, she told her husband, " that her mind was steadily fixed upon the joys to come;" and added, " I am sensible I shall not recover; and I have now been where they were singing Hallelujah's to the Highest, and it was pleasant in my ears. I have seen the beautiful situation of the inhabitants of the new Jerusalem:" with many similar expressions, which I have hardly either leisure or room to insert; but the foregoing will give thee an idea of the comfortable state her mind was in, which she appeared to preserve to the last.

The two following pieces of religious poetry appear to have been composed, the first, in the year 1778, soon after her return from a visit to some of her friends, and the latter, some considerable time afterwards; and as they are solemn and instructive lines, and describe the pious and exercised frame of her spirit, they claim a place in this collection. Though she possessed a considerable talent for this sort of composition, yet she cultivated it but little, and very rarely indulged herself therein; this may have proceeded from an apprehension, that it too often tends to draw out, and habituate the mind to a display of unfelt sentiments; a too high colouring, if not a false representation, of things; and a decoration of language inconsistent with the simplicity of truth. It is, indeed, a talent which, in its exercise, requires very great circumspection; and, in the reading to which it leads, a religious guard and limitation.

    Though clothed now with ease, tho' the pure stream
Of social converse and congenial love
Now offers me its balm, yet doth my soul,
In retrospect, far other scenes survey,
Far other sources for energic pow'rs.
How can my pen pourtray the deep distress,
How paint the anguish of a heart that bled,
Or how describe the current as it flow'd
From sorrow's briny deeps? It fails; and lost
In recollection's maze, the mind that felt,
Can only now explore the ambient main,
Which, with impet'ous haste, my little bark
O'erflow'd, and seem'd to sink it in th' abyss.

But say, why sunk it not ? by what kind hand
Was it sustain'd ? or why was it not driv'n
Against that rock, on which so many split,
And pour their mournful accents to the waves?
'Twas not thyself that did support; 'twas not
Thy strength bore up: thou canst not thus convert
Th' o'erwhelming surge of mourning into joy.
Then who ? that great I AM, that Majesty
Who made the bush his temple, and whose flames
Consum'd it not; who breaketh by his word,
And with consolatory bands binds up;
Did he not condescend to intervene ?
Did he not say ? "be still, it is enough,"
Yea, with compassionate regard, pour'd in
The wine and oil. Forget it not, my soul !
Nor seek a greater joy: yet patient be
In suffering; in seasons of distress,
When nature pours her bitters in thy heart,
When heav'n seems brass, and earth with iron bars
Doth hold its cheering goodliness from thee;
Then with a calm resigned mind give up,
Freely surrender all thou callest thine;
No longer rest on Jordan's banks, but with
Stability step in, and learn to know
That stones there are which for memorials serve;
Then bring them up from thence, as proofs where
    thou
Hast been, and therewith raise thine Ebenezer.
But ah ! how thoughtless in this prosp'rous state,
Which now I view, but not with equal eye;
Yet humbled in the dust, implore thy aid,

Thy care, thou benefactor kind! or how
Can I, amidst each smiling scene, select
And cull the chiefest and the best of all
That's offered? How render thee thy due
For benefits, "thy mercy and thy truth?"
Through ev'ry dispensation of thy love,
Through ev'ry min'itration of thy judgments,
Grant, ah! grant, a self-abased spirit;
That so, thy great supreme commands, thy will
May be obey'd, and mine as clay be form'd.

 And ye, my friends! who lately were and are
The sweet endear'd companions of my life,
Ah! may we long each others blessings share;
Soften each sorrow, intermix each joy,
With unity of spirit soar above
These transitory things, and as we rise,
Together drink the well refined wine;
And in that pure and purifying stream,
Which from the throne of the most High proceeds,
Witness our minds repeatedly baptiz'd.

My soul ascends in humble flight
 Above these transient woes,
And fill'd with songs as in the night,
 She to the mountain goes

With harp and pipe, to celebrate
 The praise of Zion's King,
And with a weaned mind prostrate,
 An humble off'ring bring.

Prepare the off'ring, sacred flame,
   And consecrate my ground,
That, by the virtue of thy name,
   Acceptance may be found.

Thy gracious majesty that deigns
   The contrite soul to hear,
Thy wisdom that forever reigns,
   Bid humbled minds draw near.

Shall I repine then to present
   The off'ring of my will,
Shall I ungratefully consent
   Th' immortal birth to kill?

Forbid it Lord! and aid my soul
   The conflicts to endure,
Which, thro' thy merciful controul,
   Make all things new and pure.

O grant thy all-sustaining arm
   My drooping mind to bear,
And with thy consolations warm
   Preserve me from despair.

Thou know'st the tribulated path,
   Which leads from death to life,
Thou know'st the baneful dragon's wrath,
   His enmity and strife.

Thy light and truth, most gracious God,
   Withhold not from my soul;
Nor yet thy wise chastising rod,
   Nor David's washing pool.

In faith and patience, centre deep
    The myft'ries thou reveals;
And, with an everlafting fleep,
    And thy immortal feals,

Envelope each unworthy view;
    That fanctified aright,
Thy glorious caufe I may purfue,
    And witnefs to the light.

Thus thro' the few fucceeding fteps
    Appointed me to run,
Thy honour may be all in all,
    Thy praife alone be fung.

1ft month 1779—The re-eftablifhment of our own, or our friends' health, from the verge of that eternity to which we are haftening, ought to excite deep gratitude of mind, and lead to a ftill greater degree of obedience and preparation for the final call. The feafons which I paffed, and the meditations with which my mind was fupported, when watching over my departing friends, are, I think I may fay, continually before me. How low and how groveling appeared every mundane thing! How infignificant the moft defirable connexions in life, when compared with that certain portion of happinefs, that unbounded fphere of felicity, which is referved for the pure in heart! even the ftrong ties of friendfhip and love were fubfervient to thefe feelings; infomuch that I have queried, when reflecting how these fetters to our diffolution were removed, whilst those important profpects were before me, " what ailed thee, oh thou sea, that thou fleddest, thou Jordan, that thou waft driven back, ye mountains, that ye fkipped like rams, and ye little hills, like lambs!" But alas! this lafted not long; for when the folemn, awful meffenger had proclaimed liberty to a captive fpirit, and tranflated it to where mine could not afcend, then arofe every natural emotion, and inftructed me, that in a continual warfare confifted my peace. But what can I now fay? for on thefe things, as on the manna that was gathered yefterday, am I too apt to live, without enough feeking the frefh defcendings of celeftial food, and patiently fubmitting to that creative power, which would form us into the ftate of a little child. The aptitude of my difpofition to rife above the humbling principle of truth, and form to myfelf a likenefs which may be compared to a marble ftatue, or an image of fubftantial good, often leads my mind into deep lamentation and mourning; with a painful fear, that I fhall never be entitled to the handing forth of the royal fcepter, the mark of divine approbation; but to that fentence of *depart*, and being fet as on the left hand: yet when we furvey thefe fleeting moments, or rather look over them to the endlefs ages that enfue, we cannot but conclude, that nothing fhort of a ftate of infatuation would lead us to exchange, or even rifque our everlafting well-being, for the very beft things of this world.

4th month 1779—Alas! how is a large degree of truth, inward excellence, and whatever conltitutes true lovelinefs, removed! how is the beauty fallen! Affecting inftance to us her friends; but to that immortal fpirit in her which has long, in profpect of a future glorious admiffion into the celeftial regions of light, been willing to defcend into the deeps, and there behold the marvellous works of Him whom fhe ferved, it is a happy lot. Though fhe fuffered much, though forrow came in the night, in the clofe of a world wherein fhe had many troubles, yet joy has, I doubt not, fprung in the morning, in the opening of an endlefs day. How juftly may we rejoyce on her account, who was counted worthy of fo early an entrance to where the aged can but hope to be, and whofe work is done: a circumftance which the impatient mind, I believe, often wifhes for. A lamentation for thofe who knew her worth, and who hoped for a future uniting with her in the covenant of life, and of that wifdom which is from above, may, with unfeigned propriety, be adopted. For my own part, all that was within me, (when I found what thy intelligence was) feemed ftruck with amazement, and was loft for a time in reflection on her great and awful change; but when I recollected myfelf, that fhe was forever removed; and that, through the intricacies of life, I was left to move without her friendly affiftances, and fellow-feeling mind, a deep fenfe of mourning enfued: for from fo fhort, and even from a long intercourfe, I think I never reaped fo much folid benefit with any. And alas! fhort fighted as I was, I imagined it an earnest of some future fellowship in this life; and that, through the various trials that attended it, a providential help might be dispensed us through each other. But now, I find it was the fulness allotted us, and that, like Jonah's gourd, it sprung to me in a night, and has withered before the brightness of the day; withered in a time wherein my weakness leads me too much to lean on such helps. But this shock relaxes the desire, and points to the strong tower, the refuge of the righteous, where alone is true safety; and oh! may we flee thither, for the habitation is quiet and sure. I very much sympathize with you in the present trial, the loss of so near and valuable a friend. Your attachment I believe was strong, and the separation hard; but how much more profitable, if, instead of an unavailing sorrow, we consider the church's loss; that one who filled an useful sphere is removed, and consequently, that that share is left to devolve upon the shoulders of some; I say, if we consider and look sufficiently at this, being willing to step, if required, into her path, (which I know was secretly exercised, not only for herself, but for the prosperity of the great and noble cause), and thereby redeem the loss, how acceptable must that tribute be, in the sight of Him who sees not as man sees; and, if it spring from a heart devoted to the work rather than the reward, how truly profitable to ourselves! The end of the righteous is desirable, in whatever stage of life it arrives; but for my own part, if I could hope mine would be such, I own I cannot help feeling a wish, that its approach might be in the early or middle part: in what the desire originates, I cannot pretend to say, but it is, perhaps, in some unjustifiable part of self-love.

6th month 1779—How acceptable was thy account of the latter, and last end of our beloved friend! My mind often recurs to it for hope, and for strength to persevere and to obtain; but there appears so much to constitute our claim to the peaceful abode, into which the righteous only can enter, that my mind enjoys but a small portion of faith to believe it will ever reach its confines; yet I am sometimes led to consider, whether our researches after happiness, are not too much actuated by principles of self-love; and whether it is consistent with the benevolence which the gospel inculcates, that in all our concerns, and the exercise of our greatest virtues, we should be continually enquiring after the reward: does it not, my friend, (for I really do not know) indicate a littleness of mind, and a want of confidence in Him who is, "just and equal in all his ways?" for in our works there is no merit to the creature; if we trust not, where is our faith? if we persevere not, where is our patience? and if in this life, we partake of the fulness of that joy which is sown for the upright, where is the glorious reserve for futurity? Should we not then, if our minds were clothed with the nobility of the spirit in which we believe, resign all things? and being humble, suffer all things? and do all things in pure love, exclusive of any selfish view?

In your county as well as ours, there are a few who have not bowed the knee, nor sacrificed to the workmanship of men's hands, yet the general depravity does so often obstruct the current of life, and thereby stagger the feeble mind, that I believe you often experience, a seeking water and finding none; but fear not, for He in whom is the fulness of strength, is your refuge.

8th month 1779—Though I am firm in the belief, that if we experience the work of true regeneration, all our attachments must be tried in a furnace, which the natural understanding cannot of itself comprehend, and that the precious must be separated from the vile, by the mysterious operations of the divine hand; yet I do also hope, that ours will be permitted to stand, and that, if we live to survive the strength of that youthful ardor with which our present union is heightened, there will be enjoyed a fellowship, better and more pure than any we have yet experienced, and against which, all the fiery darts of the enemy will never be able to prevail. This, and similar to this, is, next to the immediate influence of the divine presence, what I strongly covet to partake of, in this vicissitude and vale of tears; wherein a cup is sometimes handed, which is so repugnant to our nature, that we cannot help entreating, let it, I pray thee, pass from me. But oh! that we may be found worthy to enjoy the celestial blessings dispensed to the faithful, by obedience to that power, which in all its workings, tends to crucify self, and prepare the mind to adopt that refined language of, " not my will, but thine be done." The more a mind possesses of that wisdom and nature, which act in opposition to the true simplicity of a little child, the greater must be the exercise; and if it has long refused the clear manifestations of duty, it is no wonder if a season of painful uncertainty ensues.

9th month 1779—Art thou in health? art thou strong in Him who goeth before thee, and who hath promised that His glory shall be the rereward of the number that deal prudently, and go not by flight? Isaiah lii. 12, 13. How safe do the steps of such appear, who have this glory for a light to their feet, and the divinely illuminated lamp to attend their path! It is no wonder that a way should often open, where the human understanding (which is dark and comprehends not the things of the spirit) can see no way; and that every necessary refreshment should be interspersed therein. I sometimes think it is a favour, that an eye is opened into this path, and that though the advancement in it is small, if there be any, yet thus seeing, and pressing forward, we may obtain. I hope thou art treading this sure ground, and that thy memorials, which are brought from the bottom of the purifying waters of Jordan, are not hid; or if they be, that it is only for their refinement. But perhaps they are like the sling stones which David had ready in his bag, till the appointed time of meeting the defier of Israel was come, and are to be alike powerful in prevailing against the enemies of the poor, and the afflicted people, which may be spared in the day of general calamity. But be this as it may, obedience is still to be attended to, and the prophet's advice remembered, of not seeking to ourselves great things, but to be content with every dispensation, whether of want or of plenty. When this situation is in any degree attained, how thankful do we feel for even a small appearance of good; for if the divine presence is no more beheld, than by the putting forth of His hand thro' the hole of the door, it still sustains and refreshes, and serves as food for many days.

10th month 1779—Poor ——— I feel for her frequently, and have often thought of writing to her; but it has as often occurred, that except the great Shepherd of Israel assist her, whence shall another do it? As his voice, his crook, and his protection, are undoubtedly offered, 'tis surely weak to suppose that the language of the creature can equal the voice of this Charmer; if indeed it do not derogate, (as I am inclined to think it does) from the omnipotence and wisdom of our holy head: and I sometimes think, that nothing more proves the deep rooted depravity of the human mind, even when measureably illumined with the brightness and glory of the eternal excellency, than looking at the members for help, and craving it from that often poor, benumbed quarter, when, at the same time, it might be said, " you have an unction from the holy one, and you know these things."

1st month 1780—There appears to me, no joy like the joy of the righteous, nor any unity like theirs; and next to the immediate influences of the divine Spirit, it is to me desirable. But obedience being the terms of this great and valuable poffeffion, what numbers, for want of this, are deprived of it! Yet he who is infinite in condefcenfion, and whofe love is unutterable, deigns to reward for every little fervice, and grants, at times, a facred view of the myftery of his own church, and his marvellous work therein. My friend is, I doubt not, well inftructed in thefe things, and though I alfo believe it is a time of fuffering like Jacob's, when the fun confumed by day, and the froft by night, yet He who knows our neceffary refinements, is able to limit the waters, that they do not overflow us, and, in his own time, will fay to the operation of the furnace, " it is enough." Till then, I truft deep will " utter unto deep," and with an increafe of fuffering, we fhall experience an increafe of holy fellowfhip.

3d month 1780—My dear friend's letter was too acceptable to lie long unacknowledged; becaufe it revived in the breaft of her friend all the cordiality of an union and fellow-feeling, which I truft do not originate in the part appointed for deftruction; but are rather the offspring of minds engaged, (though feebly) to travail on as in great weaknefs and fear, and fometimes having no language to exprefs, either to the Fountain of good, or to one another, but " fighs unutterable." How infinite is the condefcenfion of that precious influence, which helpeth thefe our infirmities, and is touched with a feeling of them; aiding the mind, with a degree of holy confidence, after all its apparent exclufions from the participation of divine good, once more to look towards his holy habitation. And as it is through sufferings that our natures are refined and sanctified, they must not be of our own choosing, because the suffering might then, in a great measure, cease, and that necessary heat which attends the furnace of affliction, and which purifies the mineral, get quenched; for so depraved are our ideas of things, that I have thought, and in some measure felt, that even in our baptisms of spirit, we would wish to have a choice; so active is self, that it cannot be satisfied without a sphere to move in. Think not, my beloved friend, that I consider this as a peculiar propensity of thine; for it rather occurred as a degree of painful experience. I have often viewed your situation, (and particularly since the receipt of thine this morning) as almost too trying for flesh and blood, but He who placeth the members of his church, and appoints them their lots, does not leave their supports to flow through these corrupt sources; but marketh their steps, and, perhaps quite hiddenly, confirms the feeble knees, and leadeth them in a way they know not. My mind is frequently too much depressed, and sometimes tossed with tempests, to admit a consolatory sentiment, much less to offer my friend the language of encouragement; nevertheless I cannot help expressing my firm belief, that all your troubles will work together for good, and that the deeper they are, the greater will be the preparation for a glorious reward in the house of the one Father, with whom a book of remembrance is written.

4th month 1780—I want to hear how you feel yourselves at your new habitation, and whether it proves a Goshen to ———, whose mind has often felt to me to be secretly clad with sackcloth, even when perhaps obeying the command, " to wash and to anoint, rather than appear to men as if fasting:" and as this is a situation necessary for us, its continuance administers no cause of discontent, if we have but an evidence that we have not stepped out of the holy inclosure; finding the fence of divine appointment to be about us, no matter what we suffer. It is not for our rejoicings, and what feels comfortable to ourselves, that we can expect a reward; but rather for our trials and probations, if we endure them with patience; and even for these we have no reason to expect a full reward; for if that were the case, where would be the reserve for the fruition of joy in the life to come? Nevertheless, we do sometimes get favoured, in our wilderness journey, with a little bread handed in secret, and with an opening of the brook by the way; and the remembrance of our partaking of this together, refreshes and strengthens in some gloomy seasons. I have often reason to number your friendly regard to me amongst the blessings of my life, and I sometimes think, in the feeling of a nearness I cannot describe, that my affection to you is not less than filial. May I be preserved worthy this fellowship, and, by an increase of purity, find an increase of that union of spirit which lives beyond the grave! I think nothing has more conduced to my confidence in, and fellow-feeling with you, than the belief that your reproof and plain dealing would be as readily administered to me, as your encouragement; and I beseech you, never lose sight of this openness, for I am surely one of the weakest and most frail of the whole flock and family, if I am worthy to be included in the number: and yet, if I know my own heart, it is not myself, but the cause which I have in view; and I wish for still more of that disposition which can enable us to say, " let the righteous smite me, and it shall be a kindness; let him reprove me, and it shall be an excellent oil."

5th month 1780.—How truly valuable is this precious unity which, like the oil that was poured upon the head of Aaron, remains to anoint the very skirts of the garments of those who have obtained the mark of discipleship, to love one another! In the renewal of it, I feel greater consolation than is usually bestowed upon me from causes of this kind, because there are few indeed with whom I find myself nearly united, or whose regard affords me relief in the time of want, although I know them to be far superior to myself; insomuch that I conclude the command is certainly to me, " salute no one by the way." But glad I am that there is an exception to this, and that I hope I can in the right line salute my friend by the way, and visit him in the wilderness, where all who are united to the true church must chiefly dwell, and wait for its redemption: and if this is not found in our time, we have yet reason to hope, that having partaken in some measure of its sufferings, whether principally for ourselves as members, or for the whole body, this offering will be acceptable to the Searcher of hearts; and, then if in His wisdom some of our days should prove to be few and full of sorrow, may we not look towards the morning of a better day, and an inheritance in that country whose inhabitants never say, they are sick! Were it not, now and then, for a little of this hope which lives within the vail, I know not how things would be got through; so selfish am I that I fear the reward is too much an object, and not that perfect love which casteth out fear, and is ready to obey and suffer all things for the work's sake.

9th month 1780—I have felt a more than usual impulse to salute thee, my much beloved friend, and, according to my little ability, to strengthen thee in repeating the efforts which I trust thou art, at times, concerned to use for thy own everlasting welfare, by turning a deaf ear to the subtle insinuations of the adversary, who is evidently seeking thy destruction. I am well convinced that no language I can use, except it be blessed with the efficacy, as well as appearance, of indisputable truth, will ever be acceptable to thee, or prove profitable; and it is, I may truly say, at this time particularly, the fervent engagement of my mind, that thou mayst come to a settlement in that power which is unchangeable, and which would, if thy anxieties and destructive heat of spirit were more damped, instruct thee still further in the mystery of thyself, and that of godliness which is profitable for thee. With what manner of love hath the Father loved thee? hath often in effect been the query and exclamation of my mind, when the wonders of thy deliverance from Egyptian bondage have occurred, with an evidence of the Hand that wrought them, and of that mighty power which hath caused the bush to burn before thee, and convinced thee that the ground whereon thou stood was holy. As sure as ever he was with Israel, and with Moses their leader, he is with thee; and thy trust in him, and seeking for a passive state of mind in that wilderness travel which may be assigned, will, I believe, effect thy arrival at the Land of Promise. But think not, my beloved friend, when there is a want of water, and of that refreshment which the unmortified will is eagerly thirsting after, to use the means whereby the meekness of Moses was overcome, to strike the rock, and thereby offend that holy providential care, which will never have thee to suffer for want of true knowledge, but will be found to provide thee with food in due season; and tho' it may not always be pleasant, but, at times, may resemble Mara's waters for bitterness, yet the spiritual Canaan being in view, and not expected on this side Jordan, the river of true judgment, it will animate to still greater degrees of virtue, such as patience, fortitude, and strength, in this holy travail. Under a renewed belief that thou art in the place allotted by divine wisdom, I feel an earnest solicitude, that thou mayest be strengthened to discharge thy duty in every good word and work; and that He who hath plucked thy feet out of much mire and clay, may not only set thee upon the immovable Rock, and establish thy goings, but, in His own time, put such a song of deliverance into thy mouth, as will last to all eternity. It is, my dear friend, with a love which I trust is more than natural, that I re-salute thee, and bid thee be of good cheer, and labour to detect every delusion, for truly there is light enough for it.

10th month 1780—Animated with the effusions of much love and near fellowship, I have many times secretly saluted you since my abrupt departure from ———; where I was thankful to feel, after a long fast from sensible enjoyments, either religious or social, that there is yet an union to be attained with the spirit of pure love, and that we can in a state of mutability, in proportion to our faithfulness, partake together of its binding influence. A revival of this sense, I was and am, I hope grateful for, and glad to find a similar sentiment in my companion. I neither received, nor expected any great peace and reward for the offering of paying you a visit, which was not completely of the free-will sort; but thus much I may say, that a degree of comfortable serenity attended my returning mind.——My throwing myself in the way of meetings, in which my attendance has not appeared to be in the movings of light, is not, in my idea, without danger: for if we depend, tho' in ever so small a matter upon a putting forth which has not a little clearness for its evidence, we may likewise conclude it to be equally safe, to offer our service from as doubtful an impulse; and thus, I am apprehensive, a clouded state may ensue. And having been accustomed to adopt things through perhaps a willingness to do good, which have not borne the royal impression, our distinguishing feelings may gradually become so weakened, that the pure unmixed word may get sullied, and the powerful demonstration thereof decrease: This is a sentiment which I offer by way of apology for myself; and yet I would not have my friends to conclude, that I believe great openings are to be looked for, in every little service. If the token of rain be ever so small, yet if it be so sure as to bear the comparison of the cloud of the size of a man's hand, I am of opinion, (though not always willing to accept it) that it is as much to be depended upon, as if the clouds were opened, and we felt the showers from thence. It is certainty, though ever so little in appearance, that I wish to follow.

1st month 1781—The trials which I believe are in infinite wisdom allotted to the rightly concerned, are many; of which, I trust, we have been favoured to share; yet we have no need to make our way harder, by adding so continually our own judgments, and discouragements upon them; making comparisons which we have no right to do, and weighing things which can only be tried in the balance of the sanctuary: for we know so little of things above us, that we are very incompetent judges who stand most in divine approbation. I cannot but much wish that ———— would grow wiser respecting these things, and endeavour to shut out discouragements which do not come in the line of wisdom; and then, I am satisfied, she would find her way to be as easy as she thinks mine is, and would be convinced that her labours have been more acceptable to him who put her forth, than she will often allow.

1st month 1781—Does not Solomon say, that a few words fitly spoken are like apples of gold in pictures of silver? I think he does; but whether or not, it is so in the scripture of my heart, and your lines prove the justness of it. Feeling has no fellow, and if the address be but felt by the receiver in the covenant of true love, it is something like such a ministry as I covet, where words are lost in power. Deceitful as I know my own heart to be, I will not allow that my remembrance of you arises wholly from " an imbibed favourable impression in times past," and that a personal absence revives it. I should conclude that to be a formal attachment which hath nothing but age for its origin, and is not supported with repeated renewals of life. Is this the inward tie that no change can break? the love that many waters cannot quench, or the floods of affliction destroy? Surely it is not of that nature which can endure the fire, and be refined by it; it is more like the base metal which would rise as the scum and be lost, than the solid gold that appears afterwards, and is able to endure even the seventh purification.

3d month 1781—I think I have entered into my domestic station, with a degree of awfulness and fear, and not without an humble sense of the unmerited favours I received from divine condescension, and from my friends during the cessation of it. And notwithstanding many deep trials attend our leaving home, when under an apprehension of duty, and many painful jealousies necessarily arise, lest the most important of causes should suffer, yet when we are in a settled satisfaction, or under the cares of a family, by not being so frequently put upon a sense of our danger, and of our own unfitness to do good of ourselves, our minds are apt to lose their centre, by getting off the watch, and so become dissipated and carried away with trifling things; at least with things short of that certain treasure which is secured out of the reach of either moth or rust; and then they become to us (however plausible to that wisdom which cannot comprehend the mystery of godliness) unsubstantial trifles. Thus we see the necessity of having a foundation of our own; and we need not that another should build upon us, but by that same power which directed the first stone, similar to what was and is laid in Zion, tried, elect and precious, whereby we may be built up in the most holy faith. I often find it my duty, strictly to scrutinize into the moving cause of my steppings in various respects; and notwithstanding the greatest abasedness is my due, on viewing my own innumerable frailties, and inability often to turn my mind availingly to the invincible fortress, even in times of deep probation; yet if there was not a secret testimony in my heart, that it is much my lot to know an abstraction from human dependancies, my feelings would be insupportable, because I could not look for that peace which is preserved from human mixtures and interruptions.

4th month 1781—Weary indeed I have felt myself of this changeable world for a few days past: perhaps it proceeds from too great an indulgence to that eye, which is viewing the discouragements of the present day, and which has cause to run down with water, for the slain of the daughter of Zion. How are the Aarons removed, and removing, and such as might seem likely to receive the garments, have the work cut short in righteousness! how the standard-bearers faint, and how doth the enemy prevail in his transformations, in deceiving and drawing down even of the priesthood! In contemplating these things, I think I may say, that I never felt my mind similarly clad with a state of secret mourning and sackcloth, as since you left us; insomuch that I am ready to enquire, who shall stand? or from whence can the watchers come, that will faithfully discharge their trust upon our walls in a future day? I am daily convinced of the great need there is for me frequently to be taken throughout in pieces, that no comeliness may remain to self, nor manna be preserved from one day to another; that my own state, and the wilderness state of the church, may be (though not fully yet) clearly seen.

6th month 1781—I have, after contending my ground by inches, ventured to set off towards a place which I have often looked at with a kind of dread and dismay; from an apprehension that it strongly resembles that great city Babylon, in which it is hard to be preserved from tasting of the cup, either in a greater or less degree; and where, if there even be preservation from this, deep suffering must be the consequence; a state not likely for flesh and blood readily to enter into. I can truly say it is in great fear and abasement of mind, that I advance towards it; earnestly desiring to be kept to that power which discovereth the hidden things of darkness, and shews us the different sources of self-love.

11th month 1781—We are sometimes at a loss to account for our own actions, because they proceed from causes unsearchable to us, and which we are led insensibly to comply with for our own good, that *that* part in us which is appointed for death, and which, by means of the flaming sword, is totally separated from the tree of life, may receive no food nor vigour to support it. Since I saw thee, many and complicated have been the concerns and feelings of my mind; new causes and new anxieties have occurred, from which I have seen great need to procure a secret dwelling in a quiet habitation, and to crave daily assistance to abide therein, that my own root might not be more impoverished; but that by an inward attention to the voice of the true shepherd, a more intimate acquaintance with him might be cultivated, and a greater subjection of spirit experienced; whereby I should be more clothed with that true humility and pure simplicity which are essential to the cause of righteousness, and necessary for the preservation of our minds in a state of acceptance with Him, who sees not as man sees, but who knows what His wisdom has prohibited to us, and marks our obedience.

How affecting was the removal of our beloved ———! Silent astonishment, and secret mourning, for an individual and general loss, was all the language I could use. My heart was indeed affected, and is not less so in the fresh feeling of a dissolved affectionate tie, and of the uncertainty of all our comforts and attachments, notwithstanding they may in prospect appear durable; but as we do believe there is an union which exists beyond the grave, a fellowship unconfined to these mortal bodies, how strong an incentive is it to purchase this permanent inheritance, though at the expense of our own fervour, and that friendship which is conceived in the false refinements of the human imagination; and which being tinctured with the gilded impurities and dregs of nature, becomes of that kind which is at enmity with God, because not subject to the power of His cross. To be stripped of ourselves, to be simple, to be fools in our own eyes, and in the eyes of others, are experiences not pointed to by our own dispositions, but are indisputably the way to that kingdom which flesh and blood cannot inherit. By yielding to this way, how humbly may we commemorate that power which gives according to our advancement, the victory over a host of opposition, and dims that eye in us in which our enemies are magnified; giving a holy confidence that binds up the mind, humbly exalts it above these momentary things, and, by measureably uniting us to itself, enables to discern the origin of our feelings, and what proceeds from them, by tracing them to their spring, and proving them in the light. Our experience is small, but, I trust we mutually long for that which is good; may we each be, more and more, drawn from every mixture of self, and become as a weaned child!

12th month 1781—If I had known your plan of proceedings, it is likely I should have met thee with a few lines somewhere; but a morsel of friendly converse, or a token of true regard, may, perhaps, be as acceptable now thou art returned to a more homely fare, and feeling a little more descent to some inferior service in the house, than was then allotted. Notwithstanding those that visit the true seed in this declining day, seldom find themselves, either secretly or publicly, mounted on the king's horse, but rather have to experience a baptism into its sufferings, and a fellowship therewith; yet even in this state, if our minds are kept low enough, and in a situation ready to receive and dwell under the divine allotment, there is a strength attends it, of which the most favoured servants, we have cause to believe, are often stripped on their return. No wonder then, if we, who are infants in this service, should be suffered to feel ourselves, as the dry bones in the open valley. Under this state of humiliation before Him who knows all things, and who wisely strips us of our judgment, in order to refine it; how beautiful that reply to the query, " can these bones live ?" thou knowest oh Lord: in this humble situation, how ready are we to receive the resurrection of life, or to wait for it the appointed time, till all unprofitable moisture is exhausted, and the seasons have passed over us!——— A most affecting circumstance it is, that a man, and indeed a family, standing in apparent approbation as ——— did, should bring such dishonour to the cause, and themselves be plunged in such deep distress! It is, however, a proof how we ought, in whatever we do, to fix our eye upon the right object, and to prefer a consistency with the truth, to our appearance in the eyes of men; for certainly if this had been more the engagement of many minds, there would have been preservation experienced from many of these painful and dishonourable circumstances.

1st month 1782—My remembrance of thee was tenderly affectionate, and a solicitude accompanied it, that we may live so near the pure life of truth, having our minds frequently stripped of whatsoever is tinctured with the gilded impurities of nature, as to feel an increase of unity therein. When I am led to consider my own aptness to get from under the power of the cross, a fear is ready to enter, that the garments, the coverings of my mind, which may, in some small degree, have been washed, will again gather their spots, and I become more and more reconciled to them; so that the consequence may be an inability to distinguish betwixt the clean and the unclean. In this necessary perspective of myself, the means of preservation have, in infinite condescension, been discovered; and a willingness frequently to descend to the washing pool, has proved the request of my heart, that He in whose hand I wish to feel myself, may not only be the reprover, but the remover of every opposer of His work. Discouragements arise from without, for on every hand there is cause of mourning, and the few stakes that can be perceived amongst us are ready to fail with weakness; wherefore we see the greater need, with all the vigilance we possess, to repair to that foundation which stands sure; and truly those who are established thereon have engraven upon them that indisputable seal, and most desirable evidence, of divine acknowledgment. Our pilgrimage here seems, and will prove, of so short duration, that the sufferings which attend it for our refinement, are blessings demanding our humble acknowledgment. I have often reflected upon your situation with a sympathy which I trust is measurably of the right kind; and have felt the arduousness of your path, the stability that is required for it, and patient resignation of the cause to Him whose own works alone, or those of His own pure spirit can praise Him, and effect true and profitable deliverance to his dependant children. " What can the wrath and envy of man (if we are tried with it) do unto those that are hid in the secret places of the Almighty, and gathered under the healing wings of the Prince of Peace? since by his armour of light they shall be able to stand in the day of trial."

12th month 1782—I place little dependance on dreams; they are often a mass of confusion; but we are bound to acknowledge that they sometimes contain clear intelligent information or caution. I believe however, it is always safe to attend to the hint, " let him that hath a dream tell [it as] a dream," but the pure word should be spoken more freely, for what is the chaff to the wheat? Thine was expressive of a union with thy friend which is comfortable to her, and from which it is the fervent desire of my mind we may receive strength and instruction in the future movements of our lives; wherein perhaps, if we are favoured to be of any service at all, it may go hand in hand; but what are all the emblems of this fellowship to the thing itself? what are the branches without the Root that bears them? I often wish the great objects in my eye may be solid and permanent; that visionary and delusive gratifications may be proved, by being brought in their infancy to the balance of the sanctuary; and that nothing may resist the fire in doing its office upon that which is light, and which has not been formed and tried in the hand of the Potter and Purifier of his people; but watchfulness is our best retreat, and I find that without it, in this land as well as in our own, there is continual danger of being warped aside, and losing our attention to the secret reproofs and dictates of wisdom.

3d month 1782—I felt a satisfaction in hearing from thee, and finding that the exercises which had attended, were productive of that peace which never succeeds our moving out of the line of pure wisdom, and is therefore an evidence of the Master's approbation; and what more do we wish for? for if that is experienced when we have broken the morsel of bread given to our charge, it is enough for us, and the blessing must be left to that bountiful hand, which owns only its own works. Though poverty was the covering of my mind on my return home, yet I felt no uneafinefs from an apprehenfion of having left thee too foon, but rather a belief that it was right for thee to feel that thou waft ftronger than thou apprehended: and I now hope, that as thou haft afrefh found the divine ability allotted thee, to be fufficient for the work of the day, that thou wilt be more devoted to move alone in future, and become lefs dependant upon reeds fhaken with the wind. It is an excellent thing fimply to mind our own bufinefs, to attend to the path cut out for us individually, and let it be what it may, to be content therewith; becaufe it is only by the members of the body thus keeping their places, that they can be made truly ufeful to one another, and profperous in the caufe wherein they are engaged.

3d month 1782—I can feelingly fympathize with my dear friend in her prefent fituation of mind, and under fome difficulties, which may be encreafed by the want of feeling, baptized elders, fuch as live near the fpring of life themfelves, and whofe deep can call unto the deep in thofe whofe line of fervice varies from their own. Where there are fuch as thefe, they are felt to be ftakes in the divine enclofure about thofe I call the moft tried of the flock, the poor meffengers that blow the trumpet on the holy hill, and have to defcend from thence into the deeps, and awfully to dwell there, humbled under a fenfe of themfelves and *what they are:* and though in this day of weaknefs, each member does not keep in its own function, but numbness and insensibility have seized many, let us trust that our holy Head will not suffer us also to become castaways, if we attend to his direction.——A secret dwelling as in deep waters we know to be safe; and, my beloved friend, may we keep there, grow more and more united to the truth itself, and support one another in the fellowship thereof!

9th month 1782—When an unavailing anxiety has possessed my mind, about the situation of things amongst us, and the wilderness state of the church; I have been led to conclude that it is not consistent with the divine will, that we should be ever impatiently enquiring, " what wilt thou do for thy great name?" but that we should rather centre deep in our own minds, and resignedly and faithfully co-operate with his work in the earth; feeling our minds so reduced as only to pray for that which is the mind of the spirit, even if it required the petition, " feed thy people with thy rod!" In our late visit, we deeply felt, at times, our weakness, and when most baptized thereinto, with our eye single to divine help, we had humbly to observe, that then His strength was manifest in our weakness; and that it was only as we descended to the spiritual brook, and there received with simplicity the heavenly armour, that the battle was blessed, our heads covered therein, and ability found to discover the little ones on whom the purifying hand is turned. I believe I may say we returned under the humbling impression of being unprofitable servants, begging to be enabled to continue suppliants at the gate of wisdom, and to attend in future to the smallest of its pointings. I need not tell thee how agreeable it was to meet my husband at my return home. On our separation, the passage feelingly occurred to, and refreshed my mind; " Lord I have left all to follow thee." To be employed in the cause of truth, and to have the spirit thereof for my companion, appeared, when nature was subordinate, far to surpass every selfish enjoyment in this life, notwithstanding I might prove a vessel of least honour in the family: and on our meeting again, I found there was need of a renewed engraving of these impressions, in order to preserve a preference to the truth, and to keep in our remembrance that we have no continuing city here.

10th month 1782—It is an unspeakable favour, through all, to believe that, if we dwell in the pure life and oneness of the truth, many waters without, or floods of temptation within, will never be able to quench our love, though for a time, when they rise high, they may veil it. The prayer of my spirit is, that my dwelling may be in this hidden life, that I may prefer its substantial operations to either spiritual or temporal enjoyments, and that by it my body and mind may be preserved from running to and fro in the earth, with any blast from the wilderness. But oh the need of " standing still in the watch," the infirmities of our nature are so many and great! Remember me and crave my preservation, that my life at least may be given me for a prey; and may you and I farewel, and increase in that life and love which change not, nor end.

———— 1782—I received thy affectionate letter in due course: it was truly acceptable; and though thou wast far from being forgotten by me, it tended to revive that near sympathy with thy secret spiritual travail, which particularly accompanied my mind when near thee in person, and which I trust proceeded from the cementing influence of divine love, and gospel fellowship.

We meet with but few in this pilgrimage and state of probation, who are dipped in sympathy with us, and know what it is to be destitute of all comeliness. There are many who, were we clad in royal apparel, and had the King's signet always unveiled upon us, would no doubt acknowledge us in the gate; and, in the victory of the heavenly cause, cry, Hosanna! with us in triumph. But what was the path of the Master? Was it not the path for his servants, that they might be encouraged, and have a stedfast example therein? He trod it before them, and endured the several gradations and dispensations of the spiritual warfare; he fasted in the wilderness, till he was an hungred. Let us not then think it strange that the servant is not greater than his Master. Our safety depends upon our watchful attention, that when we are tempted we yield not; but oh! how near does the impatience of our dispositions border upon that language, " command these stones that they be made bread;" forgetting that it is not by bread alone that our hidden life is preserved, but by every word that proceedeth out of the mouth of

God, and by every turning of his divine hand upon us; whereby, in his wisdom, we grow from stature to stature, which by taking thought for ourselves we cannot do. If we are found worthy to stand as pillars in the Lord's house, in this day when there are many heavy burdens to bear, we must be first upon a sure foundation, our dispositions, like those of the disciples that discovered the love of their Master's glory on the mount, must be subservient to divine control; and we must not only learn to descend from the vision of light, but to keep the charge, and tell it to no man until the life of power arise. How hewing and forming are these things! and what instructive traces do they leave of the Master's work, because they reduce self, and convince that no confidence must be placed therein! May it be our experience, dear friend, in the few succeeding steps of our lives, patiently to suffer, and fervently to wrestle for the blessing of preservation.

1st month 1783—What has felt very desirable to me is, that in these outward separations, we may encrease in that which is good, and that whatever befals us may tend to settle us the more in the groundwork of true religion, that therein we may stand, and therein grow; then will the fluctuations of this uncertain state become sanctified to us, and being instructed in the school of Christ, our spirits and conduct will become more conformable to the purity of the Pattern. My fear of myself daily encreases, and I am also apt to think that by looking too much at any evil, we may insensibly be almost drawn into it. It is nevertheless good to survey our standings, to prove our own infirmities, and repair to the place of help. The multiplied distresses, both spiritual and temporal, that have been permitted to befal us in this land, or since I left my own, have often occasioned a secret cry for the continuance of divine preservation; and a little ray of hope that the Lord hath not forsaken us, is all the succour that my poor tossed mind has often felt. There is great need in time of outward perplexity, impartially to examine the cause, to search what there is in us that requires these things; by so doing we may often see couched under them the wisdom of a divine Hand, and that to remove the cause in ourselves, is to go to the root of the matter.

1st month 1783—I feel now, as at many other times, my mind drawn into near affection, and, I trust I may say, that true fellowship with thee, which springs when I am capable of experiencing any better enjoyment than what is natural; but as that only arises from the renewings of life, I am often afraid to speak of it, lest it should fall short of its character in the time of trial: however, I may say I feel that love which many waters and seasons of deep and secret distress, have not quenched nor diminished. A degree of this mark of discipleship reviving in my mind, has sometimes been as a temporary cordial, tending to dispel the gloom of many discouragements, and opening the view to a little pure serene satisfaction. My dear friend, many are the trials of the enemy of our peace to overset us, many have been the assaults which I have met with since I saw thee, far exceeding what I ever knew before. If divine help will condefcend to be near, and preferve me from finking in the pit of difcouragement, juft keep my fpirit alive to confide in his name, and dwell under his power, my heart, I truft, will bow in humble gratitude before him, and acknowledge his might. Our eye is now much fixed upon Yorkfhire; oh! that we may there experience the evidence of divine acceptance, and that, in our movements, or not moving at all, the bleffing of prefervation may attend us. Outward enjoyments, domeftic tranquillity, and the affectionate regard of our friends, are all in themfelves defirable objects, but without this bleffing, what are they? infipid, or fruitlefs delights.

1ft month 1783—As, (in infinite wifdom no doubt) our minds are at times drawn into folitude, fo as to refemble the Pelican in the wildernefs, having no accefs to the habitable parts of the earth, nor fubject to human obfervation, fo it appears confiftent with godly jealoufy that human confolation fhould be forbidden, and that, having our dependance only on a gracious and merciful Father, who deals with us as children who require his chaftifing hand, his rod and his ftaff, we may procure to ourfelves a fafe foundation, with a quiet habitation thereon, out of the reach of human interruptions. Surely there are none fo tried as the poor weak inftruments, that are ufed for the divine will to be communicated through. Thefe require not only the forming of the Potter's hand, but higher degrees of drying, and greater heat in the furnace to prepare them, than almoft any other veffel; nay (if I may be allowed the comparifon) they are like dishes that have to pass thro' the oven for every service, and which, after they are emptied, and the company has enjoyed them, need more washing and care than any other utensil at the table; and great danger there is that, by indiscretion of some sort or other, they will get cracked or broken. I look with dread, I am bowed down and dismayed, at the sight of the precarious standing of such, but especially of my own: the consideration of human weakness, and "how frail I am," is almost my meat and drink. How excellent is the privilege of having a monitor at home, an impartial Friend in our bosom, who, if we enough attend to Him, is able to make us as wise even as our teachers! the reproofs and wounds of this Friend are better than the kisses of an enemy.

1st month 1783—I have now continued about two weeks longer in this place, and have received very affectionate kindness, and great hospitality from my friends. Were there not something in our minds that is panting after superior, more extensive, and secret enjoyments, I have thought myself placed amongst the cordials of life: but without the seasoning virtue of truth, and an evidence (though ever so small) of divine approbation marking, or resting upon, our dwelling place, they are tasteless and insipid enjoyments. Perhaps I have deprived myself of that which is good, and am now too ready to let others share the same; a disposition which I wish not to cultivate, it being highly inconsistent with the benevolence of the gospel, which breathes no language inferior to that of,

"Glory to God in the higheſt, peace on earth, and good will towards men." But how to diſtinguiſh, at times, the grand cauſe amongſt a multiplicity of cauſes, requires wiſdom, undefiled wiſdom, that the immortal birth may be ſurrendered to the breaſt and care of its true mother, and that nothing hurt it, or diminiſh its ſtrength; but that, under all turnings and overturnings, diviſions and ſubdiviſions, it may gradually and ſteadily grow in ſtature, in wiſdom and pure underſtanding, and take to itſelf an everlaſting dominion in us. It is the "deep that calleth unto deep." I thought I felt, on reading thy laſt, ſomething of the mind of truth in reviving a little my drooping ſpirits; a degree of thankfulneſs covered my mind, and I was encouraged to wait the paſſing away of this gloomy night, in comfortable hope of the dawning of a better day, wherein the former and the latter rain may deſcend, to add ſap to the root, and to refreſh the branches. What is it in us that flinches ſo much at ſuffering? It muſt be that fleſh and blood which can never inherit the kingdom. I have beſtowed ſome pains to ſilence it with reaſoning, and arguing the nature of things; but alas! I have ſorrowfully found it fed thereby, and perceived that it is only in humbly abiding under the divine operations, that ſubjection is wrought, and the moſt ſo, when the cauſe was not fully diſcovered; for then the lowly petition aſcends, which at this time covers my ſpirit, Grant me a grain of the precious gift of faith, that I may live and walk thereby.

1st month 1783—O this root of self, when will it be subjected! It perhaps appears more to oppose thy service, but I believe it more secretly prevails in me, and is not under that control and subordination which thou hast it in more minute things. But let us not weigh ourselves by one another; let us rather bring our spirits to the balance of the sanctuary, and if there we want chipping and hewing, not think hard of the instruments that are to do it; but passively and patiently endure all things, in hope to enjoy that little which is our own in the end, having it pure and separated from the vile. My mind has been drawn into great nearness to you many times since we parted. I have feelingly remembered the seasons when, though beset with many secret probations, we might say, We took sweet counsel, and our spirits were baptized together, and prepared thereby to go up as to the mountain of the Lord, and to the house of the God of Jacob, where He has graciously condescended to teach us more and more of his ways, and begotten fresh resolutions in us to walk in His paths. Let us not faint, my beloved friends, but wrestle with Him for the renewal of this blessing; that though it may be our lot often to be separated, our spirits may unite together in holy fellowship, and that pure love which many waters cannot quench, nor all the changes of this uncertain state of being ever diminish.

6th month 1783—My mind is much with you, and I trust it is in that fellowship which can unite with the absent though in suffering, and breathe for the prosperity of the precious truth. I beg to be more and more bound to that, let its appearance amongst men be ever so mean and contemptible; for it is here that we are not afraid of human wisdom and displeasure. But is there not, sometimes, too much fear of this sort, when under that power, and the burthen of that word which, if it met with no obstruction in the instrument, would oftener break the rocks, and be a consuming fire amongst the cedars of Lebanon? May this your season of suffering be blessed to you and the church! and oh! may your hands be strong in the faith, and hold out to the end in patience, that with the church coming out of the wilderness, you may repose on the breast of the Beloved of souls, and your cause centre with Him.

7th month 1783—My best wishes accompany thee, in this stepping out into the awful service of visiting the few scattered professors under our name, and perhaps of unfolding in the fresh openings of life, further manifestations of gospel light to such as are not yet of our fold, particularly in Scotland. I remember that before we entered the borders of that land, and indeed whenever I viewed it in prospect, it was clearly impressed upon my mind, that there was no track for us to go in, nor any footsteps to be depended upon in that journey; but that our attention would be continually required to the fresh pointings and qualifications for service: and on our leaving Scotland, we had greatly to lament a deviation from this pure indwelling of spirit, and unfaithfulness to some manifestations of duty. When the mind, after being engaged in service, has got a little liberty, and feels itself as a bow unstrung, it is too apt to rejoice, and evade the next bending for service; whereby half our commission may be neglected, when we are peculiarly called to watch, to try and to feel every step that we take. Here simplicity and humility are our companions, and if a pure holy zeal covers us, in a state of true dependance, the wisdom of the creature has no part; but the life rising into dominion, and being taken for our guide in every step under the exercise of the gift, we have no need to be anxious for doctrinal arguments to prove what we assert to the people; because this life answering the life in those that hear, can expound and unfold such mysteries as have been hid from ages; and it is only by our single attention to the purity of the gift, and the milk of the word, that we can be preserved in that simplicity which confounds the wisdom of the wise, brings to nought the understanding of the prudent, and exalts the seed of the kingdom. Thus I apprehend the ministers of the gospel are led, not only to teach all nations whither they are sent, but to baptize them into the power of the gospel, however few the number of their words may be. I feel a strong desire for your faithfulness in this journey, and that as you pass through little villages and towns, it may not be without feeling for service, for in this respect we were deficient. Look not too much at your own weakness, but consider the strength of that almighty Arm which works marvellously for those that rely upon it, and gives them faith for their victory. I know there is something in us, when we occasion many people to be called together, that fears for ourselves, and for the truth; it is well, in these times of trial, to consider our own inability, and in whom help and power dwells; for then a calm sometimes allays these anxieties, and spreads upon our minds the beauty and convincing influence of a lively, awful, silent worship, which stands in need of no addition, but which, at times, is accompanied with words in the demonstration and power of the same spirit.

7th month 1783—I think I was scarcely ever sensible of more death and darkness than since I came here: if a little life and light should spring in our future sittings, it may have some reviving effects, for really my spirits are in a drooping way, and my strength also. I expected nothing but suffering on coming here, and thus far it is my portion; this satisfaction, however, attends me, that it is but for a day or two, and I endeavour to lift up my head above sinking too much; but oh for the cause! the testimony of truth seems nearly laid waste, and the pure life crucified. Here are, indeed, many valiants, but what can they do? it is not the servants of themselves, that can make the dry bones live. The little strength I feel, seems to be in endeavouring after a settled retirement of mind out of meetings, and being willing to appear foolish as I am.

7th month 1783—There is a beautiful order in the growth of the spiritual, as well as natural man: he is at first carried and fondled, and it is then generally right to give him what he cries for; in a little time, he makes some efforts to go by himself, which, sooner or later, mostly prove effectual. Presuming now on his own ability, he assumes the air and carriage of a man, and in this confidence goes forward, till his stumblings, his falls, and his wounds, have sufficiently convinced him, that he is but a child, and that his will is no more to be depended upon than his strength. As it was right to indulge the simplicity of his first desires, so now, these becoming mixed with evil instigations, either in the appearance of a friend or an enemy, it becomes necessary, in order to preserve this simplicity, and the divine impressions which may renewedly descend upon it, industriously to repel and guard against the powerful influence of self-love and self-seeking, which is the beginning of our continual warfare. I at times thankfully view some of the exercises of my mind, as a probationary childhood, frequently occasioned by indiscretion, and increased by the growth of the corrupt will with a growing knowledge in divine things; so that I have been and am frequently ready to conclude, I shall one day fall by the hand of this enemy: but oh! may we support the warfare which is mercifully begun! and by depending solely on that Arm, which cut Rahab, and wounded the Dragon, be no ways instrumental ourselves in preventing a maturity in the pure life, and preaching by good works. I hope my dear thou continuest, and will continue to feel thy habitation like the house of Obed-edom. It is indeed distant from us; but of how little consequence is that, when there is fellowship in the circulating life of truth, wherein we are as epistles written in one another's hearts, which are meditated in, at times, to the refreshment of our spirits when drooping and feeble.—It is a blessing not to be lightly esteemed, to be married to those of lively spirits, and clean conduct; not drawing back, but helping forward, that work to which there is a divine calling: and as ——— is among those who are thus blessed, it will, I have no doubt, sweeten many unpalatable cups, and render moderate some blasts from the wilderness of this world, and its corrupt fluctuating spirit.

1st month 1784—Oh the need there is, when we feel a secret divine approbation for some little faithful services, as the answer of well done, carefully to centre this treasure, and leave it in the hands of our great benefactor! for how unfit are our earthly hearts to be entrusted with riches so weighty, and so different in their nature! they are indeed found to be as bags with holes, which lose the precious gift amongst the rubbish of the house. Under these considerations, I am led at times to prefer poverty, and nakedness, and want, to an appearance of wealth, and spending my spiritual substance in riotous living: and to be preserved chaste and faithful in this state, is one of my strongest desires, yet attended, in some degree, with the certain knowledge of how frail I am.

1st month 1784—We have great need, in this day, for clean-handed, single-eyed instruments, in the work of reformation; such as demonstrate, in the particular parts, and general tenour of their conduct, that they truly fear God, and hate covetousness: for, of such only is the pure spiritual building composed; the church, against which, Satan and his agents can never prevail; whereto the nations may gather, behold its purity, and be invited to become living members thereof. But, oh how defiled is our camp! how temporizing are the spirits of those who ought to stand, as valiant soldiers, against spiritual wickedness in high places, and fight manfully under the banner of the Lamb! The world, with its gilded baits, has allured their attention, and attracted their sight, from the example of our holy pattern; it is therefore no wonder, if the work they undertake is superficially done; and that which has been their snare, passes unobserved for want of purification. From a view of these things, I have been led to prefer, and even to request tribulation, mortification, and what may be called evil things, in this life, to an unsubjected mind, being an unsound member in the church, and seeking to be heir of two kingdoms. Whether I am thus preserved or not, I believe that now, as formerly, the lame, the blind, and the dwarfs, will not be accepted to minister of the most holy things, and carry forward the cause of righteousness in the earth, till their application is uprightly, and humbly made to Him, who is the healer of all diseases, and the restorer of ancient paths to walk in.

2d month 1784—Thou hast often been in my remembrance since we parted, and both when hoping and doubting, I have wished to address thee in this way, believing it warrantable now, as in the captivity of the Jews, for thofe who are uprightly, though feebly, concerned for the profperity of truth, to fpeak often one to another; and the trufting that a book of remembrance is written, cafts, in fome depreffing feafons, something of a ray of fpiritual funfhine upon the fpirits in prifon; which, though not a promife of freedom, yet cheers a little, and renders tolerable our unavoidable fituation of mind. A multiplicity of concurring circumftances, paft and in profpect, have of late deeply affected me: the fpirit of Goliah rages from every quarter: its power I feel, the low ftate of the church is evident, and my own weaknefs ftares me in the face. I would be glad to dwell in obfcurity, and have my name blotted out of remembrance. There are many called foldiers amongft us, but oh! how few of fuch as are loyal to the King of kings, and whofe work is diligently to eftablifh his government; infomuch that fuch children as I am are ready to conclude, that if we move at all, our hand muft be againft every one, and every ones hand againft us: for though retirement is what above all things I would choofe for myfelf, yet if I apprehend myfelf called to fervice at all, it is the fervent prayer of my fpirit to be preferved therein from the fear of any man, and from doing the work deceitfully: neverthelefs, the fecret feelings of my mind feem to fay unto the feed, that " bonds await you." May we then poffefs our fouls in patience, and not fear in feafons appointed to contend for our faith!

2d month 1784—Being affected with the general causes of discouragement, and so much afflicted with some particulars, I am ready at times to conclude, I cannot hold fast my faith without wavering in this time of trial. You, my beloved friends, have your share of exercise; and whatever others do, be you faithful unto death, spiritually and naturally, and then will your services be crowned with that life which cannot be gainsayed. We have much disloyalty amongst us to the King of kings, and some who are his subjects want to take from him an improper share of rule. Seeing these things, let us be lowly, and shelter ourselves under the spirit of the Lamb, that the prevalence of this alone may be the weapons of our warfare: though we experience him to be slain as from the foundations of the world, and have to go down into suffering with him, and our faith deeply tried, yet let us remember that He lives and reigns for ever, and that, notwithstanding the combined powers of darkness, of the encrease of His government there shall not be an end.

Our passage through life is like a journey wherein are difficulties and snares; and wherein we find many who say they are going to the same port, and who think they have found out, from longer experience and superior wisdom, a better and somewhat different road; but when we believe them, and make a little trial of their path, how have we, with painful steppings, to return to our tribulated pilgrimage? I feel deeply engaged in my spirit, that I may, and that we all may, look to our own standings, not even to the most approved instruments for instruction, when our application ought to be to the Spirit and example of our Holy Head and High-Priest.

11th month 1784—I am really very poor, but whether enough so I cannot tell. I am however rather more contented than when thou saw me last, having been a short time with ———, and secretly comparing trials a little has done me good: indeed I think it is a wise way, when we imagine ourselves under suffering, to look into the pages of another's book, and meditate in their probations. Here we number our own blessings, and a language sometimes unexpectedly arises, "what shall I render unto Thee for all thy benefits?"

1st month 1785—Though outward separation, and other circumstances inherent to our peculiar stations, may sometimes blunt the continual keenness of natural affection; yet the pure cement of true religious union being more durable in its nature, and of a more preserving quality, it can never be diminished, as our spirits become more and more influenced thereby, and we so transformed by the renewings of the mind, as not only to prove what is the divine will concerning us, but to yield obedience to all its requirings. Under this holy and spiritual canopy is preservation and peace; and whilst the carnal mind, and the wisdom thereof is perplexed, and exposed to almost continual fluctuation and disturbance, they that are gathered here (not from speculation, or the line of another's experience) but from a living and heart-felt sense of the certainty of divine truth, can acknowledge, " we have a strong city " and that" salvation is appointed for walls and bulwarks." Oh! that we may more and more know our dwellings to be within this holy enclosure; for the incorruptible inheritance is no where else to be found, than in knowing the divine will, and doing it.

7th month 1785—There is a love which I trust is ours, independent of visible signs, and distinguished by that freedom which the truth gives, whether it be in speaking or in being silent. The substance of true friendship is hidden; and it is not of a corruptible nature, if we keep it in its right soil. Though its branches are often cut down by the good Husbandman, yet the stump is fastened, like that we read of, with a band of iron and brass in the tender grass of the field; and when we renewedly experience that the Most High reigneth, it puts forth again, and excellent dignity is added unto it. I feel as I write an affectionate nearness to you, and oh! may we all so dwell under the dew of heaven, and the times and dispensations appointed to pass over us, as that the joy of the Lord may fully become our strength!

8th month 1785—Perhaps this may find thee in some desolate place, where my spirit salutes thee in the renewed feeling of sympathetic affection, and comfortable hope that, through the multiplied trials of thy day, and of the present journey, thou wilt be secretly supported with the arm of Omnipotence, and refreshed after many weary steps, with the streams of divine consolation; so that thou wilt still be able to do all things, through Him that strengtheneth thee.

My mind is much with thee and thy valuable companions, and sometimes I think I feel a fellowship in some of your sufferings, not doubting but a measure of them is mingled in the cup of your present service: and why should it not be so, when we consider the tribulated path of the great Master, and that it is enough for the servant to be as his Master, and the disciple as his Lord. The wise purposes of the great Potter are not always seen; there are many things in the process of forming the clay, or a people to His praise, the necessity whereof is not always manifest to those that stand by; and I have thought that in the line you are, have been, or may be led in, some amongst you may find openings to services, which not being found in the pages of past experience, may occasion doubts and dismay, and perhaps a profitable query, hath the Lord done this? yet it is also profitable to remember, that it is not for the instrument to say to him that useth it, " what doest thou ?" I do not wonder at your feelings in being so separated in person from the visible church. I remember, though in a less degree, similar impressions which have never left me; and indeed my mind is comforted in finding an encreasing attachment to, and value for the precious fellowship of the brotherhood, though it is not always found in an entire similarity of prospects, and of ways and means of prosecuting good, so much as in an uniform, upright concern for the prosperity of the cause, which under the shadow of heavenly instruction, is one of the best cements that fellow travellers can experience. We should be glad, in our passing along, to find more of it; and were this united engagement to appear in an honest search into the real state of individuals, of families, and of meetings, some of Jericho's walls might fall in the contest, and people's attention get turned to desolated Jerusalem. But it is a land of mists and fogs, yea, in some places, of clouds and of thick darkness: may that over-ruling power which has its ways in the deeps, dispel these temporary things, and usher in a greater display of pure light, that they who are engaged to work, and are appointed for it, may work in the light, and fully approve themselves children thereof.

11th month 1785—I feel for ———, and wish her an increase of faith, or a more free exercise of that which she has, that so, it may fully be accompanied with such works as the great Father of the family has assigned her; perhaps both she and I would fare better, did we look more inward and less outward in our reflections upon ourselves, and for every future supply of wisdom and strength. It is surely a wonderful attainment to live by faith; it is deep beyond human penetration, and seems to comprehend all that is needful for a follower of Christ to experience: but the trial of it remains to be more precious than that of gold, and preferable to the best of our faculties that we can substitute for it. Poor ——— she has often felt near to my life. It is the poor that can most feelingly salute the poor, and dip with them in their afflictions;

go with them to the house of mourning; and, when the holy anointing is poured forth, rejoice together in hope.

1st month 1786—I hope that county is by this time profitably visited, or rather the seed therein, a place where I once thought it was the hardest to find (however in myself) of any I was ever in. But places and persons alter; and where death most reigned, perhaps life may now most eminently abound; and life is never more acceptable than when it succeeds a total death, nor light, than when it springs out of the greatest obscurity. To dwell with that which teaches to die daily, and to be preserved from the sleep of carnal death, is an attainment I sometimes covet; but flesh and blood had rather be sustained with a little of yesterday's manna, and retain a former evidence of life, than undergo, from day to day, in religious services, the conflicting exercise of being buried in baptism, though it is blessed with the resurrection of divine virtue and power: and the reason I apprehend is, because no flesh can glory herein; it therefore opposes this work, and the resisting of this opposition with the little strength we have, truly occasions a continual warfare to the christian traveller.———The present is a scene of conflict and probation; but when we are strengthened to look over it, to that glorious habitation, whose walls are salvation, whose gates are praise, and whose inhabitants no more say they are sick; there is something so animating in the prospect, that we are willing to endure all things to attain it. Let us then take courage in hope, and faithfully endeavour to do our present best.

4th month 1786—We have often conversed about friends in Ireland, and felt the glow of true love therein; which, tho' not much expressed to themselves, is yet a living spark in all our breasts, which many waters cannot quench; nor will long separation be able to erase those epistles which are written by the finger thereof, and in which there is a liberty sometimes allowed for the spirit to meditate, with a degree of strengthening consolation, especially when, by the clearness of the characters, we find one another as fellow pilgrims, travelling after the resurrection of pure life, and making steady advances towards that city which hath foundations. Upon this object I sometimes fix my eye, with renewed resolutions, thro' holy help, to press forward thro' the difficulties of the present scene, and to count all things but as dross and dung that I may win Christ, and be found in him; not having on my own righteousness, but the righteousness of faith in Christ, that thereby I may attain the resurrection of His power, the fellowship of His sufferings, and be made conformable to His death. The spirit is willing thus to endure, but the flesh and its inherent propensity to ease, creates a warfare, wherein I sometimes fear, the natural and best life will entirely fail.

5th month 1786—We are sometimes like pilgrims whose faith and patience are at a low ebb; and were it not for the gracious condescension of

Him who regardeth even the sparrows, and whose arm of everlasting strength is underneath in seasons of drooping and dismay, we should be ready at times to faint; but it is the renewings of holy help that become strength in weakness to those that put their trust in it; and is a present sufficiency when we are not able to provide for ourselves. May thou be fully grounded in this trust, that thereby, in times of discouragement and sifting, thy stability may endure, and thy experience encrease in the knowledge that all things work together for good, to those that truly love the appearances or manifestations of the divine will. I believe thou knowest that I dearly love thee, and, I may add, have felt sweet unity with thy spirit; and therefore hope ever freely to pour into thy mind any little hints which may in that love revive towards thee. And now, as thou hast put thy hand to a good work, let me say, look not back; and when the certainty of thy being rightly anointed for it is withdrawn, which is no uncommon trial, look not then to the sentiments of others for support and encouragement; but labour after true quietude and patience of soul, whereby thou mayest, with comfortable assurance, in the right time, have thy head raised in hope, and thy growth in religious experiences be less superficial, than I fear is often the case even with those who have been put forth by the heavenly shepherd. There is no consolation, no confidence, wisdom, or strength, like that which proceeds from the deep and hidden spring, whereunto we must learn to dig, if ever we are rightly grounded in the work of sanctification: and as the divine will is our sanctification, if we obey it; be not slack in surrendering thyself thereto. I write not these things from an apprehension that thou needs them more than others, for my sentiments of thee are very different; but I wish thee to set out independent of any instrumental help, except that which is sent from the fountain of purity; and to look to no example further than it is consistent with the holy pattern.

7th month 1786—I remember it is said, that even " when the sons of God met together, Satan came also amongst them;" so that if he did so again, it was no new thing; and we are instructed by the angel how to deal even with him; not to bring a railing accusation, but patiently, and with christian fortitude, to commit the great cause to that power which can protect it, and rebuke the adversary, but not in our way, and in our time; for it is in general most eminently displayed when the creature is reduced, and nothing left in us that can boastingly exult even over Satan himself. To behave ourselves wisely in the church, humbly and watchfully to fear meddling with things too high for us, things into which our minds are not renewedly baptized, is a care which I wish we may ever preserve; for herein a godly jea⸺sy over ourselves and our own spirits, will help ⸺ ⸺tre us in that meekness for which the pat! ⸺ ⸺rue judgement are appointed, will give a rie⸺ ⸺ of what is opposition to the truth, and ⸺ ⸺ ⸺ot, and how to use the armour of light; which, when rightly put on in meetings for discipline, unfolds the simplicity of truth, and discovers the pure disinterested foundation of those who are engaged to contend for the faith. It is becoming the nobility of the cause of righteousness, to see its warriors so unfeeling of personal opposition, as to return good for evil, and patiently to endure all things, seeking an opportunity to bless, by candidly opening each others understandings, and then generously forgiving. There is no doubt, but that, in our society, if the root and ground of christian discipline in ourselves were attained to, and abode with, meetings for the promulgation of it in the general, would be more owned by their members being baptized by one spirit into one body, and more crowned with that life which is peculiarly in reserve for those, who have been faithful to the death of the cross in themselves. I am often humblingly convinced, that whatever I do in the sacred offices of the church, if it be the fruit of speculation, a lively imagination, or only a desire to render myself useful, however suitable it may seem, yet not proceeding from some little influence of the holy anointing, which lets me see myself with others, it is sure to leave a painful corroding sense upon my own mind, which I am afraid I have sometimes charged others with being the cause of, rather than myself. Thus danger appears on every hand, except we are watchful and humble; but " the humble the Lord teacheth of his ways, and the meek he guides in the paths of judgment: "thy gentleness (said David) hath made me great."

8th month 1786—I see abundant occasion to watch the spring in myself from whence my rejoicings and depressions come. Self is a subtil enemy, insinuating itself into the company of the purest intentions, and approved services, claiming a share of their peace, and of the spoil of the most righteous victories over every enemy but itself. A furnace, however, is wisely prepared for gold, where this dross discovers itself by separation; so that if we are zealous enough to get rid of it, we must frequently retire to the test, submit to whatever degree of purification the great Refiner sees meet, and cheerfully endure hardness under His gracious protecting power; for, according to my experience, I take this redemption of the pure life from all self-seekings, to require the closest combat, and most intrepid perseverance of a christian, in order to gain access to that river which makes glad the city of God, and to inherit the promises of the gospel in their own purity; where the edge of many sorrows and trials is blunted, when they have nothing to strike at but holy humility. O 'tis a blessed experience which my soul fervently craves! I sometimes think I gain a little ground towards it, when a discovery of its animating glory, substantial feeding, and impregnable defence, is made to my understanding; but, on finding how little capacity I have to receive things genuinely divine, the acknowledgment is readily made, that I know nothing as I ought to know, which is only attained by an experimental growth and eftablifhment therein; and yet fhort of this I fometimes defire to find no reft.

10th month 1786—Experience teaches us, that it is not always we are capable of even enjoying that good and profitable communion which, by virtue of the key of David, is fometimes opened for our prefent refrefhment and encouragement, in our path of deep proving and frequent difmay; much lefs of fo refting in it, as always to be ready for the expreffion of thofe things which are not at our command. I conclude thou knoweft that ——— has been fometime in a low depreffed fituation of mind, but her company had a favour in it, of which fhe herfelf was not fenfible, as is generally the cafe with thofe who are under the moft unmixed difpenfations of purifying virtue. That ftate wherein all fenfe of comelinefs is taken away, and under which we are clothed, as the prophet Daniel thought himfelf, with corruption, is that which appears to me the moft acceptable, and no doubt is the beft prepared to receive the language of, " arife, thou art greatly beloved of the Lord;" the chaftening of thefe having been feen, and their many mournings heard, by the gracious ear of the Lord of Sabaoth. How different would things be amongft us as a people, if all thofe who wifh to be confidered as under the divine forming hand, and who are ready to ftep into fervice, were but enough emptied, and their beauty ftained in their own eyes! many fpacious buildings on a fandy foundation would then be thrown down, and there would be more exercife and care in fearch of the immoveable Rock of ages, which really in many places seems grievously neglected. My prospects are often mournful when I look at myself, there weakness and inexperience in some necessary refinements are sorrowfully manifest; and on taking a view of the state of the visible church, we see many of its members so diseased that they cannot perform their allotted functions, nor edify the body, though they retain their places there: the redeemed sanctified church how small! and in what a wilderness state! So that to look at ourselves, at the degenerate, or at the preserved church, ministers discouragement, and shews us the necessity of turning our attention another way; inward, instead of outward, and there waiting for the renewings of that power by which the worlds were made, and receiving supplies for spiritual wants at the first almighty Hand.

1st month 1787—Your joint affectionate salutation came duly to my hands, and with the sympathy expressed in it, afforded me a little of that consolation which the drooping mind sometimes longs to partake of, when meditating on its own weakness and unworthiness of the renewed proofs of friendly regard and christian fellowship. It is pleasant indeed for brethren to dwell together in unity; and O that in order to retain this mark of discipleship, our eye may be single! for this leads to a communion still more excellent and pure, than that which we enjoy with each other in this mixed state of things, even a communion with the light which discovers all things, and is the life of those that believe in it. Yes I do know your path, and that it is a tribulated one: may you run your race therein with patience; for "tribulation worketh patience, patience experience, and experience hope, and hope maketh not ashamed, because the love of God, (and not of ourselves) is shed abroad in our hearts." Here is a foundation, which the gates of hell cannot prevail against, and which, as we keep to it, will preserve us from being soon shaken in mind, or troubled with those changeable things which in the course of our pilgrimage may befal us. I hope you will continue to keep in your remembrance a poor little sister, beset with many discouragements, and sifted with many fears and doubtings, particularly respecting our future movements; for I endeavour what I can to leave the things that are behind.

4th month 1787—Your company was pleasant to us, and the remembrance of you is so, and I trust will continue as long as the sincere engagement of our minds is to be branches in the same Vine. Though, separately and unitedly, we may experience the chilling blasts of winter, and feel the dryness and strippedness peculiar to that season; yet learning in the school of Christ, in every state to be content, and perceiving with encreasing clearness, where the sap remains, we can rejoice therein, and salute each other in true poverty of spirit.

4th month 1787—I received a kind encouraging letter from thee some months ago, when, with many others, I was about the remains of our dear friend ————. We had been paying, for a few days before, the last office of friendship to him, and were witnesses to the awful conflicts of his spirit, in struggling, after many years disobedience to the openings of truth, for that eternal peace for which his soul was poured forth like water, and his bones seemed out of joint; but divine compassion was near, through the efficacy of renewed visitation, to gather into the heavenly garner. The season was altogether so deeply affecting to my mind, which was low and depressed when I went, and I got so involved in the gloomy passages of death through which he had passed, that it seemed as if many circumstances attending my continuance in mutability, were lost in the prospect of that solemn period wherein mortality must be put off. But on reading that part of thy letter wherein thou sayest, that in thy late illness, thy hope was abundantly confirmed in the invisible power of an endless life, I was favoured with a little glimpse of the saints inheritance, which, at times, has revived ever since, as a cordial to my mind: for in the course of divine wisdom, the hand of affliction, and deep spiritual probation, has lain steadily upon me for many months. Thou wouldst hear of an illness I had at Sheffield, which occasioned my dear husband's hasty return. My dwelling, for some time, seemed to be at the gates of death both spiritually and naturally; being in that state wherein I could say with the spouse, that "I sought him whom my soul loveth, yea I sought him upon my bed, and found him not," yet this invisible Arm being underneath, was graciously revealed in an acceptable time, when, through sore tribulation, a resigned frame of mind became more my experience.

5th month 1787—If the right thing does but prevail in the approaching solemnity, it may be a time of healing. Those whose spiritual faculties are alive in the truth, can hardly fail of beginning to feel an exercise on that account ; and no doubt it is necessary that it should be so, in order to prepare and reduce the minds of friends to a state of child-like simplicity, and that abasedness of self, which endureth all things, hath nothing to lose, and therefore, with christian firmness, rejoiceth in that tribulation, by which the pure lowly seed of the kingdom triumphs in overcoming evil by that which is good. Thou and others have had to drink many bitter cups in that place ; and it may be that, through patient perseverance in well-doing, in secret suffering with the seed, maintaining the faith in that power through which miracles are still wrought, the day is approaching, wherein that life which is the light of men may become more conspicuously the crown and diadem of our assemblies, and of the services performed in the church.

5th month 1787—I received thy letter, and was pleased to hear from thee, though the account of thy health, &c. was not so favourable as might be wished; but I hope that after thou got set off from home, and became resigned to what had sometime appeared right, thou would revive both in body and mind. I have frequently known it to be the case with myself, having been often worst just before setting out, when the mind was depressed with the weight of future engagements, and loaded with the sense of its own exceeding great weakness, and inability to do any good; and at the same time, having the comfortable enjoyment of divine help veiled till the needful season. This experience was never more confirmed to me than in the present journey, nor the sufficiency of that arm, which remains to be mighty to save, is strength in our weakness, and a present helper in the needful time. If we are but favoured in our future steppings, to encrease in this experience, our trials which are in the way to it will not be too heavy, in comparison of that pure consolation which they produce: and as we are endeavouring (all of us I hope) to move forward in a line of simplicity and faithfulness to what we apprehend is right, don't let us add to our difficulties, by admitting carnal reasonings, and taking too much thought for to morrow; but rather labour after that great attainment of living one day at once.

6th month 1787—You will see by the foregoing, that we are arrived at the intended place of our abode, and have ventured to ask at last for a recommendation from our friends of the monthly meeting. I trust it is with diffidence, and the humbling sense that we are liable to err, that we take this step; and yet, as it appears in the way to peace, it is no doubt safest to take it, and also most consistent with good order. We wish not to get from under that disposition which, in the feeling of creaturely weakness, " feareth always," lest the subtle, transforming enemy should beguile us, induce to eat of that which is not good, and beget a confidence in our own strength and sufficiency to preserve ourselves. A self-righteous spirit is greatly to be dreaded; and though a state of doubting and discouragement is attended with many more sorrows, yet if the faith remains unshaken, it is at times refreshed with that precious dew, and the springing up of that well of life, which make amends for all, secretly replenish the drooping, yet waiting mind, and encourage it to press forward in the way which the vulture's eye hath not seen, nor any natural fierceness ever trod therein. Well! I trust so much we may say, that our minds, since leaving England, have been bowed in contrition before him who sees in secret, and settled, sometimes, in a quiet dependance upon his almighty Arm, rather desiring to be sustained in obscurity, than to be accounted any thing amongst men.

8th month 1787—Your joint salutation was truly acceptable; for though our love was not lessened, yet the sensible feeling of it, on reading your letter, was comforting to us, and strengthened the desire, that neither heights nor depths, things present nor things to come, may ever be able to separate us, either from the love of the great Shepherd, or from any of his faithful flock; of which number, may we, beloved friends, approve ourselves in all humility and godly care, enduring hardness as good soldiers of Jesus Christ, and not in our wills entangling ourselves with the affairs of this life; but seeking above all things to please Him who hath mercifully called us into the spiritual warfare. Ah poor ———— indeed! any thing that denotes the entrance of the wolf, seems to touch my tenderest feelings; because that little part of the great Shepherd's flock has been peculiarly visited, and their welfare the object of my frequent and fervent solicitude. Oh what need there is of watchfulness! truly the wolf cometh to tear and destroy, though, in order to deceive, he may put on the sheep's clothing: so that nothing but the true light can discover the hidden things of his dishonesty.——I have had cause to say, since leaving my native country, that the divine hand is full of blessings, and that our real comforts depend not so much upon outward circumstances, as on that holy attractive influence, which at times graciously opens a passage for the humbled mind, out of the cumbers and discouragements of the present time, into a state resembling the green pastures of life, and enables to lie down in quiet resignation as beside the still waters; leaving future events, when we have done our best, to that power which can turn the wilderness into a fruitful field, and cause the fruitful field to be counted for a forest. When this good is mercifully near, and we are favoured with the common comforts of life, there ought to be a grateful acknowledgement thereof, as well as obedient returns.

8th month 1787—Thy brotherly salutation confirmed a hope I had entertained, that there lived in both our minds such a degree of true love, that whether we thus conversed together, or not, we should nevertheless be favoured to feel one another in our respective lots, and experience the truth of that saying, " deep uttereth unto deep." My dwelling, in general, has seemed so much in twilight, that meditation suited me better than action, and the increase of my acquaintance with the everlasting *Friend*, whose name is Wonderful, and whose works are inconceivably so to the natural mind, has seemed an enjoyment of the very essence of all friendship. In seasons of awful retirement, since I came this time to this land, my spirit has saluted the few fathers, the brethren and sisters, yea, and the instructors too, whose counsel is the counsel of truth, and whose joy is in its prosperity: and O! that my steppings amongst you, may be such as to bring no dishonour, nor be the occasion of stumbling to any! I wish to be the companion of such as faithfully and secretly labour for the encreasing prevalence of gospel power; that so, through its purifying and sanctifying operations, every work may be wrought, and become an object of the blessing which makes truly rich. Tribulations are undoubtedly the lot of all, who are seeking to follow their Lord and Master in the Regeneration; but He who knows what they stand in need of, in His own due and appointed time, reveals to them His consolations, if they are willing to dive deep enough for them; for thou knowest it is in the deeps that wonders are seen, and pearls procured. If I knew how to put into words, the variety of my sentiments and feelings since coming to Clonmel, the freedom I feel with thee rather urges me to it; but someway or other, they seem enveloped in an undesigned secrecy, and whenever I attempt to unfold, there is a sudden restraint, like the turning of a double lock, and a wise and gracious intimation, to keep in my tent. The Lord is the tent of Jacob. How defirable is it then to be of the wreftling feed, the Jews inward, " of the circumcifion that worfhip God in fpirit, rejoice in Chrift Jefus, and have no confidence in the flefh :" for thefe, knowing in whom they have believed, have the refuge of the righteous to flee to; and being thus exercifed and favoured, no matter how little and fimple fuch appear, how much they feel their own weaknefs, nor how proftrate they lie at the feet of their Mafter, where, with reverent attention His gracious words are heard and received.

I have often feared that, for want of faith enough herein, and a patient waiting in the abafement of felf, for the renewed revelation of the divine will, the carrying forward of the Lord's work, both in individuals, in the vifible church, and in the earth in general, fhould be retarded; and thofe defigned to be the inftruments thereof fhould forbear to follow the Lamb through fuffering, and to fight under His banner, fhould lofe that hope which maketh not afhamed (becaufe the love of God is fhed abroad in the heart) and caft away their fhield, as though it had not been anointed. Well! may we profit by thefe confiderations; and looking forward beyond the things that are feen which are temporal, to the things that are not feen which are eternal, hold faft our faith, and the profeffion of it without wavering, feeing that he is faithful who hath mercifully called us.

I obferve thy confignment of a few lovely plants to my care; but hoping and believing that they are divinely cared for, and are already taught where to feek their own bread, I feel particularly cautious of being the means of drawing their attention to any fource of comfort or inftruction, inferior to that which has been opened in the fecret of their own fouls. I wifh them to be more and more acquainted with, and fingly to rejoice in, the voice of their beloved; and I know this is all thou covets for them. But we muft both allow, that vifited minds are fometimes in danger of feizing and refting in fecondary confolations, by placing an undue dependance upon the inftrument of their good, and being thus prevented from getting down to thofe nether fprings, where, with pure and humble rejoicing, the fpirit draweth water, and no flefh glories. I do not mean that thefe dear girls are in any danger of being too much attached to me; becaufe they have neither occafion to be fo, nor are fo unwife; but though I love them, and have apprehended myfelf conftrained to demonftrate it, yet my own ftate generally feels an object of the compaffion and fympathy of the feebleft traveller Zion-wards; and this confcioufnefs makes me keep much at home, and moftly in my chamber, where the fweet fociety of my beloved Robert Grubb, and our truly valuable ———, fends back, now and then, a rifing figh, and urges me to number my bleffings; fetting before me the comfortable experience of the Apoftle, which I am zealoufly prefſ-ing after, that of learning "in all states to be content." We have been favoured with many epistolary visits from our friends in England, which are not unlike little brooks by the way; but ah, we may sit by them till they dry up! however, comforts they are in their proper places.

9th month 1787—Every blessing is at the disposal of unerring wisdom; and our true enjoyments are generally proportioned to the resignation our minds attain, to surrender whatever we possess to the turnings of the divine hand; counting nothing truly good but what is purified by it. This is a state which sweetens the bitterest cups; and sees beyond the transient gratifications of a worldly superficial spirit; and is only arrived at by a single attention to, and humble waiting and dependance upon, the secret monitions of the spirit of truth. —Pleasant prospects, or enjoyments of any kind, are often much veiled from my view, or shaded with a gloom, which the fallacy of human judgment, and the futility of all natural gratifications, cast upon the most lively and lawful ideas: having, therefore, fixed our eye upon one glorious object, O may it be preserved single to the end of the race! that our running being with patience, and the steps we take attended with light at the finishing of the work assigned us, we may then be indisputably convinced, that having had no continuing city here, we have found one which hath foundations.

9th month 1787—As the present scene is, consistent with the nature of things, chequered with a variety of circumstances and feelings, we must endeavour after that fortification of spirit, which so endures all things as to profit by them, and render ourselves objects of the care of the great Shepherd. Just to arrive at an attainment of this kind, is nearly all our drooping minds are led to desire, without any extraordinary exertions for enjoyments out of the line of divine appointment. I seem, at times, more and more encompassed with doubts and fears; faith is often deeply tried, and such depressions for a little while come over me, that conscious of having ventured, at the call, to walk as on the sea, and the supporting evidence withdrawn, my secret cry resembles poor Peter's when he said, " save Lord or I perish." Nothing short of divine compassion, and the renewed extension of holy help, can strengthen us to press forward with acceptance through the few succeeding probations of our day, and open in us that eye of faith which, looking beyond them all, brightens at the glory that shall be revealed unto those, whose garments have been washed and made white by the spirit and power of the Lamb. There is something in us so prone to settle down at ease in prosperity, that without some fatherly chastisements, we might forget from whom we receive our spiritual and temporal blessings.

10th month 1787—My mind, on returning and since, was favoured with a secret humble trust that I was not out of the way of my duty, in accompanying to Enniscorthy and Carlow, nor in leaving you at the latter place; though my stay afterwards in Waterford was not unaccompanied with that mortification, wherein no flesh can glory, and which was, no doubt, in mercy dispensed to us, to keep the poor vessel in such a degree of sanctification and honour, as to be at all fit for use in the spiritual family. I conclude that I need more of this kind of dispensations than others, because I think more of them falls to my lot, which proves there is more to mortify. But though I often imagine myself ready to faint, yet my fervent prayer is that I may not utterly; but rather be strengthened to endure the cross, and despise the shame of creaturely abasement, looking to the Author of all true faith, for such renewed supplies as to steer safely through this uncertain state of being, and for ability, in the due and appointed time, to finish the wisely allotted portion of work, in reverent dependance that that which is right, and abundantly more than we deserve, will be mercifully recompensed. In the service wherein thou art now engaged, I trust help will not fail of being afforded in the needful time, so as to give you all abundant cause humbly to acknowledge, in the winding up of your visit, that ye have lacked nothing. Perhaps the line of your proceeding, as to passing from place to place, is right; but some way my mind follows you with a sort of regret, that more time was not allowed to have visited, if truth had opened the way, the families of friends in the station of ministers and elders. There is much truth in a common saying, that the work which is well done, is twice done; and though this may be found the more mortifying and arduous part of the service, yet the necessity and propriety of it being great, the peace resulting from faithful labour therein, would no doubt have been proportioned. But this seems like an unseasonable hint, and I don't know any use there may be in dropping it, except by way of preface to an observation I was about to make, that friends upon religious visits often appear to be cramped in their passing along, from a sort of human prudence which dictates their making a long string of appointments, perhaps exceeding what is perceived by the eye of faith: thus they may be prevented from approving themselves those simple, humble followers of the great Master, which in the sincerity of their own hearts they have earnestly desired to be. Whether this proceeds from the want of faith in individuals, or the undiscerned influence of general custom, I know not, but certainly it is a safe and hidden path which the christian traveller walks in, when, in no respect, he desires to take the lead, but resignedly gives himself up to be led, step by step, through the difficulties of his allotted line of service.

11th month 1787—I received this morning, with comfort, the long retained token of thy affection; and can assure thee I am poor enough to enter, with heart-felt sympathy, into the situation thou describes, possessing nothing whereon to build hopes of divine acceptance, unless renewed by the creative word of Omnipotence, and replenished with strength to hold on my way. Let us not then cast away our confidence, nor conclude ourselves unprofitably tried, when we see ourselves as we are; but rather rejoice in this tribulation, and temptation to call in question all that selfish propriety, which human nature would subtilly suggest to us as wrought by the heavenly Hand. Count it all joy that thou art so cloathed with a secret sense of corruption, and art sensible of thy own incapacity to do any good thing; and rather desire to live long under these humbling impressions, than to be taken away from all opportunity of magnifying that " grace, by which thou art what thou art," poor as thou thinkest thyself. Should we be foolish enough to think we know any thing, the voice of Wisdom would soon inform us, that we know nothing as we ought to know: in patience then possess thy soul, and keep in view an encreasing resignation to every secret pointing to duty. We are very apt anxiously to look for that good in our own way, and in our own time, which is only to be obtained by doing the divine will, after we have known it; forgetting that they who err herein, are beaten with many stripes: if this is not now thy state, the hint will do thee no harm. He who knows what is best for us, wisely makes us weary of ourselves and all visible objects, in order to beget that hunger and thirst after righteousness, to which the blessings and promise belong; and so to attach us, in sacred union with himself, and love to His cause, as that in these days of lukewarmness in holy zeal, when the pure seed, through desertion, breathes the powerful query, " whom shall we fend, and who will go for us?" we may, in fingleness of heart, and living faith in divine fufficiency, anfwer, " here am I, fend me." Though this feems an intercourfe fuperior to what we often think is ever allowed us, yet the gentle movings of the fpiritual life, and the fubjected difpofition of our minds thereto, in my apprehenfion, ftrongly refembles it; and if many vifited young people in this land, as well as my own, had placed their dependance upon the fanctifying operation of that facred fire, which quickens the mind and prepares the facrifice, rather than confulted vainly with flefh and blood, they would have been ftronger in the faith, and more of them righteous contenders for it.

11th month 1787—It is by a fingle dependance upon that divine and creative power, by which all things were made that are made, that we find hard things made eafy, and the mixture of human events fo fanctified, as to be rendered falutary portions; the immortal part in us is ftrengthened to afcend, as with wings of faith and love, that mountain fpoken of by the prophet, where " nothing can hurt or deftroy." A true gofpel fpirit fo ftrongly refembles this defirable habitation, that when, in fome degree of its own purity, it breaks in upon our impoverifhed minds, we are renewedly convinced that flefh and blood hath not revealed it unto us; but humbly fubmiting to its operations and directions, felf becomes of no reputation, " and the Lord alone is exalted in that day." I feel, as I am writing, a fecret breathing for thy brother's and thy prefervation, and encouragement to pursue invariably the one thing needful, because it is sealed, that *that* shall never be taken away. The purity and permanency of heavenly treasure, are objects of no small magnitude to the enlightened mind, which has seen the fluctuation of visible enjoyments, and the vanity of all its efforts, without divine assistance, to obtain the smallest particle of true spiritual bread, or one drop of that consolation which is only derived from the pure gift, or well in us springing up into life everlasting. But it is not enough to be enlightened; we must also wait, in the abasement of self, for the thing spoken of and desired; and be willing to accept the Apostle's exhortation, not to be conformed to this world, but transformed by the renewing of our minds, so as to prove what is the good and perfect, and acceptable will, and then to do it, even at the loss of human approbation, and all the riches of the unregenerate will and wisdom of the creature. Here we learn the mystery of buying the truth, and selling all that we have for it; a mystery which, amongst many more, is hid from the wise and prudent, and revealed unto the babes in Christ. I often lament my unfitness to receive these things, and a disposition, out of the clearness and power of the gospel, to accommodate myself, particularly in company, to a worldly spirit, rather than suffer as a fool for the seed's sake; and yet I trust I am making war against it, and have victory in view.

1st month 1738—To be furnished with that excellent armour thou speaks of, is truly desirable, and when without it, the prayer of my heart is, quietly to keep in my tent; and even with it, to make no boast, nor to use it but by renewed commission. It is one of the essentials for the poor christian traveller in every station in life; because of the open attacks, the side blows, and crafty pursuits of our unwearied adversary. I feel them daily, and long for an increase of strength to resist him, stedfast in the faith. He many times seeks to make our hearts sad, when the Lord has not made them sad, and to perplex and embitter our passage through life, when he perceives that *that* is the length of his chain. We propose setting off for Cork in the morning. Even that is a burden; and I might soon work myself up to believe that I am not able to go half way to Clogheen. How admirably wise, and adapted to the weakness of our frame, was that exhortation of the great Master, " take no thought for to-morrow :" this, and such like compassionate counsel, sometimes drops into my mind in the midst of my conflicts, and proves to be words of that kind which both winds and waves obey.

2d month 1788—Though the root of any good affection be alive yet there is but one right season prescribed in divine œconomy for it to manifest itself in the branches, by causing them to bud, blossom, and bear fruit; and that being the spring-time of divine favour, when the Sun of Righteousness breaks forth upon the Lord's plantation, we must wait for it in patient, though earnest expectation, that as our abiding is in the allotment of pure wisdom, the winter (however long) will in time be past, the rains and tempests will subside, the time of the singing of birds come, and the voice of the turtle be heard in our land: then, though we enjoy it in but a small degree, we can falute each other in fpirit and word, and hail all thofe who, like Mary, are bearing precious feed, let their ftations in religious or civil fociety be what they may. A falutation of this fort fprings in my heart to my endeared friends; to the parents who have known Him that is from the beginning, and to the younger branches who have meafurably been ftrengthened to overcome the wicked one; fincerely defiring, that as we have, through abundant mercy, been begotten again to a lively hope by the power of the firft refurrection, we may, through our varied exercifes, keep our eye fingle to the preferving power of divine love, and to that inheritance which is incorruptible and fadeth not away, referved in heaven for thofe who are kept by the virtue thereof, and the precious gift of faith unto the laft day. For herein is great joy, when outward circumftances, and the accufer of the brethren fpeak trouble; here the tribulated chriftian traveller finds an undefiled reft, and by the light commits his fpirit in pure refignation to the guiding hand of Omnipotence; feeling to the confolation of his afflicted foul, that for all his omiffions and commiffions, he has an advocate with the Father, not an High Prieft that cannot be touched with a feeling of our infirmities, but one tempted in like manner, and who knows how to fuccour thofe that are tried. Well might the Pfalmift, who was fo largely acquainted with the dealings of infinite wifdom, exclaim, " how excellent is thy loving kindnefs, O Lord; becaufe thereof, the fons of men put their truft under the fhadow of thy wing."

3d month 1788—We were at their week-day meeting here yesterday, and had a large public meeting in the evening, in both of which, I trust, we were owned by the Master of all rightly gathered assemblies, and might have been more so, if resignation, and a willingness to appear weak and foolish as we are, had been more experienced. I often think that if, in this respect, we were sufficiently humble, we should fare better than we do; and that, whilst we were preserved from foolish preaching, the foolishness of preaching (as the worldly wise esteem it) when in the demonstration of the spirit, would be blessed beyond our conception, and made something like the barley loaves by which the multitude were fed. We know our own employments; but the mysterious workings of the heavenly hand, in carrying forward the redemption of the nations from the fall, are wisely concealed from us: yet the inquisitiveness and judgments of the creaturely part, often lead us into discouragements when we should, in the simplicity of little children, do as we are bidden, and leave the event to Him who knows best how, and when, to use the weak and foolish things of this world, to confound the wisdom of the wise.

3d month 1788—By way of apology for my silence let me say, that writing, in many respects, less suited the disposition and qualifications of my mind, for many months back, than a silent meditation upon the nothingness of self; which was far from always obstructing the sweet circulation of christian fellowship, and solicitude for the preservation, under the shadow of the Holy Wing, of all those who, by dispensations unerringly wise, are involved in the depths of discouragement and dismay, with respect to their own ability to promote any good word and work, and yet whose diffident minds are often assaulted by the accuser of the brethren. These have, however, no occasion of casting away their confidence, when they reflect upon the many deliverances which they have received through the communication of eternal help, and remember the gracious promise of the great Master, to those who dwell under his righteous government; " lo! I am with you always, even to the end of the world."—You are as epistles written in my heart, wherein I often meditate with secret comfort, under the belief that you are, in unerring wisdom, designed to be fellow-helpers in promoting the cause of truth and righteousness, and fellow travellers in the way thereof. If you meet with trials and difficulties, you know there is nothing new in that; they have ever attended the footsteps of the flock; and when we are careful not to multiply them by any default of ours, they are so many proofs of our being the followers of a suffering Lord, which are sealed by our extracting benefit from them, and sanctified by obedience. Hold on then as you have begun; " count nothing too near, or too dear to part with for Christ's sake and the gospel's;" fear not that humiliating baptism, which crucifies us to the world, and the world unto us; and may the Shepherd of Israel lead you as his own sheep, convey to you the indisputable intelligence of his own will, and so preserve you in a state of fidelity to himself, as that none shall be able to pluck you out of his holy Hand!

——— 1788—It is a favour that the best root needs no great profession, or specious words to nourish it; it is not strengthened by a multitude of luxuriant branches, though, if it be alive, it will discover itself by little buddings, blossomings, and fruit. Whilst therefore we are not unprofitably anxious, in time of winter, for that which is not to be had, neither let us be too unconcerned, when the full time is come for the manifestations of the life of the tree, nor count them of little value, but cherish and protect them, lest some indiscreet hand, or spirit in ourselves, should rub off that wherein is hiddenly contained the choicest fruit, and so render the coming of the spring, and the genial influence of the Sun of Righteousness, ineffectual to us. Many cautions are necessary under this simile, for even when a tree bids fair for profiting and enriching those who possess it, if that which it is to produce in the fulness of time, be gathered before it is ripe, it sets the teeth of the eater on edge, and causes the tree to be evil spoken of. Thus, on many hands, dangers occur to us in the conduct of our gifts, in religious and civil departments. How needful is it then, to ask wisdom where it is to be had, and to use it when we have it; and also to cultivate that prudence which is her sister in service, and which often opposes plans of our own contriving. These are sentiments which, though thrown out to you, tend to shew me where, and how, I often miss my way; and excite me to review the consideration of that merciful kindness, which is sometimes extended to us in a very low estate; when, in our own eyes, we seem most undeserving of that help which can alone lift up our heads in hope, when the floods of affliction prevail, and the billows pass over us. May we deepen in our experience of the Lord's fatherly dealings with us; that so, approving ourselves more and more babes in Christ, our knowledge of the mysteries of the kingdom may be pure, and of that preserving nature, that never puffeth up.

———— 1788—It is not because thou and thy dear wife were forgotten by us, that neither my husband nor I have, since our return from England, dropped you a line. Silence, on my part, has chiefly originated in a consciousness that I have not been deep enough in my spirit, so to draw water out of the wells of salvation as to be able, in true religious sympathy, profitably to visit thy often discouraged mind. To feel our incapacity to minister, in a spiritual sense, a cup of cold water to ever so feeble a disciple (unto whom we may nevertheless be bound in a constant friendship) is a merciful impression; because it humbles us, and seals upon our spirits that invariable truth, that " there is none good but one." What is this sense, but the anointing itself, which has holy certainty in it, seeing that it is no lie. Except it abide in us to this effect, our profession of being believers is vain; we shall grow weary in the christian life, and our own righteousness will soon exhaust our strength: for supplies from the eternal Fountain would soon cease, were we to appropriate them to the prosecution of ends which the Lord never required at our hands, and neglect that life of faith, of humble dependance upon the pure gift, and thofe precious influences, hope and charity, which conftrain us to render unto the great Law-giver, in His time only, whatfoever he requires at our hands, though incomplete and foolifh to the unfimplified mind. I often wifh, on my own account, to be more in fubftance than I am. That infinite kindnefs has made me a partaker of the common falvation, has fhed abroad in my heart a meafure of his love, and ftrengthened me, at times, to lay hold on eternal life, I truft the deceivablenefs of unrighteoufnefs will never be fuffered to draw me from the belief of: but I look at the office of a gofpel minifter with an awfulnefs which convinces me, that there are baptifms, humiliations, and deaths peculiar to it; and that, except thefe are often renewed, in order to ftrip off the plumage of paft experience, and of that knowledge of heavenly things, which, being like yefterday's manna, cannot fuftain, but fubtilly puffs up the mind, that babe's ftate, unto which the myfteries of the kingdom are unfolded, is unattainable, and the infcription of holinefs unto the Lord is withheld, becaufe they are not cleanfed through the word fpoken unto them. What will it do for us, even to be called to the work of the miniftry, if we fubmit not to thofe purgations which unerring Wifdom appoints? We may become veffels marred on the wheel; or, to ufe another fimile, if we fuffer not ourfelves, in chriftian patience, to be bundled up as with the dry rods, and to be as deftitute of verdure as they, we may, for want of complying with the appointed means of fruitfulness, frustrate the divine purpose to distinguish those who are invisibly preserved by the hidden life. Perhaps it may not be unsafe to conclude, that in our society there are such defects; but, as an individual, I find it safest, in conformity to the great Master's command, to judge not, except, through the spirit of the Son, the judgment of the everlasting Father is known; and at such seasons, the mind is too much humbled vainly to feed on this revealed knowledge.

9th month 1788—Thy letter saluted us two days after our arrival at home, and was truly cordial, reviving with great sweetness our love and friendship with thee and thy dear wife, and also strengthening our hope, that He who, we trust, directed our steps to your parts, and mercifully preserved us through many jeopardies, will, as you and we surrender ourselves to His all-wise disposal, so carry on the eternal purpose of his will as to increase our fruitfulness to His glory; and tho' very remotely situated one from another, make us partakers of the same living fountain, whose waters purify and gladden the baptized members of the church of Christ wherever scattered, or however obscured by the general cloud of darkness which the professors of christianity are too apt to content themselves in. But as the eternal purposes of God are, the election of His own precious seed in us, (the Lamb that was slain) and the reprobation of that spirit or seed of the serpent, which with all the wrath and artifice of a fallen son of the morning, is ever seeking to oppose the coming of the kingdom of the Messiah, how ought we to watch and be sober; considering ourselves no longer safe, nor objects of divine favour, than whilst our spirits and affections are dedicated to His righteous control, cleansing and sanctifying by the converting influence of His own power. The seed of the kingdom, through divine mercy remaining in us, and a disposition to cherish and embrace it, preserves from the sin which grieves the Spirit, and leads into death. Wherefore, to stand in that which is elect, and to experience redemption from that spirit which wars with it, ought invariably to be our aim; and if, in a pursuit so essentially necessary, we meet with suffering and deep spiritual conflict, yet remembering how inferior it all is to what He met with, who being truly the good Shepherd, laid down His life for the sheep; and experiencing Him to be in us the hope of glory, the afflictions of the present time are counted light, and the omnipotence of the Lord's everlasting arm (as we singly depend upon it) found to give victory over the enemies of our own hearts; to lead, in the meekness of wisdom, through persecutions from without, and to build up in the true faith and stedfastness of the great Captain, who goes forth conquering and to conquer. I know that religion is in a state with you, as well as with us, which requires a patient waiting and quiet hoping for the salvation of God; which is often near to be revealed when we faint in our minds, and therefore fail of inheriting that blessing the patriarch Jacob wrestled for, through a night of faithful and succefsful exercife. Thy increafe in heavenly treafure, my beloved friend and brother in the truth, is fecretly and ftrongly coveted by me; my heart often meditates upon thy folitary fituation; and, in the renewings of gofpel love, thou and thy valuable wife are made like bone of my bone, and flefh of my flefh. May the God of all grace and confolation ftrengthen and fuccour you! and I moft affuredly believe he will, as your love of His inward and fpiritual appearance, and glorious work among men, grows as a tree of righteoufnefs, bringing forth fruit in its feafon, and enduring with humble fubmiffion, every wintry and pruning difpenfation. We have heard fomething of thy profpect of devoting thyfelf to the education of children; a work peculiarly wanted in your fociety, and which, if thou enters into, in the fimplicity and fincerity which truth gives, will, there is no doubt, be a bleffing to many, and thou thereby rendered a feeling fubfcriber to that truth, " he that watereth, is watered himfelf." Thou mayeft find it an arduous undertaking, and attended with mortifying circumftances; but the liberal foul (though it may fuffer) knows beft how to travel profitably through them all. It is not human approbation that we ought to depend upon, or have fingly in view; but our ftudy fhould be to fhew ourfelves approved unto God; and then, whatever vocation in His wifdom we are placed in, or however weak we may feel ourfelves, we fhall have no juft caufe to be afhamed.

11th Month 1788—I can feelingly subscribe to the truth of what thou sayest, that it is good to spend one's days in the bands of a free and sincere friendship, and in the unity of a solid and constant faith. We are favoured with many in these parts, who have been mercifully gathered to the pure spring of eternal life, where true love and unity originate, and from whence they bring forth acceptable fruits; but, as those consolations sometimes abound, so do tribulations, on account of the spirit of the world, and many other snares, by which the enemy of all good is daily seeking to draw aside; and for want of watchfulness and care, he prevails to the great hurt of some, and casting a shade over the purity and simplicity that there is in the gospel of Christ. So that, notwithstanding we are encompassed with many blessings and advantages, we are not without our portion of trials; and can therefore, in much sympathy and love, dip in spirit with thee, and feel thee as a fellow traveller in that path of suffering and probation which, in infinite Wisdom, is cast up for the regeneration and establishment of all those who walk in it, and hold out unto the end. Fear not, neither be dismayed, though thou feel thyself as a solitary bird, as a pelican in the wilderness, or a sparrow upon the house top; He that is in thee, is greater, than he that is in the world; His wisdom will direct thee, His counsel guide thee, and His everlasting omnipotent arm sustain thee, as thy faith is stedfast therein, and thy patience maintained in travelling through the abasing dispensations which may fall to thy lot: for

I do believe thou art intended to be a man for God, and no wonder then, if thou suffer persecution and affliction: remember they are but for a moment, and light, compared with that exceeding and eternal weight of glory, which is revealed to the poor distressed mind, when it looks beyond the " things which are seen, to the things which are not seen." I feel much love to the dear young people amongst you, and shall be glad for them to be told so; and that the good account thou sent respecting them has rejoiced the hearts of many. If they follow on to know the Lord, their minds will increase in holy stability; the enjoyments of this world will fade in their view; and an inward acquaintance with the Spirit of Truth will become most precious to them; they will not do their works (like the Pharisees) to be seen of men, but the solidity and weightiness of their spirits, will demonstrate that they have been with Jesus, from whom they receive all their qualifications to perform true worship, or to do any thing that is good.

10th month 1788—Thy letter, which arrived about a week ago, was sweetly refreshing and truly salutary to us; and I may now tell thee, that though acceptable, as an individual I needed it not to revive the strength of affectionate attachment; for my spirit often embraces thee in the flowings of increasing love and fellowship, and feels thee, according to my small measure of true knowledge, in that precious unity which is better than all words (though ever so frequently and freely expressed) without it. Were it not for this cordial drop, which, like oil, sometimes swims on the top of our bitterest cups, our faith would hardly be strong enough to make us victorious over even the little perplexities attendant upon this pilgrimage and state of probation; but He who knows that we are " feeble folk," and graciously compassionates our case, becomes to us not only the shadow of a mighty rock in a weary land, but teaches us so to build our nest therein, that, in times of storm and trial, his holy inclosure preserves us, his faith stays us, and this rock pours out precious oil. May our dwelling ever be here, and our inheritance be enlarged in that which is pure! then, let our allotments be what they may, whether our bodies inhabit the dark, or the more illuminated parts of the earth; whether we are encompassed with sorrow and travail, or have to rejoice more sensibly in the revealed salvation of the Almighty Arm; all will work together for good, and we grow in qualification to worship and magnify that great and excellent Name, which only is worthy of the incense that in every place and situation is to be offered.

11th month 1788—If I know my own heart, it is my desire to know my business, and simply to do it, whether it is taken cognizance of, or not, by the truly wise and honourable; whose friendship, though strengthening, consoling, and therefore acceptable, may (if the heart be not in some degree redeemed and redeeming from the mysterious workings of self-love) be perverted, and instead of nourishing the pure immortal part, build us up in an airy notion of our own merits and attainments, and prove a snare instead of a blessing. A little acquaintance with one's own human nature, a frequent detection of its corruption, and the perplexities into which it introduces us when its subtil arguments prevail, are enough to weary out a mind blessed with the least sincere aspiration after permanent good, durable riches and righteousness; and to content us in the most obscure situation, if, through unmerited mercy, it may but be in the courts of the Lord; with the coarsest food, if but ministered to us from the hand which is full of blessings; and under the most unpleasant work, if faith is vouchsafed, that in love and pity it will be accepted. Some of us here feel it to be a low time; my knees often are ready to smite together, and my soul is exceeding sorrowful. That there are causes in myself, and circumstances attending our present situation, I doubt not; " give me wisdom, and reject me not from amongst thy children," is my secret petition.

11th month 1788—We have twelve girls, and expect more soon; so that thou wilt believe cares multiply upon us: but, all our endeavours will be ineffectual, both in this, and all other undertakings, except the blessing which makes truly rich, in unmerited mercy, rests upon them. Did the world know, how dependant all substantial comfort and permanent joy are upon this heavenly gift, people in general would toil less, think less of their own wisdom, and more simply follow that day star which ariseth in the heart, and directeth to the pure life, in which the Father is well pleased. It is a comfortable belief to my mind, that thou art arrested by this precious principle of divine light, which discovers things as they really are. Be not afraid to be led by it, into ways thou knowest not, and into paths thou hast not seen; for, in due time, it will dispel the darkness before thee, and make crooked things straight. One of the most beautiful, though most abasing dispensations, in the true christian progress, is that of becoming as a little child; the judgment is here taken away for purification, and to be made truly useful in the Lord's work, the soul breathes only to the parent for food, and depends upon no other for counsel. It is generally weak, but knowing itself so, it is safe : O happy state to be rightly brought into! May we never be ashamed of it, but for our encouragement remember, that of such is the kingdom of heaven.

—————— 1788—Self-gratification in our own way and time, has not been allotted us for the path to solid peace; and if increasing humiliation should prove the food most convenient for us, we wish to accept it from that hand, which has an indisputable right to do with us as seemeth good in the sight of infinite wisdom, and which has power to convert the greatest trials into true spiritual refreshment.

—The ways of infinite Wisdom with those He chooses to bring through, and redeem from the fallacy of human understanding, and corrupt nature, are so incomprehensible and humiliating as indeed puts us out of the capacity of saying, " what doest thou?" for who hath been his counsellor? seeing he giveth not account to any of his matters, till the simplicity of a babe in Christ is attained unto, when he reveals, according to his purposes, those mysteries unto them, which are hid from the wise and prudent.

—That junction between the monthly meetings is comforting, if only from the strength which the few living members may be suffered to feel in the unity of one another's spirits, and the blessing which may be upon their endeavours to wash one another's feet, and to bear up one another's hands. That love which has heretofore flowed in my heart as a river, to the poor in spirit on that side the county, sweetly revives as I am writing, under a renewed hope, that the eternal fountain of life will not be closed among them, however low and unworthy they may sometimes feel themselves to be of its pure refreshment. And if it be in abundant mercy kept open, and they that are acquainted with it gather to it, having their qualifications from it, and use them under its influence, they will be a blessing one to another, and more may be gathered to an inward experience of the same purifying unction, than, in some seasons of discouragement, they have an idea of.

12th month 1788—We have been sitting in a friend's family, where ——— demonstrated that her mind, through all these storms and tempests, has found where to anchor and unload her vessel, with an increase of simplicity and obedience. I wish she may now leave the things that are behind; and that we may all become more and more, not only as children, but as weaned children. To be reduced to this humbled ftate, has not only its mortifications, but its joys. The chriftian's life confifteth not in the abundance of the apparent confolations and gratifications he poffeffes; but in the renewal from time to time, of the hidden manna which the golden pot contains, within the veil of perifhing things. Thou knoweft enough of fuch fituations as ours, to make thee believe we are not without a portion of trials, (no doubt wifely proportioned to us;) yet I dare not complain, having thus far, as we have paffed along, found Him whom my foul loveth, in whofe prefence no murmuring has a right to appear. Childlike fimplicity is an experience which every chofen fervant, however feeble, ought to endeavour for. We get nothing by the contrary; for by ever fo much taking thought, we cannot add one cubit to our ftature, or make one hair of our head white or black. May you proceed on this family vifit, in the faith, nothing doubting. It was not the abundance of bread, nor yet the finenefs of it, which fed the multitude formerly. For want of faith, we lofe many miracles which the bleffing would ftill effect. Remember poor David's fling and ftone, and out of whofe mouths, ftrength and praife are ordained.

12th month 1788—I received thy affectionate fifterly falutation, which, like a little help to the weak and feeble, was falutary and acceptable. Be affured I am one of the weak and feeble; may I therefore be wife enough, like thofe little creatures fpoken of in fcripture, which being feeble folk, build their nest in a rock! and truly, dear friend, were it not for the shadow at least, of this Rock, amidst the conflicts between nature and grace, the mind would often be overwhelmed, and make the sorrowful conclusion, "there is no hope." Ah this Rock! how safe a residence is it! and methinks its obscurity from the worldly wise, and the selfish mind, adds greatly to its safety. I seldom get to it but by combat, which shews that my enemies are lively; and though it is sometimes my lot, in the cross, to set before others their inherent infirmities, and transformed adversary, yet I humbly trust I shall not, and pray that I never may, forget mine own.

12th month 1788—My heart was favoured to enter a little into thy affecting account of dear M. G's. decease, and your united visit previous thereto. That valuable woman's last days being so memorably employed in her Master's service, (after a life of diffidence and obscurity, compared with her religious qualifications, and attachment to the cause of truth) was a distinguishing mark of everlasting love and favour to her. Her close seems so lively, and her sun set in such brightness and serenity, that it conveys something animating to those who are far behind in fitness, like myself, to count not their lives dear unto themselves, if they also may so finish their course with joy. And that humble tribulated disciple L. H. appears also ready to rise triumphant above death, hell, and the grave: all that is covetous within me exerts itself in the prospect of the joyous settlements of such travailling souls, in undefiled mansions where there is no more change. Oh that I were but as willing to commit my spirit into the divine hand, during my residence in this poor frail tabernacle, (where there is most need of help) as to inherit the rewards of those who, through more tribulations, more effectual washing, and better occupation of their gifts, enter into the joy of their Lord! Well! dear friend, fear not though thou hast made an exchange so unsuited to thy natural disposition in thy present station, He who knows the sacrifice, because Himself prepared it, (how little soever thou mayest think due to thyself) will proportionably enrich thee, and present thee with the blessings of His goodness, and crown thee the more with that humility and self-abasedness which are so precious in His sight. Were it not that He loved us before we loved Him, peradventure we might sometimes think our lot a hard one, and find some cause to despair of His mercy, or conclude that His holy eye penetrates not into our lonesome and obscure dwellings (however raised up as spectacles to angels and to men) neither marks the way that we take. That sacred prerogative of the everlasting Father, of attracting and quickening the soul, opening and shutting the heavenly treasury, is, I do believe, the very thing which distracts that mind wherein patience has not had its perfect work, though it is the very thing wherein it ought to glory.

——— 1788—My husband and I received thy letter of affection for us, and lamentation over thy self. Our minds are drawn into near sympathy with thee, and we believe that this afflictive dispensation, is designed for thy encreasing acceptance with the Father of spirits, who knows best how to purify the vessels of His own house. These, thou knowest, are not only to be of gold, but of beaten gold, in order to fashion them according to His good pleasure, and render them fit for the inscription of holiness. Now, my dear friend, as thy heart's desire is to repose thyself in the joys of God's salvation, endeavour to attain that holy quietude, wherein the delusions of the grand enemy are baffled, and the tribulated spirit is strengthened to receive the bitterest cup with thanksgiving. We are of ourselves very weak, and it is sometimes consistent with infinite Wisdom, that we should be left to a deep sense thereof, that no flesh may glory in His presence; but that the hunger, the thirst, and the humiliation of the soul, may be fully proved. Therefore marvel not, as though some new thing had happened unto thee. It was the path which the holy Apostle was led in, when he declared on his own, and his brethren's behalf, that they had the sentence of death in themselves, that they should not trust in themselves, but in God who raiseth the dead: and we have many instances in our society in these parts, of upright hearted advocates of the christian religion being tried with deep poverty of spirit, and discouragement in the prospect of the Lord's work, and of their own incapacity to perform it. We have also instances of these humiliations tending to root them deeper in the experience of that fundamental truth, that the true believers in Chrift have received an anointing which abideth in them, and need not that another fhould teach them, but as this fame anointing teacheth them, which is truth, and is no lie. And being thus led on to a higher degree of union and fellowfhip with the Father, and with the Son, their qualifications have increafed to endure, for the precious feed's fake, the watchings, the faftings, and the deaths many, unto which, according to our meafure, we are all, in this mixed ftate of things, called. And when their mouths have been opened again in the congregation of the people, they have depended the more fingly and fimply upon divine impulfe, and the puttings forth, and ftrengthening virtue of the Shepherd of Ifrael. Thus the exercifed have been benefited, and the Lord's heritage comforted. I humbly truft, that thefe bleffings will refult from thy late tribulations; and that thou wilt have to fay, hitherto the Lord (and not man) hath helped me. It is to be lamented when, for want of thefe baptifms of fpirit, a fuperficial miniftry, and activity in the church prevail; for thefe are like blafts from the wildernefs, which, inftead of cherifhing, chill the hidden life, and build up in the notion, rather than in the humbling experience of true religion. It is much better to appear nothing when we are nothing; that we may be emptied and cleanfed from all felf-love, and learn patience and contentednefs therewith. I falute thee in chriftian love and fympathy, and as a tribulated fellow-traveller encompaffed with manifold infirmities, remain thy friend and fifter in the truth.

1st month 1789—My mind has often secretly visited and sympathized with thee, under the various and deep exercises which I do believe have fallen to thy lot, in the course of unerring wisdom; but it has as often seemed more my business, thus silently to feel thee under the precious influence of that love which the children of the one Almighty Father feel towards each other, than to be forward in expressing it. He who has graciously called thee out of darkness, into his marvellous light, turned his hand upon thee for good, and thus far, sustained thee thro' many refining dispensations, will not now leave thee, when Jordan may rise high, and seem to overflow its banks; but in his own due and appointed time, which must be waited for, he will divide the waters, and discover to thee, with indisputable clearness, a way where thou hast seen none; yea, according to His promise to His own seed, He will make darkness light before thee, and crooked things straight; these things will he do unto thee, and will not forsake thee. I think I know, (if I am dipped into a right sense of thy state) that the enemy of all good is exceedingly envious against the precious life, or seed of the kingdom, which is divinely intended, through suffering, to be so brought into dominion, as to establish thee in the liberty of the children of God, whereby thy usefulness in the church, in this dark and cloudy day, will encrease. Like the woman that brought forth the man-child, seen by John in the vision of light and life, thou mayst have to flee into the wilderness for preservation, because of the persecutions of the dragon, and the floods he may be permitted to pour out of his mouth. His enmity remains to be with the pure seed; and they who desire to cherish this excellent treasure, in their earthen vessels, and to live godly in Christ Jesus, must expect many of his cruel assaults, in temptations, provocations, and insinuations: but the Rock of ages remains to be their refuge, and as their tribulated spirits endeavour to retire here, and place no confidence in the flesh, notwithstanding it may be with sore conflict they gain this sure dwelling place, they will be amply rewarded, and have, in humility of soul, to rejoice in the impregnableness of the defence, and to magnify the power through which all things are possible. Whatever has a tendency to subject and reduce the creaturely part in us, however bitter its operations may be, is gratefully to be received by the upright soul, as one of the means whereby the adoption, and inheritance of the glorious promises of the gospel, is attained; and one of those bitter things which to the truly hungry soul is sweet. Therefore, let me say unto thee, fear not, thy God is with thee, and will work for thee, as thou art willing to have all the resistance of thy nature to every of his holy requisitions, wrought upon and subdued, in the day of his power. The just are to live by faith, that faith which gives the victory, and triumphs over death, hell, and the grave. Mayst thou fight the good fight thereof; and may I be thy companion in this necessary warfare; that so the attacks of our grand adversary upon such christian virtues as have been mercifully conceived in our souls, may all be rendered frustrate; and we abiding under the sacred influence of the powerful word of patience, may often have our spiritual eye opened to look beyond the things which are seen, to the things which are not seen; and for this joy set before us, count not our lives dear unto ourselves, neither love them unto death! Though my heart, as I said in the beginning, has secretly visited and saluted thee, yet I had no thought of expressing so much on these solemn subjects, when I took up my pen; but only just to convince thee that thou hast in me (though I acknowledge I was restrained in thy company lately from shewing it) a sympathizing friend and sister, according to my measure. Though, dear friend, we may be led in silent travail, and as by the gates of hell and death, yet let us remember, that this is the way in which inscrutable wisdom has ever led his redeemed children in all ages.

1st month 1789—There are seasons wherein the Bridegroom of souls withdraws himself, or, as to the sensible enjoyment of his sacred soul-enriching presence, is taken away, and then the children of the bride-chamber cannot but fast and mourn: and as I do believe thou art one of these, thou must learn more and more to endure hardness, and to bear such dispensations with christian fortitude, in that hope which anchors the soul on the invisible Rock of ages. That which is seen is not hope, and therefore, remember that this is the season wherein thy confidence in almighty help, thy faith, patience, and fervent charity, are to be tried, rather than when the bridegroom is obviously with thee, when thou canst not fail to rejoice.

2d month 1789—Thy letter addressed to my husband, M. D. and myself, was very satisfactory to us; as we found thereby that the precious unity of the spirit was mercifully preserved in thy mind and ours, notwithstanding our remote situation, and our own peculiar impediments to the growth of this immortal plant. We all feel, at times, our faith to be closely tried, and this hath been the experience of those in all ages who were pressing after a city which hath foundations; the spirit of this world, and the corruptions of our own nature, with great subtility, oppose the government of the Son of Peace in the heart, wherein the unity of the one spirit consists. These enemies of our own houses, are the great objects of the spiritual war; and as we maintain that by the aid of spiritual weapons, our faith will grow stronger by its manifold provings, and a victorious fight will at last abundantly compensate for every afflictive dispensation, and conflict of soul. Let patience then have its perfect work, that thou mayst " be perfect and entire, (as saith the Apostle) lacking nothing." Many friends here, who love you in the truth, have sympathized with you on account of your late prospect of suffering, concerning what some of you apprehend to be the law of your God; and your relief therefrom is equally rejoicing. Is it not cause of humble thankfulness, that some weak minds are spared from giving public demonstration of their fidelity to the christian religion, at a time when, peradventure, their faith therein was not strong enough to be accompanied by such works? A query of this sort to themselves ought deeply to convince them of this renewed obligation they are under to their heavenly Father, "whose eyes run to and fro in the earth, beholding the evil and the good; and that nothing short of increasing faithfulness to known duty, and watchfulness thereunto in spirit, can render them approved in the sight of so gracious a Being. We are glad to believe there are sincere-hearted men and women amongst you; may these be of one heart and one mind, walking " by the same rule, and minding the same thing," gathering together in the sacred Name, and diligently waiting therein the time which infinite wisdom prescribes, (though in ever such humiliation to the creature) before the people's minds are drawn to outward testimonies. Oh strengthen one another in this holy exercise! It is essential for gospel ministers to experience; that therein the spirits may be tried, every transformation of the enemy judged down, and the suffering seed of the kingdom only exalted. If this reduction of self, and all selfish working, were the object of your strong and feeble members, your assemblies would be solemn, your feeding would be upon the bread of life, and your souls would worship and adore the divine Presence, which delights to dwell in you, and amongst you. Thy account of the young people's faithfulness was acceptable; and, with thee, " I wish it may be a sincere step towards virtue." Hearing of the two marriages likely to be so agreeably accomplished, is also pleasant; and I hope that the reflection will be lastingly comfortable to the parties when their minds are growing under the influence of heavenly dew, and in obedience to the cross of Christ.

2d month 1789—If you fully knew the state of our minds, and how closely they have been occupied since our parting from you, I am ready to conclude, that sometimes you could hardly have refrained from dropping us a word in season. Perhaps it is self-love which directs to this vein of consolation; an hunger after sensible enjoyments, which generally manifests itself to be insatiable, and the feeding of which seldom strengthens the root and ground of true christian fellowship. It has been our lot, and I doubt not but it has been yours, since we saw each other, to pass through trials inward and outward; wherein nothing short of the Arm of Omnipotence could profitably sustain and bring through : O! that our faith may be strengthened in it; that as our race will soon be run, we may, during its humiliating course, invariably pursue the one thing needful. Then will our steps, amidst the briers and thorns of this world, and all the chilling blasts of its spirit, be rewarded in the riches of the mercy of Him who trod the path before us. I remember the unity we were favoured to feel in our little services, and the uninterrupted harmony of our connexion as companions; and these things have left upon my mind impressions too sacred to be lost in forgetfulness. Instead of their dying, I think of late they have been replenished with a degree of the best life : and as we endeavour simply to move in the lots assigned us by our all-wise Creator, however distant our outward dwellings may be, the immortal part will not fail to assimilate us in the precious covenant of love and life. It is a wonderful union which christian travellers enjoy, when they meet one another in spirit. Though their communications be mournful, yet understanding each other's language, and being companions, they are encouraged and strengthened thereby, to proceed on their journey towards a city which hath foundations, whose peace is everlasting.

3d month 1789—The precious evidence of peace, is one of those rare and valuable flowers, that seem in danger of withering with too much display in the open air. The shade, we are sometimes favoured to retire to, when the world may judge us in its own fluctuating spirit: " when thou prayest, enter into the closet and shut the door," &c.

3d month 1789—It is a very low time with me. There are few I believe that need such baptisms as myself, and therefore it is, no doubt, best for me to bear them as quietly and profitably as I can. He with whom we have to do, afflicts not willingly the children of men, and therefore, if our afflictions are not of our own bringing on, they are a part of the work of that righteousness which produces quietness and assurance for ever. We must not expect to pass through the present vale of tears, without bearing our proportion of suffering, for the body's sake, and those abasements which are so necessary for our own preservation in the truth. Wherefore let us be patient, and establish our hearts, that so we may not be moved or turned away from the hope of the gospel, but through all, stand in the faith that the day of the Lord draweth nigh.——We often find, to the mortification of the creature, that times and seasons are not at our command, nor even for us always to know: it is the divine prerogative to dispose of them; and the human mind is taught thereby its own dependency, and driven in quest of that faith by which the just live. Faith removes our doubts, anchors the soul when upon the fluctuating waters of uncertainty, " is the very substance of things hoped for, and the evidence of things not seen." Fight, my beloved friend, the good fight thereof, and give no place to the accuser; so will thy possession of this heavenly gift increase, thy offerings will continue to be acceptable, and victory become sealed to thee when the combat is over.

3d month 1789—If thou and I are really favoured with the precious evidence of gospel union, let us be tenacious of its purity. On thy part, do not fail to " exhort and reprove with all authority," even when the deceitfulness of my heart judges itself better than it is. What signifies that part in us which cannot inherit the kingdom? I cannot say that I am light hearted, though it is comfortable to believe thy burdens decrease; nor do I wish to cast a gloom upon, and cloud that sky, which, after much tempestuous weather, and a frequent oppressive atmosphere, may attract the strengthened sight to greater heights of clearness and purity, than, in some past seasons, the nature of things would allow. I congratulate thee as one, not only beholding the vision, but gradually and effectually ascending the ladder which reaches from earth to heaven; on which, methinks, the descending angels are sent to strengthen poor weary pilgrims. May I be thy companion; not so much for the sake of thy company, though that is truly pleasant, as for the glorious rest within the pearl gates, when the tribulated steps to it shall for ever cease. I believe I do not so frequently write to any one on this subject as to thyself; and I would not have thee think that my conversation is proportionably in heaven. These prospects animate the soul; but the discouragements and persecutions from that which is born of the flesh, seem as if they would drag every holy aspiration into the mire and the clay of the horrible pit.

5th month 1789—It just occurred to me as I took up the pen, that probably there is a greater similarity in our exercises, than we are generally aware of, and perhaps we are oftener dipped into sympathy one with another than we are capable of perceiving. Religious sympathy is I am persuaded a great mystery. The apostle sought to fill up that which remained (of his portion) of the sufferings of Christ, for the church's sake; and may we be like minded respecting those baptisms, which introduce into a fellowship with the effectual sufferings of the Lamb, and work in us a conformity to His death; thereby qualifying, through the power of His resurrection, to demonstrate, that they are not only for our own, but also for the church's sake. Under these dispensations, can we fail, at times, of feeling ourselves alone? We should not be exercised according to our measures, in his tribulated path, if, in the awful moment when the crucifixion of our wills is approaching, our associates and friends stood around us with the cup of consolation; no! it were his enemies then who, hastening their own destruction, pierced him, and ministered the vinegar and the gall. Let us then seize the comparison for our humiliation. Christ in us can unseal the mystery, and amidst His holy leadings in the regeneration, can renew the drooping mind with the consoling language of, " fear not, greater is He that is in you, than he that is in the world." I wish that thy mind may be encouraged, without unprofitable reasoning, to labour onward in the hidden paths and pilgrimage of the Jew inward. Thou hast put thy hand to a good work, for which I do believe thou art chosen. The enemy of all good, will, as formerly, seek to destroy the immortal birth, and not fail to cast forth floods out of his mouth, and represent them to be the ministration of just condemnation. To be preserved from this attack upon thy best life, peradventure thou mayest be induced to flee into the wilderness, where methinks I now visit thee, and where thou wilt not be suffered to fall; but thou wilt be sustained with the bread which the world knows not of, and come forth in the appointed time, more and more weaned from all human dependencies.

5th month 1789—Few sources of comfort presented at the opening of these mixed assemblies, and unless the one great source of light and purity produces to the believers the newness of the spirit, they cannot but fast; and well is it for them, when, to their fasting, they can acceptably add mourning.

For my part, I have in general thro' the course of the sittings of this meeting (which are mostly gone through) felt myself something like Mary, who sat at the blessed Master's sepulchre, with a language similar to that of " they have taken away my Lord, and I know not where they have laid Him." To thy sympathetic mind, this may be a sufficient description how things have gone with thy Sarah Grubb. Perhaps in the last moment of extremity (for sometimes we are wisely tried to the last) the joyful tidings may salute the spiritual ear, " thy Lord is risen, and behold he goeth before thee." this is the crown of all true rejoicing; this is the blessing of which the creature must ever acknowledge itself unworthy. It is a knowledge which indeed puffeth not up; and were it not that Lucifer, that fallen son of the morning, is seeking to intrude, and sometimes does intrude himself, and attracts the unwary mind to some mountain of self exaltation, peradventure the manifestations and consolations of the Spirit, would more often, and more eminently abound amongst the Lord's visited and adopted children. " Feed me then with food convenient for me, lest I be full and deny thee:" O desirable resignation!

5th month 1789—I was sorry to hear that thy mind was still in so dejected a state. Causes for situations of this sort cannot always be comprehended by us, and therefore we ought to be careful how we conclude that they either are, or are not, in the ordering of best Wisdom. One thing however affords consolation to the truly contrite mind; that all things shall work together for good to those who love and fear God. As I do believe, thou art one of those, and that thou sincerely desirest also to walk acceptably before Him, learn more and more, patiently and thankfully, to receive from His holy hand, whatsoever He appoints or permits, as dispensations which he only can sanctify. It is a sort of school the mind has to enter into, when sensible of its own infirmities, it pursues the things of the kingdom, and the knowledge how to discern them from the mysterious workings and cogitations of corrupt self. It has many lessons to learn, hard to flesh and blood; and perhaps one of the most difficult is, to think nothing too hard, nothing too near or dear to part with, for the sake of the prize in view. And were we thoroughly to learn it, I believe it would clothe us with many amiable and profitable dispositions, which murmuring Israelites have seldom time to discover.

6th month 1789—Thou art often very near and dear to me; and I have felt it renewedly during the course of the exercising meetings we have had here: for true love sometimes springs up, and attracts our attention to some suffering object, when we are ready to think ourselves destitute of its sacred virtue, and too much scattered in mind from its hidden track livingly to converse with it. So, my dear friend, it has often been with me since we saw each other; believing that thou hast trials peculiar to thyself, and peradventure, art too much depressed therewith. Let not any discouragement sink thee below an holy confidence, that the everlasting Arm is underneath;

and that, if thou " deal thy bread to the hungry, and thy water to the thirsty soul, thy light shall break forth out of obscurity, and thy darkness become as the noon day." Believe not the most subtle insinuation, that thy passage through life will continue thorny as it is; for it is in the deceivableness of unrighteousness that these things are suggested to us, in order to remove us from that stedfastness and hope of the gospel, in which visited minds are designed to be established.

7th month 1789—My heart and eyes have been afresh affected by a lively revival of days that are past: days of sore tribulation, when the old heavens and old earth were passing away, and a capacity unbegotten to rejoice in the discovery of the new. Yea, they were days when the battle was hot between flesh and spirit; and for want of being accustomed to the weapons of warfare, mind and body were wearied, and the vitals of both nearly overcome. When I reflect upon the kindness of infinite goodness many ways manifested to my weak state, and the ingratitude of my heart, I wonder at the long forbearance, and continued effusions of the quickening and purifying virtue of the immortal Word: I wonder at my present backwardness in the christian life; and my want of zeal in the pursuit of the one thing needful. May thy bosom friend and thyself, be so helpful and blessed to each other, as, in the sacred covenant wherein ye are bound, unitedly to stretch forth your hands, unfettered by any thing of your own, and let another bind, or gird you, even though you may be carried thereby whither ye would not. The inexpressibly near unity and affection which I felt with, and for your spirits, in our late and short junction, has left a sweet and consoling savour behind; which now, and sometimes, when a different influence would prevail, springs up as under the threshold of the door, and rises till it becomes a river, which my often tried mind measurably rejoices and swims in. Count not your lives dear unto yourselves, when called for at your hands; and when not, labour after tranquility of soul; remembering, that, however little and poor ye may be, ye cannot, by taking ever so much thought, add one cubit to your stature. But resignation itself is a gift. Oh that ye may covet the best gifts! for it is as we have them in view, and pray for them, according to the mind of the spirit, that we receive.

8th month 1789—Thou art, dear friend, an epistle written in my heart, where I sometimes read thee, and thy mournful, humble steppings with joy; consistent with the divine command, to rejoice in his new creation, of which, in infinite mercy, thou art happily a part; having known old things to pass away, and new ones to be brought in, where the righteousness of the creature is beheld to be as filthy rags; and where the righteousness of God, the obedience of faith, dwells. Let it dwell, and more and more abound in thy experience; for thereby thy strength will encrease, and nothing, in divine appointment, will be found too hard for thee to perform. In true simplicity, to lean upon and follow the Beloved of souls, is a wonderful preservation from that reasoning, and vain consultation with flesh and blood, which distracts the mind, and often causes it to err from the faith. It is true our spiritual guide, for wise purposes, conceals himself from us, the bridegroom is taken away, and then the disciples cannot but mourn; and better it is for them that they should mourn, than enter into the remotest confederacy with his enemy against him, call in question His manifestations, and doubt whether He is to us that friend, of whom He has given us, in broad day light, living proofs. An unbelieving heart is a temptation most subtle, and often very plausibly presented. Beware of it, dear friend! Be not afraid to have thy foolishness for Christ's sake perfected; for His gospel, which is the power of God unto salvation to all them that believe, is a fund of requisites for the christian traveller; from the babe's to the strong man's food, the cloathing of the lilies in the heavenly garden, to the accoutrements and victorious armour of the Lamb's soldiers. Fear not therefore, though thou be a child, and seem to thyself that thou canst not go; for the Lord hath anointed thee, and will therefore strengthen thee for His work, and feed thee with food convenient for thee.

8th month 1789—You are very often remembered by me in sisterly sympathy and affection, though seldom told of it; and I trust that nothing relating to my silence will be able to make different impressions. I find it very difficult in our large family, and amidst other duties than those which relate to it (though but few of them comparatively fall to my lot,) to sit down and quietly converse with my friends; and yet they come upon, or rather arrest, my mental attention, when in the very thick of cares and anxieties; so that I hope the invisible intercourse of kindred spirits, is less dependent upon outward and visible signs, than we sometimes imagine; and peradventure, the more we look beyond the things that are seen, to the things that are not seen, the more we then possess the very thing which our natures prompt us to toil for. Nevertheless, as a secondary consolation, it is lawful thus to commune. Your last joint epistle was to me a pleasant repast, though some of its ingredients were bitter herbs: you know so well how, in every new dispensation, to look to " the great first cause," and to wait for that sanctification of the Spirit, which causeth all things to work together for good to them that love Him, that it seems unnecessary for me to remark upon it; an entire freedom clothes my mind respecting you; yea, and I may add, a belief that your bitterest cups will be sweetened in the due and appointed time. To wait for that, has often been hard duty to the hastiness of my desires. But were we not to be so exercised; where or how could we obtain profitable experience in the christian's path? how could we live by faith, when all things were accountable to us? or when arrive at the quiet and safe harbour of pure resignation, if the storms of carnal reasoning were never to rise? There is a great and an attainable purity in that state of mind, which forbears to judge even in its own cause; which, in singleness, casts its burden upon the Lord, and accepts every permitted tribulation and chastisement, as a renewed seal of adoption, and evidence of our being intended to be joint heirs with Christ; and therefore bound and induced, by the unfailing mercies of God, to follow through all, our holy Head; and by the increase of his spirit, not to fear humbly to breathe the language of Abba, Father. I look up with an emulous eye, to an experience which I generally live far short of: but let us press forward, for we shall reap if we faint not.——You are a collection of chosen vessels at that place. Oh suffer not the enemy to put in his cloven foot amongst you, for he mars the purest designs; and to frustrate the gracious intention, of the Lord's children being helpmeets to each other, is one of his most subtle attempts. When there are storms at sea, vessels are often scattered, and hid one from another; perhaps all equally tossed: but there is a voice which both winds and waves obey, and which unites them again. Have faith in it, and wait for it, and ye shall do well.

8th month 1789—As children of the same family, I believe it allowable for us to commune together at times, as we walk in the way and are sad; for, methinks, the master has herein joined himself to us, and I trust will graciously continue to do so, as we hold fast our integrity, and become more and more skilful in lamentation. Elijah, in a time of deep revolt, thought himself alone, and saw Israel with an eye clouded by discouragement, till He who knows all things revealed to him his own preserved seed. In the word of eternal life only, is certainty. Well! they that feared the Lord spake often one to another: I look at thee, dear friend, as having very few to speak to who understand the Hebrew tongue;

one of the characteristics of many in this day who are called christians is, that they are half Jew and half Ashdod; but even at this be not too sorrowful: " when father and mother forsake thee, the Lord will take thee up," and become Himself the supplier of all thy wants. Who knows but He may make thee an instrument for the turning of many to a pure language, and inducing them to call upon the sacred name, the refuge and sanctuary of the righteous; that so they may be preserved in the secret places of the Almighty, until His indignation be overpast. Be a faithful watchman; yea be willing and thankful to become the most menial in the spiritual family. This humility will, with the blessing, insure thy preservation, and at times furnish thee with that bread of eternal life, which the world knows not of.

9th month 1789—I wish we could more frequently converse upon our various concerns, believing that each of us finds them at times awfully important, and attended with their peculiar perplexities. A little company in such paths has a cheering effect, as it seldom happens, in the right ordering of things, that all are sinking under discouragements together; and therefore they can the better speak comfortably when some one or other sensibly possesses the precious gift of faith, which peradventure all are nevertheless living by.

My head often seems dropping below water; yea, there are seasons when the billows actually pass over; and, through unutterable mercy, they do pafs over, and beyond the prefent trials. Sowing as in tears, in the variety of ground which we find amongft the children, my ftrength gets renewed; and my foul begotten again to a lively hope, that infinite kindnefs will, in His own time and way, blefs our feeble endeavours to prepare fubjects for the kingdom of the Prince of peace. It is little we can do; but that little let us labour to perform acceptably to the Almighty Father, and leave the world to gaze upon us, and judge of us, as it may: for when we take its fentiments into confideration, or put them in competition with our foul's peace, it is like that falfe balance which is an abomination to the Lord; whereas the juft weight (an implicit attention and obedience to divine requifition) is His delight. I wifh, dear friends, that your hands may be ftrengthened, in the faithful difcharge of your duty towards the numerous family you prefide in: for the more you erect the ftandard of truth there, the more your fervices in fociety will encreafe; and what is ftill better, the deeper your fpirits will get in the undefiled confolations of the humble followers of Jefus. Thefe are worth fuffering for, and they abound in proportion to our tribulations for His fake.

9th month 1789—I am truly glad thou ftands fo dedicated to pour water on the hands of this fweet fpirited friend; believing fuch a difpofition, conceived in the integrity of the heart, is often acceptable to, and blefsed by, the good Spirit which renews the hope of the humble, and revives the minds of the contrite ones. Let not the ufual difcouragements to thefe little furrenders, fo prevent thee from following on to the full performance, as to rob thee of the reward of enriching peace, and the increafe of thy experience in the work whereinto thou art, beyond all doubt to my mind, rightly introduced. Having put thy hand to the plough, it is not now a day for thee to look back. "Remember Lot's wife," has often been an inftructive caution, and leffon of peculiar inftruction to my mind, when in danger of giving up my fpiritual travail, and, rather than diftinguifh myfelf from thofe to whom my fteppings appeared foolifhnefs, tempted in the bitternefs of my fpirit, to fay, "I will fpeak no more in thy name." The old heavens and the old earth will (I truft) yield thee no more of their forbidden delights; and therefore, how unwife would it be, through an imperfect obedience, to deprive thy tribulated fpirit of that undefiled rejoicing, which is peculiar to the new creation of God. I mean not, by this folicitude refpecting thee, to be the means of promoting an activity from under the renewed influence of pure wifdom, or even the premature difclofing of openings into the undoubted myfteries of the kingdom; for it is a great but neceffary attainment, to know how to keep the Lord's fecrets, and when to reveal them. But a truly refigned and humble ftate of mind is a continual facrifice, and will produce the fruit of the Spirit; fo that I wifh for thee and myfelf, that this root of the matter may be found in us; then, as fteady and uniform travellers we fhall gain ground in the new and living way; and leaving the things that are behind, shall reach forth to those that are before, having our eye single unto Jesus, who also took up the cross and despised the shame.

10th month 1789—I feel myself nearly interested in thine and thy wife's welfare, and am pleased with every renewed capacity to sympathize with you in spirit, knowing, that if you dwell in that faith which overcomes the world, you must often experience trials of it, and, for its refinement, be baptized into a sense of your own weakness; perhaps so much so, as to acknowledge, with the holy Apostle, that we have the sentence of death in ourselves, that we should not trust in ourselves, "but in God who raiseth the dead." If this is your exercise, be encouraged to faithfulness herein. There are many who willingly cry, hosanna to him who cometh in the name of the Lord, but who are not bound enough in heart to the pure seed of divine light, to watch and to suffer with it, at a time when there is no form nor comeliness in it; and when it seems no otherwise to operate in the soul than by making the creature abhor itself. These take not that root in religion, and have not that holy communion or fellowship with the Father and with the Son, which qualifies the watchful christian soul undoubtedly to know when good cometh; to rejoice in themselves, and not in another; yea, and to bear testimony, in the quickening virtue of truth, that the Lord is risen. I greatly desire thy preservation, dear friend, believing that thou art designed for an instrument in the Lord's hands, to carry on his work, his great and marvellous work, amongst a benighted and rebellious people, and to be the means, in the little society thou art joined to, of drawing them, by thy example as well as precept, from the " lo here is Chrift, and lo he is there," to the kingdom of heaven in themfelves; and of inftructing them in patient waiting for its coming. This being a part of thy office, I know thou muft endure much hardnefs, and meet with perfecution in thyfelf, and in others; becaufe the enemy of all good will tranfform himfelf as into an angel of light, and try to beguile both the fimple, and thofe who are meafurably inftructed in the kingdom: but take for thy example a faithful fervant * of Jefus Chrift, who fled as the dove to the window of the ark, and ftood ftill in that watch. Then wilt thou be rewarded with the fulnefs of joy, at the coming of thy Lord, without whom thou canft do nothing; ftrength will be given thee faithfully to bear thofe chriftian teftimonies, in which thou haft moft furely believed, and alfo to suffer for them, if it be the Mafter's will. Then will the light in thee be more and more ufeful in the houfe, and the weightinefs and reverence of thy fpirit, excite the beloved youth alfo to purchafe the field where the pearl lies. May I be thy companion in thefe exercifes! my attainment in religious knowledge is fmall; and without frequent baptifms of fpirit, and watchings unto prayer, I find even that little might foon be taken away. Let me have thy prayers and the fympathy of thy fpirit, when ever the pure light teaches thee fo to do. It is a comfort

* See William Leddra's epiftle in Piety Promoted

to us to feel thee, and some others of your little flock, in the precious covenant of love and life, wherein we desire to be remembered by you and by them.

10th month 1789—Thy peaceful return is matter of joy to me. I wonder not at it, because thou wast strengthened to humble thyself as a little child; and therefore, on the wings of faith and love, art thou exalted to behold and aspire after the hope of thy calling, and even to rejoice in the renewed prospect of the land which is very far off. Ah! how often our spiritual eye wants purging and re-anointing, in order to see these things, and in our measure, to "behold the King in his beauty;" and even when it is so prepared, wisdom, infinite wisdom, presents it at times with objects more conducive to the establishment of the mind upon the Rock alone, by leaving it so destitute of sensible enjoyment, that it loaths itself, feelingly cries out, "without thee I can do nothing," and panteth, like the hart after the water brooks, for Shiloh, the River of life. Here (in another metaphor) is Christ the Rock found, whereon a truly religious weariness (not impatience) of this world, and the things thereof, tend to build, stablish and strengthen us. We are but sojourners here; let us then, with becoming earnestness of spirit, invariably seek a city which hath foundations; the very knowledge of whose Builder and Maker is life eternal. Thou art right, my dear friend, in believing me to be in a tried low state of mind, though thou art the first that seems to know any thing of it. I mourn over myself, not knowing why it is so with me. As to opening my mouth in our meetings, it seems as far from me as if I had never known such a concern. A painful gloomy exercise, or a wandering imagination, is what I have principally to travail through; and yet, having been acquainted with a situation of mind much more destitute than this, I dare not but consider the invisible support my soul is blessed with, as an object of reverent gratitude. Well might David (who knew the various dispensations of the Lord) pray that His holy spirit might not be taken from him, at the same time that he craved the restoration of the joys of His salvation. But let our allotment be what it may, there is some attention to be paid to that precept of the gospel, " to wash and to anoint, rather than to appear to men to fast." My situation in this large family, where many have their own exercises to pass through, calls upon me for the practice of every christian virtue which I have, through unmerited mercy, been taught in the school of Christ; and much complaint, or conversation about our inward state, except truth opens the way for it (which I trust is now the case,) rather decreases than increases our strength. We have a friend, blessed be the great and ever worthy name, that sticks closer than any brother; may we then cleave to Him with full purpose of heart! He can renew our resignation, and abundantly prepare us to say, " not my will, but Thine be done."

11th month 1789—I am, through infinite kindness, convinced that the immortality of the soul is manifest in the spiritual communion which, according to our measures, we experience in these mortal bodies, independent of every medium originating in the invention of man; and though a very defective purity occasions with me a very defective enjoyment of it, yet I feel at times a holy resolution to hold fast that which I have of the unspeakable gift of faith, and to accept it as an earnest of the inheritance, until, by greater degrees of light, love, and life, the redemption of the purchased possession is obtained. That thou art my companion herein, and in hidden conflict for this glorious prize, I seem assured beyond a doubt; and greatly desire that the present dispensation of unerring Wisdom may, in proportion to the depths of sorrow which thou hast experienced, lead thee up, on consecrated ground, to this dignified attainment. Ah, my friend, these are humble ascendings, because they are the consequence of descending: but they are safe; therefore fear not, O daughter of Zion; lo " I am with thee, saith the Lord; be not dismayed, I am thy God; I will strengthen thee, I will help thee, yea, I will uphold thee with the right hand of my righteousness."

11th month 1789—These are low trying times with us, and particularly to my mind, feeling myself often as one that has abundant need to go down again to the potter's house; and, through divine favour, strength is at times afforded to descend in spirit to where a right and true sense of myself, and the purity of the cause I am sometimes engaged to advocate, is obtained. We often have need of the prayers, and sympathy of each others spirits, and oh! that we may be kept in that faith which gives the victory, fo as to wreftle effectually for the renewed fupplies of the Spirit, that none of the difcouragements of our day may prevail againft us. I know thou haft thy fecret provings; but fear not, "greater is He that is in thee, than he that is in the world." We have champions in this land, who feem to defy little David's fimplicity; but if thofe who go forth againft fuch in your parts, as well as here, do it in the name of the Lord God of the armies of Ifrael, and with thofe weapons which He approves, victory will finally be on their fide.

11th month 1789—I have long feen it neceffary to watch my own heart, left while I nourifhed an approved chriftian fympathy with my fellow pilgrims, and manifefted it in the line of apprehended duty, I fhould alfo draw their attention and affections to myfelf, and thereby wound the pure life by ftrengthening the root of felf love in both; and inftead of building up in the moft holy faith, and in a fingle dependance upon the one true and everlafting Lawgiver, make fuch a compofition of nature and grace, as would keep the mind in fermentation, rather than in perfect peace; rob of His honour the Captain of our falvation; and prevent thofe mighty works being done in His name which call for the finglenefs of the believing heart. I have beheld an evil like this in our camp, and its impediment to the growth of vifited minds to that ftature in Chrift, to which their peace affuredly called them. Do not miftake me; I reverence the bond of chriftian fellowship, and in a sense of the fellowship itself, with its sacred consoling unction, my spirit has often been dissolved, and fervently craved its increase in myself and others: yea, I have rejoiced in the flowings of that language, which I can now feelingly adopt to thyself (not from partiality so much as from a renewed concern for thy preservation) "My longed for and joy, stand fast in the Lord, my dearly beloved." In seasons like this, we perceive where the mixture lies; the natural part (which cannot inherit the kingdom) blending with a rightly begotten exercise and sympathy with each other. If our most amiable qualifications, and affectionate endearments, are not subservient to, and sanctified by, the refiner of hearts, they are encumbrances to the gospel, and the services of it.

12th month 1789—Accept the expressions of my renewed love and sympathy for, and with thee; the remembrance of thee is precious to my heart, because I comfortably feel thee to be a fellow traveller towards a city which hath foundations. We must not expect the weather, the roads, and the disposition of our minds for prosecuting the journey, to be always pleasant; but we must ever be careful to keep in the way; to travel when light is upon the path; and to rest in the night. We are not to conclude every thing lost which is out of sight; the most valuable grain the earth yields, passes through a temporary death. We are most of us senseless enough, at times, to be objects of the Apostle's rousing address, "thou fool, that which thou sowest is not quickened except it die." Human nature is so subject to deception, that it can frustrate, by some pollution or other, almost every dispensation, but death: therefore, be thou faithful unto that, remembering the consequent promise; " thou shalt receive a crown of life."

12th month 1789—I assure thee my heart feels for thee a cordiality, which at times does myself good: for in loving those who love the truth, (as I believe thou dost) we unite ourselves to a chain, the end of which, however remote from the perfection of the divine life, happily connects us with all the living, in seeking after those things which excel in purity and duration. One comfort that attends those who are simply, and singly pressing after the hope of their calling is, that they are not bound to tell all they feel, neither with respect to themselves, nor others; it is not essential that they should seek eminence, even in the religious world. They are happily spared the trouble of such vain objects, and find that, in solitude of spirit, the Beloved of souls speaks most comfortably to them, and enriches them with most spiritual blessings, which he causes them to enjoy in heavenly places. Oh, how often I covet for myself, and my friends, that we may keep sacred, to these " heavenly places," the gifts of the spirit! Nature is apt to feed upon them, to bask itself in their influence, and congratulate itself in the possession of such treasure; when alas! the gold, the precious gold, this way becomes dim, and is often unwisely tinseled over by the unsanctified affection of the creature. I wish,—that thou and I may possess that love or charity which boasteth not itself, nor is soon extinguished by the changeableness ever to be found in the face of perishing things; but may cherish in ourselves the root from whence every christian virtue springs. Then we may have rejoicing in ourselves, rather than in another, and our mental salutations herein be more frequent than our expressions of them. Thy account of dear ——— is comfortable, she is a truly valuable woman, and will I hope, more and more, shew herself to be what she is. Obscurity is not always granted to those who most seek it: it is sometimes a favourable climate for the fruits of humiliation's valley; but these are in wisdom, and for the good of mankind, often exposed for those that thirst, and have nothing wherewith to buy.

12th month 1789—A week or two after our return from Dublin, A. S. departed this life. We hear she had sore conflict of mind for some days, greatly fearing her future welfare: so pure did that kingdom appear, when her admired liveliness, and faculty of pleasing ceased; when pleasant pictures of spiritual things were torn to pieces, and the day that burns as an oven came upon them. But this heaviness of spirit was a merciful dispensation; the chastisement yielded peaceable fruit; for before she finally took her leave of visible things, she had to acknowledge unfailing mercies.

12th month 1789—I have seen, in my short life, so much fallacy in human wisdom respecting matrimonial connections, and so much blessing showered upon an attention to simple uncorrupted openings, which have not at first appeared most plausible, that

I seem to have no faith left in any direction but that which the devoted heart finds to make for peace. In concerns of this sort, it is often very difficult for such to judge, because prepossession and inclination are apt to influence our best feelings. Natural affection bears some resemblance of sacred impulse; and therefore, methinks that this seed, though ever so right, must die in the ground before it be quickened and sanctified. In short there are few openings, for our and the general good, which have not to pass through this temporary death, few gifts but what are designed to be buried in baptism: and I wish thee, if ever thou possess a female companion, to obtain her as a fruit of the new creation; that so thou mayst reap those spiritual advantages which those enjoy, who, through the effectual working of the grace of God, drink together into one spirit, whether in suffering or in rejoicing; for without this experience, Zion's travellers must find such connections to be secretly burthensome and insipid.

1st month 1790—I rejoice that the Keeper of Israel, who sleeps not by day, nor slumbers by night, hath thee under his providential care. This is a sustaining persuasion, a hope in times of trial, which settles the otherwise tossed mind on the consecrated ground of pure dependence: mayst thou never doubt it, Satan will not fail to assault thee, sometimes in roaring about thy dwelling, and sometimes, with the subtilty of the prince of the air, seeking to take possession of all within thee, which can possibly incline to disobey the commands of inscrutable and infinite wisdom. Remember he was a liar from the beginning; and invariably opposeth the exaltation of the mountain of the Lord's house. He prefers any hill to this; and had rather we were gathered to the heights of our own imaginations, and the seat of judgment, there to condemn ourselves, and reason out of doors the convictions of truth, than that we should die daily to the will of the creature, and sit in reverent dependence at the feet of Him who bruises the serpent's head.

1st month 1790—I want thee to be encouraged, and to put all thy confidence in the everlasting arm. Leave, as much as possible, things that are behind; be content with the present emptiness (when it is thy portion) and neither toil nor spin for future supplies. He that cloaths the lilies and the grass of the field, is abundantly able and ready, in his own time, to reveal his gracious providence, and minister, from the treasures of wisdom and knowledge, to his flock and family, even through the weak and foolish things of this world; so that things which are not, (minds reduced to a sense of their nothingness) may bring to nought things which are. The christian's strength consists in the favour and countenance of his Captain; and the obtaining of this leads the mind into that abasedness where Satan finds himself discomfited, and his head bruised. "He shall bruise thy heel." Little indeed is in his power, if we maintain the humility, the simplicity, and holy dignity of a converted soul. Many words are unnecessary at present. The Master, who knows what thou canst bear, will I doubt not give thee thy meat in due season, waken thee morning by morning, and cause thine ear to hear as the learned : in all things may he instruct thee to discretion, and preserve thee in the way whereinto he hath led thee, even that way which truly no fowl knoweth! I know, from a degree of experience, that the farther we get from a dependence upon instrumental consolation, the more likely we are, with holy certainty, to discover (amidst inward conflicts) the indubitable evidence of being upon the true foundation, the seal of adoption, the white stone with the new name, &c. The very chastisements which introduce the mind to this humbling knowledge, are (when passed by) sweet to the new taste, as the honey and the honeycomb.

1st month 1790—I did not forget thee; but truly self was at that time so much the object and subject of my cares and exertions, that if I could but any way keep my head above water thereby, it was more than my doubting mind could at times hope for. Ah, my dear friend, I have a heart prone to rebel against, and live above the pure principle of truth; and because thereof, my spirit is at times covered with mourning as with a garment; and more especially, when I consider the greatness, and the holiness of that Name, of which I venture to make mention in the congregation of the Lord's people. It is mercy, nothing short of mercy, so marvellously displayed in the choice of vessels for sacred services in the church. " He will have mercy on whom he will have mercy :" this truth baffles human reasoning : and therefore, let thee and me covet an increase of the increase of God, and ask in faith for the best gifts. Being afflicted with the impurity of struggling nature, let us come boldly to the throne of grace, to help us in the needful time, and to settle our spirits in calm acquiescence with, and resignation to, the dispensations of infinite wisdom; that so, from every temptation and tribulation, our souls may be restored, with this immortal and unadulterated song, " thy will be done." If we are but as the ram's horns, through which the Shepherd of Israel speaks at times to his people, (in concert with his inward and more despised teaching) let us be content, and simply seek an holy conformity to, and adorning of his doctrine.

2d month 1790—It is not by might or by power, but by the spirit of the Lord, that His work prospers, or his praise is effected; and therefore a little one may be made " a thousand, and a small one a strong nation." Under this persuasion, the faith is strengthened in the Omnipotence of the smallest revelation of the Lord's Arm in our little services, and our trust removed from the appearance of strength, to strength itself. The rich man cannot glory in his riches, nor the strong man in his strength, but the cause of glorying is found to be in the righteous government and dispensations of our Holy Head. Thy letter brought you all so much to my mind, that it seemed as if I was with you, sharing in your concerns, and feeling in part that weight of exercise with which dependant servants are introduced into their field of labour. Now perhaps I may congratulate you on the completion hereof, and participate in that humble rejoicing wherewith Ebenezer's are set up. I fervently desire to possess an increasing capacity to feel with the members of the mystical body, wherever scattered, or however concealed in the depths of the wilderness from the human eye; for I am persuaded that, as our spirits are regulated by the president of this church, they will, at times, be carried beyond the bounds of observation, to visit the seed in prison.

3d month 1790—Though my heart sympathizes so nearly and tenderly with thee and thy dear wife, as that I could mingle my tears with yours, yet I dare not utter the language of commiseration, for your late loss of a lovely plant out of your garden; but rather of congratulation for the blessed experience, that " the eternal God is your refuge, and that underneath are the everlasting arms." Herein I rejoice, and will rejoice that such unadulterated consolation is ministered to the poor in spirit. You have a fresh opportunity, my beloved friends, by pure resignation, to commit your spirits, your children, and your substance, into divine keeping. May nothing impede the progress and perfection of this work, this glorious work, whereby the song of the redeemed is learned, and qualification wrought to unite with the heavenly host, in proclaiming, that " worthy is the Lord God and the Lamb, to receive riches, honour, and power, both now and for ever." A mind centred to the source of instruction, wisdom, and strength, can receive little more by such communications as these, than an outward and visible sign of that inward and spiritual grace, wherewith the soul is replenished, and wherein it finds the substance of all that is truly good. It is nevertheless an allowable accommodation to the weakness of sense, thus to commune; and having, in moments of drooping, been refreshed by thy tender sympathy and salutations, my heart is bound in christian affection to share thy griefs, and hail thee on every renewed accession to the Master's cross, and participation of his crown. Oh my friend, what nailing we take, before we are bound to it! how nature opposes that holy experience of being led as a lamb to the slaughter, and as a sheep that is dumb before its shearers. Hard as the work is, with God all things are possible; and therefore let us watch and be sober, adding to our faith virtue; that when the power is revealed by which we can do all things, we being in readiness, may advance from strength to strength, and finally appear before the Lord in Zion, amongst those who are fully sanctified. We are now returned from our quarterly meeting, where I trust the gospel cause did not go backward. We ought not to look for great things; we do not deserve them. And I perceive that when we are most dipped into this sense, life and immortality (being graciously in waiting) are the most sure to be brought to light. Therefore let us be humbled under the mighty hand, that we may be thus truly exalted in due time; yea, in all our provings, let us sink down into our own nothingness, and value every dispensation which clothes us with it; for then, methinks, we shall learn in every thing to give thanks.

3d month 1790—Thou hast, my dear friend, of late appeared to me to be preparing to set out, according to the sacred counsel of the great Master to His disciples, without scrip or purse, or two coats, reduced to a simple dependence upon renewed supplies from the holy treasury, and learning, in a new line of service, to live by faith. Mayst thou encrease in the certain knowledge, that the Lord is gracious unto such humble faithful walkers before him. I feel a confidence that it will be so, and that thy feet will grow more and more conspicuously beautiful upon the mountains ; because they are, beyond all shadow of doubt, shod with the preparation of the gospel of peace, and through adorable kindness, washed for the service on which thou art now set out: therefore gird up the loins of thy mind, and hope to the end. Do not be afraid of the gloomy exercises into which thy mind may often be baptized. Remember that even the great Master, who knew without fear or doubting that he should glorify the Father, groaned in himself before he raised Lazarus from the dead. Do, I intreat thee, offer thyself up freely, and do not seek to cut thy matter shorter than is consistent with thy peace. Look forward and not backward ; for if I am not mistaken, thy progress in the work whereunto thou art called, is not designed to be as slow as some thou mayst esteem thy cotemporaries ; and it is as great an evil to take from the words of the prophecy of the book, as to add to them.

3d month 1790—Your many testimonies of affection for us, your repeated accounts respecting yourselves, and, above all, your steady increase in saving knowledge, of which we are persuaded, are frequent occasions of humble thankfulness to the Father of mercies, whose blessings, variously showered upon you and us, are worthy of reverent commemoration, and grateful enquiry, what we shall render unto him therefore. It is little, very little, that we can do for so bountiful a Shepherd; nor does He, blessed be His name, require at our hands what He has not furnished us with ability to perform: but that little, let us present at, or cast into the secret treasury, not doubting His compassionate acceptance. An humble resigned spirit is a gift which, I believe, was never refused at the altar. It is, whilst preserved, a continual offering, a sweet smelling sacrifice, the savour of life unto life in those that believe; it is a bulwark or fortress, where, in times of desertion, temptation and tribulation, the weary soul finds shelter, and all the armour of light against Satan's attacks and fiery darts. Now, my beloved friends, my heart feels you as companions in the christian path; and in your exercises, your discouragements and poverty of spirit, I participate; though distant in the outward, yet as the Apostle said, " present in spirit." —Be assured that the same afflictions are measurably accomplished in every true member of the mystical body. You have companions therein, and need not be told, that all these things are intended for our refinement, and encreasing usefulness and service in the church militant here on earth: that when this mortal shall put on immortality, the tribulated spirit may obtain an eternal residence, in the glorious church triumphant, where all tears are wiped away: these are animating considerations, and prompt us to endure hardness like good soldiers of Jesus Christ, and to receive with thanksgiving every humiliation and spiritual baptism. I know, dear friend, that if thou art mercifully kept quick in understanding in the fear of the Lord, the weak, unconverted state of many of your members will occasion thee to go mourning on thy way, at the same time that thou finds a necessity to attend to that command of the great Master, to wash and anoint rather than appear unto men to fast. This hidden exercise of spirit will espouse thee more closely to the heavenly bridegroom, who hath the spirit of wisdom and understanding, and who judges not after the sight of the eye, or the hearing of the ear. I do hope, my beloved friends, that your labours will be blest though yourselves think them very weak and small. If our treasure is but laid up in heaven, no matter how little our corrupt hearts are entrusted with the knowledge of it. Be not afraid of leaving the sheep and lambs, when the good Shepherd calls to any duty; His care is better than ours, and He can supply all your needs, by the riches of His grace in Christ Jesus our Lord.

4th month 1790—I am comforted in finding that your hearts are knit together like David and Jonathan's, in opposition to every stratagem which Satan may use. As I do believe the cement is composed of materials acceptable to the penetrating eye of the great Preserver of men, so I trust you will feel your union to be a balm through the future steppings of christian and social travel, however it may please infinite Wisdom to dispose of you, as to your outward settlements, or journeyings in the present world.— Settle it in thy heart, to expect a mixture of bitterness in that cup of comfort, which the great Master may minister to thee. No deadly sorrow is in the blessing; but evil things, and mutable things, till our purification is complete, have a power over us which keeps our spirits in a state of profitable groaning; and if we do but experience the fulfilling of that gracious promise, that for the cryings of the poor, and for the sighings of the needy, he will arise, let us thank him and take courage.

My beloved ———'s letter came at a time more acceptable than would be prudent for me this way to describe. It renewed that precious participation of each other's exercises and consolations, which I do believe originates in the Fountain of everlasting love. I look with humble admiration at that holy hand which is leading thee about, and instructing thee; and my faith is strong that the Lord will keep thee as the apple of his eye, and, in his own time, make all clouds of discouragement as the dust of his feet. Thou knowest, and thou wilt more and more know, that, for the right performance of any religious service, we want emptying from vessel to vessel; and when we consider how many have suffered by an imperfect experience of this great work, we ought not to lament at any dispensation, or change of seasons, which brings us, in the least degree, nearer to that state and stature, for which infinite kindness designs us.

5th month 1790—That measure of conversion which is essentially necessary, rightly to introduce us into every new line of service, bears a strong resemblance to the first step of the great apostle into the christian religion: a light shone around him; such conviction seized his soul, that whilst he asked, "who art thou," he called him Lord; he consulted not with flesh and blood: happy resignation! which however, did not keep him out of *the street called Strait*, neither for a time were his eyes suffered to be opened.—We have each our peculiar exercises, as we have each our peculiar infirmities; all which, through sanctification and purification of heart, may help us forward to a final settlement in that glorious city, whose inhabitants no more say they are sick. —I hope thou wilt not draw back from any opening to duty, which thou mayst be favoured with. The right time, and our time, do not always agree; but we ought invariably to bear testimony to the first, by the subordination of the latter. " Wisdom is justified of her children;" and therefore do not reason unprofitably upon thy duty.

7th month 1790—It was pleasant to be informed of thy safe landing in Ireland. I hope thy drooping mind has been refreshed, not only by the strengthening sympathy of fellow-travellers, but also by the composing, and yet animating virtue of Shiloh's streams, and that thou hast been enabled to lie down beside these waters which run softly. Thou knowest that when we can get here, it is like getting home, to a joy with which no stranger can intermeddle. The increase of such a capacity is what my soul longs for; that in this exercising journey before us, wherein creaturely efforts can do little for the promotion of the great cause, the pure seed may, from place to place, be at least secretly visited; and that whether effects may be seen or not, the work, in divine condescension, may be hid with the Lord.

11th month 1790—The comfortable evidence thou mentions, of there being a power strong in proportion to thy weakness, strengthens my declining faith, and encourages me to lay hold on the same blessed hope, because it met the witness in my heart that says it is the truth. A confidence so precious is not to be cast away; it is designed for an anchor to the poor vessel, secretly attaching it to eternal help, when, in divine wisdom, its course is restrained on the waters of affliction and uncertainty. Then let me say, cast not away thy confidence, for therein is great recompence of reward. We are often tempted to do this; sometimes, in the multitude of objects, forgetting the great source of good, and means of preservation; and at others, looking so timidly and doubtfully at them, as to lose our interest in both. May thou and I, watch against these and other evils; and pray, according to our measure of faith, that that spirit may preside in us, which can rejoice in God alone, though none else regard it, or can own its life.

——————— 1790—I cannot know that thy sufferings and temptations are so deep, without feeling an affectionate, sisterly solicitude about thee, at the same time that I perceive with joy thy steppings are in the footsteps of the flock. But with the greatest cordiality do I find, that thou canst not draw thy consolations from even the springs of fellow disciples. The well's mouth being closed in thyself, thou sittest mourning at it, and every drop of water brought thee from thy neighbour's overflowings, serves but to augment thy lamentation; for thy thirst cannot be satisfied with that, which is not the " well in thee springing up into everlasting life." I am glad thou art resolved to be patient; if thou holdeſt thy integrity herein, and letteſt patience have its perfect work, thou wilt find more perfection in this diſpenſation than is manifeſt at preſent, and moreover thou wilt lack nothing. Then be of good cheer, my beloved friend : believe in the fatherly care and compaſſion of Him who is the Lord Almighty; and doubt not that all His chaſtiſements are the more indelibly to fix the ſeal of adoption upon thy ſpirit; whereby thy qualifications may be ſtrengthened to cry Abba, Father! in proportion to the increaſe of thy ſervices in and for His Name. Were not the experiences of the Lord's dealings to us as individuals ſomewhat deep, there might be more danger of ſtumbling in the paths of judgment, when, for the welfare of others, we may be turned into them; and marvel not if, after this baptiſm with which thou art baptized, the Maſter, who is rich in mercy, and inſcrutable in wiſdom, calls upon thee for ſome new act of dedication. Till then, fight the good fight of faith; now is thy time to prove the ſufficiency of thy ever victorious Captain. Reſolve if thou periſh, it ſhall be at His footſtool. Let not out thine ear to the accuſer of the brethren, believe him not, even reſpecting thyſelf, when he tells thee that thou art not what thy friends take thee to be. But if the Father chaſtens, and draws thee from man's judgment, by ſhewing thee the fallibility thereof, cleave to him as to thy beſt friend. Experience will convince thee, that whoever ſtand thro' the ſtorms attendant on their pilgrimage for the honour of the great Name, muſt learn to paſs through good report, as well as evil report; with an equal neglect of it as such; for the weapons of their warfare being spiritual, they must not fail to apply them to the spiritual wickedness in the high, but secret places of their own hearts. Self is apt to feed upon the manifest unity of our friends, and to draw our attention from the pure and strengthening virtue which supplieth every joint of the mystical body; rendering us less capable, than we otherwise should be, of eating that bread which the world knows not of.

———— I have a comfortable hope respecting thy prosperity and preservation, and already rejoice in the symptoms thereof. That one especially, of the passing away of the old heavens and the old earth, is so favourable, that I trust thou wilt fully resign thyself thereto, that so they may be remembered no more, nor come into, to way-lay thy mind in any of its preparations for gospel service. Yes, my heart can feel with thee, in thy frequent incapacity to rejoice in even the purest friendship, or to support it by the effusions of natural affection. Oh that all whose hearts and tongues have been animated with the live coal from the sacred Altar, had fully passed through dispensations of this sort; methinks the priesthood, and other living members in the church, would be more burning and shining lights, have more true christian sympathy for each other, and oftener meet one another in the field of spiritual exercise, or, in other words, enjoy the true communion of saints. We miss many of the excellent promises of the gospel, for want of coming to, and dwelling in, that humbled situation of mind to which they belong. How many sit in judgment, who never sufficiently, by virtue of the meekness of their spirits, were guided in the midst of its paths! How often do we hear attempts to sing the praise of Zion's King, by those whose general conduct bears no testimony to a fervent travail of their spirits after deliverance from the enemies of their own houses, and who consequently cannot stand upon its banks. Though I often fear it is the case, I dread to settle down (because it sometimes appears to be my duty to shew unto others their transgressions) as if the work was done at home, and my soul's adversary overcome; when, peradventure, his force is redoubled, and his artifice herein more than ever effectual. "Watch and pray," sweetly occurs to my mind, and for this good end, "that ye enter not into temptation;" that the vessel may be preserved in sanctification and honour, and that the immortal birth may have its habitation in a purified temple. Then may the new heavens, the new earth, and the holy mountain, in times of refreshing, break forth into singing, because the Lord comforts his people, and hath mercy upon his afflicted.

F I N I S.

www.ingramcontent.com/pod-product-compliance
Lightning Source LLC
Chambersburg PA
CBHW020535300426
44111CB00008B/672